IDEOLOGY AND ECONOMICS

IDEOLOGY AND ECONOMICS

U.S. RELATIONS WITH THE SOVIET UNION, 1918–1933

JOAN HOFF WILSON

UNIVERSITY OF MISSOURI PRESS
COLUMBIA, 1974

FOR MY FATHER, JOSEPH HOFF
AND IN MEMORY OF MY MOTHER
PEARL LAWRENCE HOFF

PREFACE

Why did the United States delay sixteen years after the Bolshevik Revolution of 1917 before recognizing the USSR? A number of books and articles have discussed this question, but most of them have overemphasized the U.S. business community's effect in first delaying and then bringing about recognition.[1] At the same time, they have underestimated the increasingly bureaucratized and ideological position Washington officials took on the issue, preferring to describe the Government's opposition in conventional individualistic and moralistic terms.[2] Certainly, people at all levels of U.S. society voiced considerable personal and moral indignation about the emergence of a Communist regime in postwar Russia; however, the U.S. Government's nonrecognition was more than an unreflective moral stand instinctively assumed by incompetent political leaders to satisfy unorganized public opinion.

Instead, the policy of nonrecognition represented one of the United States' first postwar diplomatic acts primarily based on the conscious consideration of economic and ideological factors by Government leaders who, in turn, were subjected not only to the direct pressure of interest groups, but also to the impact that the systematic institutionalization

1. See Paul F. Boller, Jr., "The 'Great Conspiracy' of 1933: A Study in Short Memories," *Southwest Review* 39 (Spring 1954): 101–2, 104–6, 109–12; William Appleman Williams, *American-Russian Relations, 1781–1947*, pp. 236–38; Donald G. Bishop, *The Roosevelt-Litvinov Agreements: The American View*, pp. 7–10; Peter G. Filene, *Americans and the Soviet Experiment, 1917–1933*, pp. 227–39; Edward M. Bennett, *Recognition of Russia: An American Foreign Policy Dilemma*, pp. 101–4; Robert James Maddox, *William E. Borah and American Foreign Policy*, pp. 210–13. Only Robert Paul Browder, in *The Origins of Soviet-American Diplomacy*, pp. 108, 219, explicitly questions the significance of business pressure, but even he assumes the existence of strong interest-group activity on the part of a united business community (pp. 75–82, 120).

2. Maddox, *Borah and Foreign Policy*, p. 191; Filene, *Americans and the Soviet Experiment*, pp. 90, 105, 129; Bennett, *Recognition of Russia*, pp. 53, 68; Boller, " 'Great Conspiracy' of 1933," p. 100; Browder, *Soviet-American Diplomacy*, pp. 3–24; Daniel M. Smith, *Aftermath of War: Bainbridge Colby and Wilsonian Diplomacy, 1920–1921*, pp. 55–62.

of such factors had on them as they performed specific bureaucratic tasks that related to the Soviet Union.

After World War I, U.S. policy makers encountered economic considerations in the formulation of policy toward the USSR that frequently were geared to maintaining the unprecedented economic opportunity facing the United States as the world's leading creditor. The policy makers also confronted ideological considerations in the same process that had been forced upon them for the first time by the appearance of hostile foreign ideologies in the course of the war, namely, German imperialism and Russian bolshevism.

In diplomatic relations with the Soviet Union from 1918 to 1933, the United States never reached a balanced or coordinated political and economic foreign policy because the reaction against bolshevism prevailed in the State and Commerce departments while U.S. businessmen participated in a relatively steady increase in trade with the Soviets after 1923. The refusal of Government officials to admit this basic contradiction in the first half of the 1920s allowed it to become an ideologically institutionalized aspect of U.S. diplomacy in the second half of the decade. Concurrently, the disunity created by disagreement among different companies and business organizations about the advisability of trading with an unrecognized nation prevented large and small economic interests alike from significantly influencing the process that ultimately led to the establishment of diplomatic relations.

While the policy of nonrecognition was being formulated and implemented, the executive branch of the Government and most individual corporations and interest groups were participating in the general search for a new political and economic order—a search, semiconscious at best, that had begun in the 1880s. The first phase of this quest for more efficient governmental and economic organization climaxed just before and after World War I with the appearance of federal regulatory agencies and departmental restructuring, along with the revitalization of specialized trade associations and such broadly based, influential national business groups as the National Association of Manufacturers, the American Bankers Association, and the Chamber of Commerce of the United States. The impact of all these organizational changes on the Government and on business circles, as well as the ideological and economic points of view the changes reflected, have generally been overlooked in previous studies about the reasons for the delay in recognizing the USSR until 1933.

The subject matter of this book is, therefore, a familiar one, but in some places, the methodology and interpretation differ significantly from those found in other works. Among other things, an attempt has been made to assess the degree to which the increased bureaucratic structure of authority that permeated U.S. society influenced the formulation of economic and foreign policies toward the Soviet Union. Viewed as part of the pervasive thrust toward greater rationalization of society, which was common to all industrialized nations at the turn of the century, this search for a new order in the form of socioeconomic organization, followed corporatist lines in the United States.[3]

Such terms as corporate liberalism, corporatist ideology, or simply corporatism describe the specific kind of political and economic rationalization that U.S. leaders developed in response to their growing fears about "destructive competition" and "social anarchy."[4] Corporatism generally refers to a

3. For a discussion of this search for order and corporatism, see Robert Wiebe, *The Search for Order*; Rowland Berthoff, *An Unsettled People*; Ronald Radosh and Murray N. Rothbard, eds., *A New History of Leviathan: Essays on the Rise of the American Corporate State*; Grant McConnell, *Private Power and American Democracy*; Alfred D. Chandler, *Strategy and Structure: Chapters in the History of American Industrial Enterprise*; Andrew Shonfield, *Modern Capitalism*; James Weinstein, *The Corporate Ideal in the Liberal State*; William Appleman Williams, *The Contours of American History*; Louis Galambos, *Competition and Cooperation*; Galambos, "The Emerging Organizational Synthesis in Modern American History," *Business History Review* 44 (Autumn 1970): 279–90; Samuel P. Hays, "The Social Analysis of American Political History, 1880–1920," *Political Science Quarterly* 80 (September 1965): 373–94; Mathew Elbow, *French Corporative State*; Ralph Bowen, *German Theories of the Corporative State*; Cyril Black, *The Dynamics of Modernization*, pp. 175–99; Kenneth Barkin, "Populism in Germany and America," in Herbert Bass, ed., *The State of American History*, pp. 373–404; John A. Garraty, "The New Deal, National Socialism, and the Great Depression," *American Historical Review* 78 (October 1973): 936–44.

4. Eugen Golob, *The Isms*, pp. 541–97; Robert Brady, *Business as a System of Power*, pp. 21–188; McConnell, *Private Pow-*

kind of political economy that represents a middle course between state socialism and monopoly capitalism. It was often advocated after World War I as a substitute for both. Corporatism calls for the organization of society along the lines of functional economic units that include both labor and management, that are voluntary and decentralized, and that are simultaneously self-governing and self-regulating. Theoretically these industry-wide units would work together in harmony out of a sense of community, social responsibility, and devotion to efficiency. As a blend of democratic liberalism and the corporate state, it was proffered by men like Herbert Hoover in the 1920s as an ideological and economic means for preserving individual initiative while taking advantage of the latest technological advancements. Despite the association often made between corporatism and national socialism, there was nothing inherently fascist in the theory, nor was it incompatible with democracy.

It was evident from the first appearance of corporatist ideas in the United States that there were two distinct ways of implementing them. One stressed completely cooperative economic organization and regulation along neoguildist lines. The other stressed federally directed and enforced organization along statist lines. Hence, the type of corporatism that first emerged in the United States was essentially an ambiguous and often contradictory conglomeration of federally regulatory agencies and procedures purported to preserve liberal democratic concepts about private property, individualism, voluntary effort, and local control, despite an increase in monopolistic or oligarchic economic practices and the appearance of large-scale, national organizations at all levels of society. The more voluntary, decentralized aspects of this kind of corporatism, which involved informal cooperation between private and public segments of the political economy, were abandoned in the panic of the Great Depression for an equally ambiguous, neopluralist brand of welfare statism. However, this shift did not entail any basic departure from corporatist ideology within the Government or business cir-

---

er, pp. 54–70; Otis L. Graham, Jr., *The Great Campaigns: Reform and War in America, 1900–1928*, pp. 1–51, 97–169; Samuel P. Hays, *Response to Industrialism*; Weinstein, *Corporate Ideal*; Galambos, *Competition and Cooperation*; Edwin Layton, *The Revolt of the Engineers*; Wiebe, *Search for Order*.

cles; it simply represented a shift from guildism to statism in the continuing attempt to work out a corporatist order compatible with American ideals and traditions.[5]

Corporatist ideals and the resulting military-industrial complex fostered by them since the advent of the Cold War have inevitably and irrevocably influenced U.S. foreign policy. Particularly, they, and the accompanying organizational forces that were formally set in motion by the Progressive movement and World War I and finally institutionalized in the 1920s, have affected U.S. attitudes toward the Bolshevik Revolution and the USSR.[6] Thus, in addition to analyzing individual business and Government personalities, traditional diplomatic and commercial correspondence, and trade figures, an attempt has been made to describe those few, but significant, organizational and ideological factors influencing the formulation of policy about Russian recognition.

The definition of the term "ideology" is discussed in detail

5. Ellis W. Hawley, *The New Deal and the Problem of Monopoly*, pp. 35–52, 472–90; Herbert Stein, "Pre-revolutionary Fiscal Policy: The Regime of Herbert Hoover," *Journal of Law and Economics* 9 (October 1966): 189–223; Garraty, "The New Deal," pp. 907–36; James Olson, "The End of Voluntarism," *Annals of Iowa* 41 (Fall 1972): 1104–13; Joan Hoff Wilson, *Herbert Clark Hoover: Forgotten Progressive*, chaps. 2, 4, and 5; Galambos, *Competition and Cooperation*, 199–202.

6. Robert D. Cuff, "A 'Dollar-a-Year Man' in Government: George N. Peek and the War Industries Board," *Business History Review* 41 (Winter 1967): 404–20; G. Cullom Davis, "The Transformation of the Federal Trade Commission, 1914–1929," *Mississippi Valley Historical Review* 49 (December 1962): 437–55; Carolyn Grin, "The Unemployment Conference of 1921: An Experiment in National Cooperative Planning," *Mid-America* 55 (April 1973): 83–107; Burton I. Kaufman, "Organization for Foreign Trade Expansion in the Mississippi Valley, 1900–1920," *Business History Review* 46 (Winter 1972): 444–65; Burton I. Kaufman, "The Organizational Dimension of United States Economic Foreign Policy," *Business History Review* 46 (Spring 1972): 17–44; "The War Bureaucracy and Foreign Trade Expansion, 1917–1921," paper read at the April 1973 meeting of the Organization of American Historians; Paul A. Koistinen, "The 'Industrial-Military Complex' in Historical Perspective: World War I," *Business History Review* 41 (Winter 1967): 378–403; Koistinen, "The 'Industrial-Military Complex' in Historical Perspective: The InterWar Years," *Journal of American History* 56 (March 1970): 819–35; Gerald D. Nash, "Experiments in Industrial Mobilization: WIB and NRA," *Mid-America* 45 (July

in the last chapter. What should be noted from the outset is that it is not used with a negative connotation in this work, except when ideological considerations limited diplomatic options or perverted common sense in the conduct of foreign affairs. The comprehensive orientation-guidance definition employed here views ideology positively as an "ordered system of cultural symbols" that may or may not correspond to reality, depending on the function it is performing for the individual or group. This broad definition obviously encompasses political and socioeconomic viewpoints. It has been used to demonstrate the existence of an ideological predisposition among U.S. policy makers following World War I—a predisposition often matched in intensity, if not in schematic coherence, with that of Communist ideologues. Until recently, most diplomatic historians have been reluctant to deal with domestic ideological concepts or to admit that the foreign policy of the United States has been as ideologically motivated in this century as that of its most feared enemies.

This broad definition of ideology has not been employed to obviate the need for analyzing and evaluating economic motivation on the part of businessmen or Government officials. Although difficult to determine, each time self-serving economic considerations appeared to dominate actions or policy, they have been distinguished from the cultural and political aspects of the prevailing business ideology of the 1920s that functioned as a general orientation guide in a time of postwar transition for the vast majority of Americans. Hence, I have referred to ideological *and* economic motivation of certain actions and policies whenever the relative importance of the pecuniary intent could be determined. The same interaction between general ideological predispositions and elusive economic self-interest continues to

1963): 157–67; J. Richard Snyder, "Coolidge, Costigan and the Tariff Commission," *Mid-America* 50 (April 1968): 131–48; Wiebe, *Search for Order*, pp. 222–23, 235–36, 295–302; Galambos, "Emerging Organizational Synthesis," pp. 279–90; Charles Norman Fay, *Business in Politics: Considerations for Business Leaders*, pp. 1–21, 135–53; Thomas C. Blaisdell, Jr., *The Federal Trade Commission: An Experiment in the Control of Business*, pp. 287–311; Nellis Stalker, Jr., "The National Association of Manufacturers: A Study in Ideology" (Ph.D. dissertation, University of Wisconsin, 1950), pp. 276–85, 292–96, 313–20, 420–24.

affect the formulation of U.S. foreign policy, most notably when that policy concerns relations with the Soviet Union and other Communist nations.

Diplomatic developments in Soviet–U.S. relations since 1917 have exhibited certain consistent features. For example, recognition in 1933 did not resolve the discrepancies in the economic and political treatment of the USSR by the United States, because departmental rivalry and bureaucratized anticommunism continued to hinder the formulation of a cohesive policy. Moreover, literature about Lend-Lease and the origins of the Cold War clearly indicates that cooperation between the two nations during World War II offered no solution and that there is still a strong tendency for the United States to overestimate probable Soviet response to proffered American credit and commodities.[7] Since the 1920s, the aim of U.S. policy makers appears to have remained rooted in ideological preconceptions while their methods have remained essentially, and at times most crudely, economic in terms of execution.[8] The $1,000,000,000 Soviet wheat deal of 1972 is only one of many indications of continued lack of coordination between U.S. economic and political policies, especially in their implementation.[9] Others are the tendency to encourage developing trade relations in such times of economic adversity as the early years of the Depression and the early 1970s, when the United States experienced its first unfavorable international balance of trade since 1894; congressional opposition to trading with the USSR during the 1930s because of purported Soviet use of forced labor and during

7. For a review of the literature on Lend-Lease, see Warren F. Kimbal, *The Most Unsordid Act: Lend-Lease, 1939–1941* and Robert Huhn Jones, *The Roads to Russia: United States Lend-Lease to the Soviet Union*; for a review of the literature on the Cold War, see Robert James Maddox, *The New Left and the Origins of the Cold War*, Thomas G. Paterson, ed., *The Origins of the Cold War* and Joseph M. Siracusa, *New Left Diplomatic Histories and Historians*.

8. Bruce Kuklick, *American Policy and the Division of Germany: The Clash with Russia over Reparations*, p. 229.

9. For reports of the confusion and mismanagement involved in the 1972 political détente with the Soviet Union, the subsequent wheat deal, and attempts to liberalize trade arrangements between the two nations, see O. Edmund Clubb, "New Horizons in U.S.–Soviet Trade," *The Progressive* 37 (June 1973): 41–44; *The New York Times*, "The Week in Review," May 28, 1972,

the 1970s because of reported restrictions on the emigration of Jews; and finally, the continued haggling between the two nations over credit, most-favored-nation treatment, and above all, debts resulting from nationalization of property after World War I, loans made to Russia during that war, and those remaining from the Lend-Lease programs of World War II.

* * * *

I wish to acknowledge financial assistance for expanding and rewriting this work, which was originally part of a much larger study on United States economic foreign policy in the 1920s, from the University of California, Berkeley; California State University, Sacramento; and the American Philosophical Society. Most of the primary material came from many business publications, the Library of Congress, the records of the departments of State and Commerce in the National Archives, Yale University Library, the Franklin D. Roosevelt Library, the Butler Library at Columbia University, and, most important, the Herbert Hoover Presidential Library at West Branch, Iowa, and the Herbert Hoover Archives at Stanford University. Two graduate students, Sandi Pelose and Frederick J. Mayer, typed the original manuscript, and many invaluable friends and relatives provided other technical assistance and basic emotional support. I thank them all.

J.H.W.
Sacramento, California
October 1973

---

p. 1. *San Francisco Chronicle*, October 5, 1972, p. 14; "This World," July 15, 1973, p. 10; July 20, 1973, p. 11; July 22, 1973, p. 10; October 30, 1973, p. 1; November 2, 1973, p. 6. Even the Soviets' alleged resale, for a profit, of wheat originally purchased from the United States in 1973 is not without precedent. It also occurred in 1922 and 1923 when they exported surplus wheat obtained from the American Relief Administration, much to the consternation of U.S. officials. See Benjamin M. Weissman, "The American Relief Administration in Russia, 1921–1923: A Case Study in the Interaction Between Opposing Political Systems" (Ph.D. dissertation, Columbia University, 1968), pp. 325–32.

CONTENTS

I

PERSPECTIVES: GENERAL VIEWS
OF U.S. BUSINESSMEN
AND SOVIET OFFICIALS

Relations with a Bolshevik-dominated Russia posed the most threatening ideological problem for U.S. businessmen immediately following World War I. Although the impact of the Bolshevik Revolution on international affairs in the 1920s has often been underestimated, and its impact on U.S. foreign policy has been ignored until recently,[1] one of the best ways to measure it is through a study of opinions within foreign and domestic business organizations. The views about the USSR held by U.S. businessmen and their organizations, for example, were in a state of flux between 1918 and 1933 and at no time reflected any clear understanding of the economic and social viability of either communism or socialism—even after recognition was granted. In fact, on the eve of recognition most individual businessmen and business groups were still expressing doubts about the Soviet Union's future under communism, even though that country was apparently surviving the Great Depression better than the United States, emerging as a world power under Soviet rule, and presenting an impressive example of economic planning through the First Five-Year Plan. Thus, during the period under consideration here, fear, doubt, distrust, ideological arrogance, and organizational vacillation all underscored the

1. Notable exceptions include William Appleman Williams, *American-Russian Relations, 1781–1947*; Edward Hallett Carr, *The Soviet Impact on the Western World*; John M. Thompson, *Russia, Bolshevism, and the Versailles Peace*; Beatrice Farnsworth, *William C. Bullitt and the Soviet Union*; Ronald Radosh, *American Labor and United States Foreign Policy*.

several attitudes assumed by the U.S. business community toward Soviet Russia.[2]

Like most people in the United States in 1917, businessmen naïvely and mistakenly believed the establishment of the provisional government after the March Revolution indicated that Russia was on its way to establishing a lasting democracy.[3] President Wilson contributed greatly to the creation of this illusion. Of all his statements on the subject, his eulogistic reference to Russia in his War Message on April 2, 1917, probably remains the most historically inaccurate and unrealistic characterization of the country and its people. He made this statement and those that followed during the summer and fall of 1917[4] despite the official reports and personal warnings that he and the State Department received about Russia's increasing internal instability. News of Russia's exhausting war effort and the growing influence of Socialist and Communist elements within the so-called democratic Provisional Government (discounting the laconic and often erroneous reports of the U.S. Ambassador to Russia, David Francis) gave Wilson and his administration little reason to believe that the March Revolution would, or could, act as a panacea for all Russia's ills. Yet official sources in the United States cast the March Revolution and the Provisional Government in just that role between March and November 1917.

2. Meno Lovenstein, *American Opinion of Soviet Russia*, pp. 111–49; Peter G. Filene, *Americans and the Soviet Experiment, 1917–1933*, pp. 101–29, 211–29.

3. Lovenstein, *American Opinion*, pp. 13, 16, 49–50.

4. President Wilson's public messages concerning Russia during the summer of 1917 consisted of the following: War Message, April 2; message to Baron Rosen (chairman of the Society for Promoting Friendly Relations between Russia and America), April 30; message clarifying war aims to Russia, May 22; message expressing objectives of Root Mission, May 26; welcome to the first ambassador of Free Russia, July 5; reply to the Pope's peace proposal, August 27; cable to Moscow Assembly, August 27; answer to Madame Bressovsky's appeal for funds, October 18; remarks upon sending Sisson to Russia, October 23. In none of these statements did the President give any indication that he thought Russia unable or unwilling to continue along the road to democracy that he had so eloquently described in his War Message.

Even before the March Revolution, in fact from the beginning of the war in 1914, the President had been repeatedly cautioned about the instability of Russia's war effort. One of the first to do so was the U.S. Ambassador to the Court of Saint James's, Walter Hines Page, who had pointed out to him on October 29, 1914, that the Russians lacked "staying qualities," and three years later Page wrote about the "considerable ignorance and anxiety among the representatives of the Allies as to what Russia is doing or can do." Again and again the close friend and personal adviser of the President, Col. Edward M. House, disclosed to him his suspicions about Russia. Early in 1917 Lloyd George had publicly acknowledged that the assistance offered to Russia by the Allies and the United States fell "very far short of her undoubted requirements."[5] The May 8, 1917, report of North Winship, the consul at Petrograd, was especially insightful. His very detailed, objective account of the "imminent and tremendous danger of the situation" apparently went entirely unnoticed, as did U.S. Ambassador David Francis' May 17, 1917, report of Socialist activity against the war effort. But the public, including the business community, was never accurately informed about the internal situation in Russia by the United States Government.[6]

Therefore, when the Bolshevik Revolution occurred in November 1917, the business community in the United States was no more prepared to accept or appreciate its significance than were other groups in the society. Businessmen across the country reacted with immediate and overwhelming hostility to the new Soviet government because they expected economic and ideological disaster in Russia. The economic chaos there was cited time after time as a point in proof of the failure not only of that Communist experiment but of all such experiments. For example, when Herbert Hoover

5. Burton J. Hendrick, *The Life and Letters of Walter H. Page*, 3: 168; Charles Seymour, ed., *The Intimate Papers of Colonel House*, 2: 121, 129, 157, 174–75; David Lloyd George, *War Memoirs*, 3: 463.

6. North Winship to Robert Lansing, May 8, 1917, U.S. Department of State, *Papers Relating to the Foreign Relations of the United States* (hereafter cited as *FRP*): *1918, Russia*, 1: 42–51; David Francis to Lansing, May 17, 1917, *FRP: The Lansing Papers, 1914–1920*, 1: 338.

referred to Russia as a cesspool, he was firmly convinced that socialism and communism were bankrupt philosophies: It made little difference to him whether the Soviet experiment was Communist or Socialist because he already believed that it had "proved itself with rivers of blood and suffering to be an economic and spiritual fallacy and to have wrecked itself on the rock of production."[7]

Businessmen in the United States may well have considered the almost total disruption of industrial production in Russia between 1917 and 1921 the most damning feature of the Bolshevik system. During those four years, 90 per cent of Russian industrial and agrarian production was disrupted or destroyed, but most contemporary observers did not realize that this economic disintegration was a product more of the war than of Bolshevik rule. Moreover, the significant, if erratic, industrialization of the Russian economy in the late nineteenth century had made substantial progress by the eve of World War I, and that progress ultimately gave the Bolsheviks a solid base upon which to build, once they brought the revolution, civil war, armed intervention, and famine under control. Any new government would have faced economic chaos for a few years; the Bolsheviks under Lenin proved no exception.

These extenuating circumstances, however, were not admitted by the business community in the United States immediately following the war or later in the 1920s. Business spokesmen did not try to analyze or understand Soviet economic disintegration, but simply used it as a contrast to bolster their own particular ideological position. Because of a basic lack of understanding of bolshevism or communism as a social and political, as well as economic, system (and because the Soviet Union did not begin to appear economically sound until much later in the decade), Russia's political system was more seriously criticized before 1920 than was its economic philosophy, which was usually summarily dismissed as an obvious failure.[8]

---

7. Herbert Hoover, "What Thinking Men Are Saying," *The Magazine of Wall Street* 25 (December 27, 1919): 191; Hoover, address delivered September 16, 1919, Speeches and Addresses, 1915–1923, Hoover Papers, Stanford University.

8. Lovenstein, *American Opinion*, p. 47.

Therefore, the Bolshevik experiment represented a serious ideological threat to the American way of life; it was essentially a rebellion that challenged liberal democracy's tenets about property rights, individual liberty, nationalism, representative government, and even traditional diplomatic procedure.[9] The U.S. business community, along with the U.S. Government and the Allies in general, found itself forced to defend the *status quo* in the face of what appeared to be the rapid spread of bolshevism in western Europe immediately following World War I. So from a naïve optimism for the democratic future of Russia, American businessmen turned to an equally naïve defense of democracy and capitalism. Russia's withdrawal from the war under Bolshevik leadership and its later repudiation of all debts contracted by the tsarist regime further increased businessmen's suspicion of "pandoric" Russia. Only privately did a few members of the business world assume any hopeful view of the Russian situation between 1918 and 1920. Publicly, most businessmen routinely predicted, especially before the Armistice, that the war would actually destroy Soviet socialism.[10]

Business journals also quite confidently forecast that the Soviet government could not last, both because the majority of the Russian people were opposed to it and because it was a proven economic failure. According to this line of thought, once the Bolsheviks were overthrown, Russia would realize her latent democratic and capitalistic predilections and in addition would become a "vast potential market" for raw materials and investments.[11] Aside from these few optimistic convictions about Russia's distant future, business comments on Russia were primarily negative and ill informed between 1918 and 1920. The Red Scare of 1919–1920, while greatly aggravating criticism and fear of bolshevism, did nothing to change or improve the basic arguments against it.

Not only was bolshevism never clearly defined by the

9. See Chapter II and Herbert Hoover, *American Individualism*.

10. *The Wall Street Journal*, March 18, 1918, p. 1; *Pacific Banker*, March 30, 1918, p. 1; *Iron Age* 102 (August 15, 1918): 402.

11. See Chapter II and Lovenstein, *American Opinion*, pp. 13–14, 47.

business community, but also it was associated with anything and everything deemed incompatible with traditional American ideals as they were then embodied in the business creed. For example, Bolsheviks at one time or another were described as mad dogs, rats, anarchists, thieves (especially after the nationalization decree), fanatics, cowards, traitors, insidious propagandists, tyrants, reactionaries, murderers, pacifists, liars, and—perhaps worst of all—subversive internationalists. At the same time, the ideology of bolshevism was characterized as a theory opposed to Western civilization, as the key to all postwar European political and economic instability, as a threat that was un-American, impractical, unworkable, utopian, and, most significantly, as a contagious disease.

To stop the spreading sickness of bolshevism U.S. businessmen generally agreed by 1920 that the answer was, most simply, a "bread and butter" cure.[12] The business community predicted and believed, using arguments very similar to later ones favoring the Marshall Plan, that the United States could take positive and effective action against bolshevism by helping Europe recover economic stability. Unemployed populations, inflated currencies, and war-ravaged industries, as well as the general postwar uncertainty caused by the delay in negotiating the treaty and the lengthy debate over ratification in the United States, were cited as catalysts for social and economic discontent in Europe. This discontent created an atmosphere in which Bolshevik propaganda techniques were most successful.

The "bread and butter" solution seemed an easy and sure one in the years 1918 to 1920. It consisted of relief aid to Europe's starving populations, to be supplemented first by short-term credit and later by long-term loans and investments. By putting Europe in a better economic position (and incidentally by quickly settling the ratification dispute in this country), the ideological threat of bolshevism would assured-

12. *The Wall Street Journal*, November 13, 1918, p. 1. *The Magazine of Wall Street* 24 (June 21, 1919): 383; 25 (November 29, 1919): 6. *Nation's Business* 7 (March 1920): 12; *Pacific Banker*, July 6, 1922, p. 1; William Diamond, *The Economic Thought of Woodrow Wilson*, pp. 177–78.

ly be removed, according to this thesis. Hoover bluntly stated the solution in relation to U.S. economic self-interest:

> I do not believe that we can, with such a surplus of bread-stuffs in our hands, sit down in the U.S. and see millions of people starve merely because we exact cash instead of credit. Unless we take some immediate action in the matter we shall have a breakdown of stable government in Central Europe. If we look at it from the most selfish point of view of our own future interests we cannot expect to have peace and a recuperation of the world if we allow the creation of another cesspool like Russia.[13]

That "bread and butter" might not be sufficient to wipe out the contagion of bolshevism was not seriously considered by the business community in years immediately following the war. In fact, in addition to propounding it as an aid to Europe, Hoover and others in business and the Government also promoted the concept as a panacea for all of Russia's internal problems. Thus, while Russian relief had been discussed in vain at the Paris Peace Conference, it was finally undertaken unilaterally by the United States between 1921 and 1924 as a cure for revolution. Among businessmen, Russian relief was a popular substitute for two unacceptable choices, namely, recognition of, or armed intervention against, the Communists. Although Hoover and other business and Government leaders quickly perceived the limitation of the relief approach from a pragmatic, if not ideological, point of view, rank-and-file businessmen did not realize the limitation until the 1929 Depression.[14] By that time they thought of the Red Scare as no more than a dim disagreeable memory. Moreover, they knew that the Communists had not succeeded in taking over any major European country since World War I. Finally, they were then aware that trade possibilities with the Soviet Union were greater than any time before or after World War I.

By 1929, therefore, many of the views held by a majority of businessmen between 1918 and 1920 concerning Russia

13. Hoover, "What Thinking Men Are Saying," p. 191.
14. J. Thompson, *Russia and the Versailles Peace*, pp. 222–67; Filene, *Americans and the Soviet Experiment*, pp. 75–82; Farnsworth, *Bullitt and the Soviet Union*, pp. 47–54. See Chapter II for Hoover's views on Russian relief.

had changed or were in the process of changing because the Soviet Union was beginning to emerge as an economic, as well as a political, reality. And as the complexity of Soviet development slowly revealed itself to the businessmen of the late 1920s, the "bread and butter" cure so confidently espoused earlier no longer seemed to fit the disease—a disease that had become chronic, rather than curable, and that had gained strength and respectability in the process. As a result, people in business circles increasingly questioned the original economic assumptions of the nonrecognition policy, but as subsequent chapters indicate, they did not subject the original ideological assumptions supporting nonrecognition to the same pragmatic scrutiny.

Ultimately this discrepancy between U.S. economic and ideological views of the USSR misled Soviet officials, who had originally initiated commercial contacts with the United States following World War I in the hope that the USSR would obtain diplomatic recognition in the process of participating in trade. There were also other reasons for this consistent Soviet desire for improved economic relations with the United States in particular. First, U.S. goods were considered of better quality.[15] Also, the United States represented a greater potential source of capital and credit than Germany, France, England, and Japan combined.[16]

While these were immediate and practical considerations, there was still another fundamental reason for the many postwar Russian attempts to establish substantial economic contact with the United States. It was a somewhat abstract notion often expressed by Soviet officials and by Russian sympathizers in the United States but seldom acknowledged by anti-Soviet businessmen or the U.S. Government. It was, as Lenin is reported to have said to Armand Hammer, a U.S. concessionaire in Russia, a desire to come into contact with

15. Louis Fischer, *Why Recognize Russia?* p. 149; Elisha M. Friedman, *Russia in Transition: A Business Man's Appraisal,* p. 305; Calvin B. Hoover, *The Economic Life of Soviet Russia,* p. 166.

16. Hopper (Hamburg) to State Department, March 24, 1923, U.S. Department of State, Records Relating to Internal Affairs of Russia and the Soviet Union, Record Group 59, File 861.63/40; Armand Hammer, *The Quest for the Romanoff Treasure,* p. 63.

the material and pragmatic achievements of the American experience in the New World. "This is what Progress means," he exclaimed to Hammer in 1921, "building, inventions, machines, development of mechanical aids to human hands. Russia today is like your country was in the pioneering stage. *We need the knowledge and spirit that have made America what she is today.* [Emphasis added.]"[17]

This desire and need of the Russians not only to acquire U.S. recognition, goods, and credit, but also to come into contact with the technical superiority and materialistic mentality of the American people, was recognized in U.S. articles and books that favored either greater commercial contact between the two countries or outright recognition of the USSR. Such works also had other themes in common, such as the similar geographic and climatic features shared by the United States and the Soviet Union. One of the earliest public business acknowledgements of the physical similarities between the two countries and of Soviet dependence upon U.S. technology can be found in *Iron Age*. In a July 1926 article, Stewart McCulloch Marshall, a consulting engineer, stated that because the United States and Russia had similar geographic and demographic problems, "American practices in railroad and industries . . . are perfectly adaptable to Russian conditions." Later that same year at the National Association of Manufacturers convention, in a discussion concerning Russian trade a New York businessman asserted that more than U.S. money, the Russians needed "good advice . . . American brains, American experience, [and] American engineering knowledge."[18]

Another indication of the Russians' general underlying interest in the United States can be found in the popularity of what the Russians called "Fordismus" or "Fordizatsia." These terms referred to assembly-line production and mass distribution. Both concepts were eagerly being accepted and praised in Russia by 1926 and 1927, according to *The New*

17. Hammer, *Quest*, p. 62. For details about the technological aid the Soviets obtained from the United States, see Anthony C. Sutton, *Western Technology and Soviet Economic Development*, Vol. 1, *1917 to 1930*.

18. *Iron Age* 118 (July 1, 1926): 3; National Association of Manufacturers, *Proceedings*, October 6, 1926, p. 39.

York Times, and Ford's *My Life and Work* and *Today and Tomorrow* were in popular Russian translations by 1927.[19] Bernard Knollenberg, a New York attorney, may have exaggerated only slightly when he wrote in *Nation's Business* for April 1930 that the Soviets admired anything "American-sky" to the extent that "if Lenin is Russia's God today, Ford is its St. Peter."[20] During World War II the president of the Chamber of Commerce of the United States confirmed in retrospect this trend, so evident in the Soviet Union in the 1920s, when he said, "The Russians have a great desire for co-operation with America; they almost revere production, and to them America signifies production . . . [and so] they want to imitate America especially with regard to her standard of living."[21]

By the early 1930s many statements had appeared in U.S. writings that noted the Soviets' conscious emulation of U.S. industrial attitudes and techniques and the common belief the two nations had in "the Future of the Machine Age."[22] Contemporary statements also described other similarities. James D. Mooney, a vice-president of General Motors, talked about a most abstract kind of similarity after returning from a visit to the USSR in 1930. "The two countries," he said, "both have broad horizons that induce a vision of the future;

19. Allan Nevins and Frank Ernest Hill, *Ford,* Vol. 2, *Expansion and Challenge, 1915–1933,* pp. 601, 603–4, 673, 682n. 2; Dorothy Thompson, *The New Russia,* p. 163. See Chapter IV and Appendix C for details of Ford's activities in Russia.

20. *Nation's Business* 18 (April 1930): 266; Hammer, *Quest,* pp. 104–5. Hammer points out that Ford was temporarily unpopular among Soviet leaders in the early 1920s because of his proclaimed antisemitism. Also see Stetson (Warsaw) to State Department, July 29, 1926, U.S. Department of State, Records Relating to Internal Affairs of Russia and the Soviet Union, Record Group 59, File 861.008/429.

21. Quoted in Hans Heymann, *We Can Do Business with Russia,* p. ix.

22. Gerhard Dobbert, *Red Economics,* pp. 282, 319; Thomas D. Campbell, *Russia: Market or Menace?* p. 147; C. B. Hoover, *Economic Life,* p. 166; Hammer, *Quest,* p. 62; Heymann, *We Can Do Business,* p. 220; D. Thompson, *New Russia,* pp. 160, 165, 169; Samuel Haber, *Efficiency and Uplift,* pp. 150–59. Haber confirms U.S. Socialist, as well as Soviet, interest in the scientific management techniques of the Taylorites in the early 1920s.

neither of us is afraid to work or to take a chance." U.S. engineers in Russia were also attracted by the hard-working nature of Soviet officials and the "work ethic" that seemed to prevail under the First Five-Year Plan. By the end of the decade U.S. engineers tended to ignore the political and social aspects of communism and simplistically to equate the industrial goals of the Soviets with the aims of scientific management in a capitalist system.[23]

The most commonly cited similarities, however, remained the climate, the large population, the vast territorial expanse that encompassed a single free-trade zone, the great natural wealth, the lack of imperialistic designs, the desire for peace, and the suspicion of Japan's intentions in the Far East.[24] What was not usually admitted or recognized by those Americans who favorably compared the two nations was that some of these common characteristics might well promote serious competition in the future.

U.S. businessmen even occasionally acknowledged, albeit grudgingly, that capitalism and communism were very much alike in certain respects. According to Virgil Jordan, president of the National Industrial Conference Board in 1933, the Soviet Union was

> the most capitalistic country in the world because it spends a larger part of its working energy in creating the means of production, and it has put itself under a spartan communist regimentation in order to compel its people to consume less and save more. In fact the communism of Russia in its deepest sense is merely an expression of its intense determination to make itself more capitalistic, for in view of the Oriental temperament of its people it could never persuade them to make the sacrifice necessary to accumulate capital rapidly otherwise than by subjecting them to arbitrary and

23. *The New York Times*, October 8, 1930, p. 11; Stuart Chase, *The Nemesis of American Business and Other Essays*, pp. 172–73; Lewis S. Feuer, "American Travelers to the Soviet Union, 1917–1932: The Formation of a Component of New Deal Ideology," *American Quarterly* 14 (Summer 1962): 136–43. For further details about the attitudes of U.S. engineers working in the Soviet Union, see Chapter V.

24. Fischer, *Why Recognize?* pp. 150–51; Friedman, *Russia in Transition*, pp. 250–53; Dobbert, *Red Economics*, p. 324; Hammer, *Quest*, p. 234; Alcan Hirsch, *Industrialized Russia*, p. 263.

tyrannical discipline. When you look at the problem in this light, it appears that one reason—perhaps the main reason —why Russia has suffered relatively less severely during this depression is that she has been so much more capitalistic than the 'capitalistic' countries . . . because in this country . . . [the] slowing up of saving and real investment beginning as early as 1925 was in my opinion one of the deep-seated sources of the depression.[25]

Although this statement was an exaggeration resulting from frustration and disappointment over the Depression, the idea that capitalism and communism were similar or virtually the same had been expressed earlier by Senator Borah, *Nation's Business, Iron Age,* and even Herbert Hoover.[26] The uncommon business argument was that communism resembled capitalism because the Communist state was a "gigantic corporation" in which all working citizens were considered stockholders. Communism was also sometimes described by U.S. businessmen as capitalism "enormously magnified," the "most extreme type" of capitalism in which the government ended up being the only capitalist. Comparisons of monopoly capitalism with state socialism have become much more common in recent years.[27]

Socialists or Communists, on the other hand, often drew very different conclusions after recognizing these same kinds of similarities. Anna Louise Strong pointed out in a foreword to one of Lenin's works that "socialism itself can only succeed if it produces wealth more efficiently than capitalism." This same idea was stated much more bluntly by a young Bolshevik who supposedly told Dorothy Thompson, "Russia will be more efficient as a producing mechanism than America, because there is not so much waste in our system. Here everything is controlled; everything is planned. We will not

25. *Journal of the American Bankers Association* 26 (December 1933): 64.

26. *The Wall Street Journal,* January 8, 1925, p. 1. *Nation's Business* 15 (January 1927): 46; 15 (October 1927): 60; 18 (January 1930): 12. *Iron Age* 107 (March 31, 1921): 881; Filene, *Americans and the Soviet Experiment,* p. 109.

27. *Iron Age* 107 (March 31, 1921): 881; Campbell, *Russia,* p. 46; George Lichtheim, "What Socialism Is and Is Not," *New York Review of Books,* April 9, 1970, pp. 41–45; Hannah Arendt, "Thoughts on Politics and Revolution," *New York Review of Books,* April 22, 1971, p. 8 ff.

overproduce here, underproduce there, but everything will be regulated. That is why, in the end we will *beat you at your own game.* [Thompson's italics.]" Perhaps Stalin's interpretation of the similarities between capitalism and communism most succinctly sums up the Soviet point of view: "The union of the Russian revolutionary spirit with the American practical spirit," according to Stalin, was "the essence of practical Leninism."[28]

These admissions of the similarities between capitalism and communism were not completely accepted throughout the U.S. business community by the time recognition was granted to the Soviet regime in 1933. Indeed, the statements in business journals in defense of capitalism that stressed its unique features, particularly the idea that economic cooperation between government and business and between different firms did not in any way resemble socialism or communism, were much more prevalent before 1933 than were statements pointing up the similarities between capitalism and communism. Nevertheless, the common economic features of the two systems were on occasion expressed and can be considered that part of the business rhetoric between 1920 and 1933 that helped to clear the way for U.S. businessmen's acceptance of recognition for practical, rather than ideological, reasons. In the long run, however, such statements on the part of a minority of poorly organized businessmen and certain Russian sympathizers would not have had even this marginal influence upon the general business community if they had not been accompanied by increased trade with the Soviet Union during the second half of the 1920s.

28. Anna Louise Strong, quoted in Haber, *Efficiency and Uplift*, p. 151; Stalin, quoted in D. Thompson, *New Russia*, pp. 166, 168.

II

RATIONALIZATIONS: VIEWS OF
HERBERT HOOVER AND
CHARLES EVANS HUGHES

The two most important Russian problems that concerned the U.S. business community immediately following the war and during the 1920s were the related issues of diplomatic relations and trade relations with the new Soviet regime. Although trade between the two countries steadily increased, very few U.S. businessmen advocated recognition of Russia during the years 1918 to 1932. This strong and consistent opposition to Soviet rule was in keeping with the confused and unenlightened business attitudes toward bolshevism already described. It was also completely in accord with the United States Government's refusal to grant recognition first to the Russian Soviet Federated Socialist Republic and later to the Union of Soviet Socialist Republics when it was formed in 1922. The business community did not, however, play a significant role either in formulating the initial nonrecognition policy or in bringing about formal diplomatic relations in 1933, when that policy was abruptly changed by Franklin Delano Roosevelt.

The original policy of nonrecognition remained essentially the same under the administrations of Wilson, Harding, Coolidge, and Hoover, although it did become more rigidly institutionalized within bureaucratic circles over the years. Unofficially expressed as early as December 4, 1917, in a memorandum by Secretary of State Robert Lansing to President Wilson, nonrecognition was not officially proclaimed until August 10, 1920, in a statement by Lansing's successor, Secretary of State Bainbridge Colby, to the Italian Ambassador to the United States, Baron Camillo Avezzana. While the famous "Colby Note" was later elaborated upon, it remained the basic statement of policy throughout the 1920s. Basically, it stressed the friendliness of the United States for the Russian people, as distinguished from their leaders, and expressed faith in their ability to "overcome the existing anarchy, suffering and destitution" that they were experiencing.

The nonrecognition policy on the part of the United States, the note went on to insist, had "nothing to do with any particular political or social structure" that the Russian people might adopt; nonrecognition stemmed from the belief that "the existing regime in Russia is based upon the negation of every principle of honor and good faith and every usage and convention underlying the whole structure of international law—the negation, in short, of every principle upon which it is possible to base harmonious and trustful relations." Under such circumstances the United States could not see "any common ground upon which it can stand with a power whose conceptions of international relations are so alien to its own, so utterly repugnant to its moral sense." The note also opposed the dismemberment of Russia by specifically reaffirming that the United States did not intend to recognize the independence of the "so-called Republics of Georgia and Azerbaijan" because this violated the "territorial integrity and true boundaries . . . of the former Russian Empire."[1]

The ideological base for nonrecognition was laid with this document. Especially important was that portion of the statement objecting to the "alienation of Russian territory." That this position was devised and defended by the Demo-

1. Bainbridge Colby to Baron Camillo Avezzana, August 10, 1920, *FRP: 1920*, 3: 463–68; Daniel M. Smith, *Aftermath of War: Bainbridge Colby and Wilsonian Diplomacy, 1920–1921*, pp. 55–71; Robert Lansing, *War Memoirs*, pp. 343–44. After the November 1917 revolution, Secretary Lansing was much more convinced than Col. Edward M. House that bolshevism represented a serious ideological threat to U.S. liberalism, capitalism, and nationalism. His success in convincing President Wilson of this threat presaged the strong ideological overtones of the Colby Note, even though Lansing was out of office when it was drafted. For details of the differences between Lansing and House on Russian policy and of their respective influence on Wilson, see N. Gordon Levin, Jr., *Woodrow Wilson and World Politics: America's Response to War and Revolution*, pp. 57–73.

crats is somewhat surprising, because it clearly violated Wilson's proclamations on self-determination. Although the United States probably would not have protected the boundaries of formerly tsarist Russia with military force, the principle contained in this section of the Colby Note was extremely significant because it was based on practical strategic diplomatic arguments, as well as impractical ideological ones. The policy is, therefore, one of the first examples of modern diplomacy following the First World War.

The major practical reasons for the U.S. stand against the dismemberment of the Russian Empire at the beginning of 1918 were largely influenced by the following wartime considerations: the conviction that self-determination would further weaken Russia's fighting capabilities; the fear that the Allies, in particular France and England, intended to divide Russia into respective spheres of influence; the suspicion that Germany had encouraged the peoples along Russia's western border to proclaim their independence in order to create a "chain of vassal states . . . as a means of establishing economic control over Russia"; the desire to neutralize Japan's expansionist designs in Siberia and Sakhalin; and the view that, because no one group could claim to represent all of Russia and because Bolshevik rule was unacceptable, the most expedient policy for the duration of the war seemed to be to wait and continue to recognize the defunct Provisional Government, since the demise of the Communist regime was inevitable anyway.

Ideological opposition to dismemberment was self-evident. Since the Bolsheviks had come out in favor of independence for nations formerly within the Russian Empire, the United States could not agree, even though the Wilsonian principle of self-determination might well be the victim of such opposition. Accordingly, Secretary of State Lansing had told Wilson that the Bolshevik policy of allowing every community to become independent meant "international anarchy," citing, among other things, the specious example of the Federal Government's position during the American Civil War to justify his position. In the long run, ideological considerations against dismemberment outweighed the practical diplomatic ones, because once these questions of wartime strategy no longer existed, the United States clung to the idea of not alienating Russian territory.[2]

The business community supported this portion of the Colby Note because it shared with the Government two assumptions about Russia. One was that the refusal to agree to the territorial dismemberment of Russia would prevent the Bolshevik regime from making a false appeal to Russian nationalism. The other was that the protection of the Russian people "from invasion and territorial violation" would hasten the day of their inevitable revolt against Communist tyranny and thus earn the United States their future gratitude and, it was hoped, trade. Russia was to be preserved intact in order that it could later be brought into the fold of democracy and capitalism. Anticipation of future commercial expansion, then, as well as sociopolitical values, characterized business and governmental opposition to the partitioning of Russia following the First World War.[3]

In retrospect it appears quite probable that, if the United States had recognized only the small European portion of Russia actually controlled by the Bolsheviks in 1920 and if it had actively encouraged the establishment of non-Communist regimes elsewhere, the revolutionaries might ultimately have been deprived of valuable natural resources and might have been contained by a host of new, antipathetical

2. Claude E. Fike, "The United States and Russian Territorial Problems, 1917–1920," *The Historian* 24 (May 1962): 331–46. A selective group of states formerly located in the Russian empire was recognized by the United States in the 1920s, but the non-dismemberment principle of the Colby Note was not formally renounced until the spring of 1933. See Edgar B. Nixon, *Franklin D. Roosevelt and Foreign Affairs*, Vol. 1, *January 1933–February 1934*, pp. 53–54. By that time, however, ideological opposition to the Soviet regime was so ingrained in U.S. policy that not even recognition could modify it.

3. American-Russian Chamber of Commerce policy statement, December 23, 1920, U.S. Department of State, General Records, Record Group 59, File 661.1115/315; *The Annalist* 17 (March 7, 1921): 299. *Bradstreet's* 48 (August 14, 1920): 529; 48 (August 28, 1920): 560; 48 (October 9, 1920): 656. Levin, *Wilson and World Politics*, pp. 3, 13–15, 197, 219; Ronald Radosh, *American Labor and United States Foreign Policy*, pp. 241–44, 250.

neighbor states. By ideologically holding out for an entirely democratic, capitalistic Russia, the United States pursued a policy that resulted in the loss of the entire nation to Western political and economic traditions. At the time, however, Wilson and Colby were advised to oppose dismemberment and recognition of Bolshevik control of part of Russia by men with such different points of view and backgrounds as the business internationalist Norman H. Davis and the re- pentant ex-Socialist John Spargo. In fact, all of the major principles set forth in the Colby Note were recommended by these two men. It was Spargo's draft, however, that Secretary of State Colby incorporated almost verbatim into his state- ment.[4]

The Colby Note did not specifically mention trade, Bol- shevik repudiation of tsarist debts, or the nationalization of property after the November Revolution, but Government officials and businessmen did cite these economic issues when they defended the policy of nonrecognition and criticized the Communist experiment in Russia. Nevertheless, by not officially stressing economics, the Colby Note left the door open for future trade relations without formal recognition. This has since become a common characteristic of modern ideological diplomacy. Instead of relying exclusively on specific economic arguments to support nonrecognition, Gov- ernment officials said that trade was not affected by diplo- matic status and used primarily broad ideological arguments against recognition for the next sixteen years.

This basic ideological approach, established under Wilson, was institutionalized by succeeding Republican administra- tions of the 1920s and figured prominently in the Democratic negotiations leading to recognition in 1933. Originally, it also perfectly mirrored a questionable diplomatic concept that had strongly emerged during the war. The major tenet of the concept was that "international intercourse was impos-

---

4. Fike, "The United States and Russian Territorial Problems," pp. 333–34, 345–46; Norman H. Davis to Colby, August 7, 1920, Box 8, Davis to John Spargo, August 12, 1920, Box 53, Davis Papers; Ronald Radosh, "John Spargo and Wilson's Russian Pol- icy, 1920," *Journal of American History* 52 (December 1965): 548–65. The only section of Spargo's draft that Colby chose not to include in his note was the one against trading with the Soviets.

sible between nations of radically different ideologies." As Norman Davis told Colby, "It is utterly impossible for two systems based on such diametrically opposed principles to work in peace and harmony."[5]

Herbert Hoover and Charles Evans Hughes elaborated upon both the economic and the ideological implications of the Colby Note immediately upon taking office. For example, on March 21, 1921, Secretary of Commerce Hoover issued a widely publicized and extremely influential press release about relations with Russia. In it he unequivocally maintained that the exchange of goods between the two countries was limited by the entire philosophy of communism, not by any policy on the part of the United States. At the same time he specifically called upon the Bolsheviks to abandon "their present economic situation." Hoover explained that no normal commercial relations based on credit could develop with Russia "under a government that repudiates private property." Further, no moderation of communism by the Bolsheviks would bring about a "real return to production in Russia," and production was the key to recovery. Speaking specifically to inquiries that he, as Secretary of Commerce, had received from foreign trade associations in the United States, he emphasized that trade with the Bolsheviks was limited to their current gold reserves and, in the absence of internal production, these would not expand. Estimating these reserves at anywhere from $60,000,000 to $200,000,000, he concluded that even if Americans traded their commodi-

---

5. Davis to Colby, August 7, 1920, Box 8, Davis Papers; Christopher Lasch, *The American Liberals and the Russian Revolution*, p. 218. According to Lasch, "It was not only with regard to relations with Russia that Americans were misled by this peculiar conception of international affairs. The converse of this proposition—that just as opposite ideologies repelled, similar ideologies attracted each other—was responsible in the early years of the war for the fear of a rapprochement between militaristic Germany and Tsarist Russia. . . . It followed from this premise . . . that if Tsarist Russia was irresistibly attracted to Germany, revolutionary Russia would be as irresistibly repelled by her. . . . All of these attitudes toward revolution originated in the assumption that the ideological alignment of a nation dictated its foreign policy. Since these attitudes, in one form or another, persisted for decades, the importance of the original assumption can hardly be exaggerated."

ties for "this parcel of gold," Russia's production would not be improved, for improvement required the abandonment of all aspects of communism, not simply its economic manifestations. An inconclusive survey conducted by the Commerce Department on April 4 indicated that 26 newspapers across the country had commented favorably on Hoover's March 21 policy statement while 17 had not. More significant was the endorsement it received from a group of prominent citizens on March 25, including such businessmen as the presidents of the U.S. Steel Corporation, the National City Bank, the Baltimore and Ohio Railway Company, in addition to the president of the Carnegie Institute, the former president of Harvard University, the entire executive board of the International Longshoremen's Association, and the American Legion Committee on Anti-American Activities.[6]

This press release clearly indicates the predominance of ideology in Hoover's view of Soviet Russia. Within a year he was writing in his *American Individualism* that communism was a "social philosophy" that challenged "the physical and spiritual forces of America." *American Individualism* was Hoover's attempt to present in outline form a socioeconomic philosophy for the United States that could counter the various ideologies he saw emerging in Europe. In particular he envisaged using this American ideology abroad to counter Bolshevik propaganda. It was not that he feared the spread of bolshevism to the United States—he had made this clear to Woodrow Wilson as early as March 1919—but he was convinced of the potential impact of bolshevism in Europe, "where the gulf between the middle classes and the lower classes is large, and where the lower classes have been kept in ignorance and distress." Under these conditions, Hoover believed, Communist propaganda would be most effective and "do violence to normal democratic development." Therefore the United States could not "even remotely" recognize "this tyranny that is the negation of democracy . . . without stimulating actionist [*sic*] radicalism in every country in

6. For the endorsement, the complete text of Hoover's press release, and the department's survey, see Russian File, Official File, Herbert Hoover Commerce Department Papers (hereafter cited as HHCD), Herbert Hoover Presidential Library; *The New York Times*, March 25, 1921, p. 2.

Europe and without transgressing on every National ideal of our own."[7]

Hoover's sophisticated analysis of the receptivity to bolshevism of people living in countries where there was a great difference between the living standards of the lower and upper classes was matched by his protests against interference with the civil liberties of Communists, as well as other radical groups, during the height of the Red Scare from 1919 to 1920. Although he tried to discredit pro-Soviet groups in the United States, he did not simplistically blame the Bolsheviks for labor unrest in the United States during the immediate postwar years of nationalistic hysteria and depression. Instead, he admonished the leading Red-hunter of the Wilson administration, Attorney General A. Mitchell Palmer, that his "policemen could not overtake an economic force allowed to run riot in the country."[8] Yet he remained convinced of the necessity to promulgate an American ideology because bolshevism, more than of the other foreign ideologies, threatened the traditional American concepts of individualism, materialism, private property, mobility, frontier neighborliness, equality of opportunity, competition, democracy, and economic expansion abroad. Most important, he instilled this point of view throughout every division of the Department of Commerce, especially during his first years in Harding's cabinet when he directed the activities of the American Relief Administration (ARA) in Russia.

Hoover saw no contradiction between his ideological denunciation of bolshevism and his support for Russian relief programs during the Paris Peace Conference and his first two

7. Herbert Hoover, *American Individualism*, pp. 1–13; Hoover to Wilson, March 28, 1919, Herbert Hoover Pre-Commerce Papers (hereafter cited as HHPC), Herbert Hoover Presidential Library.

8. Edwin T. Layton, "The American Engineering Profession and the Idea of Social Responsibility" (Ph.D. dissertation, University of California, Los Angeles, 1956), p. 170; Hoover, press release, "Views of Bolshevism," April 25, 1919, 19-Herbert Hoover Public Statements (hereafter cited as HHPS), Herbert Hoover Presidential Library; Benjamin M. Weissman, "The American Relief Administration in Russia, 1921–1923: A Case Study in the Interaction Between Opposing Political Systems" (Ph.D. dissertation, Columbia University, 1968), pp. 252–55, 436–37.

years as Secretary of Commerce. In fact, he prided himself on being the "truest friend" of the Russian people because of these relief activities. Obviously, given the time and energy Hoover put into relief plans for Russia, they were important to him for many reasons—none of them devoid of economic and ideological overtones. Beginning in March 1919 as Director General of the Inter-Allied Council for the Relief of Europe, he suggested to President Wilson "that some Neutral of international reputation for probity and ability . . . be allowed to create a second Belgian Relief Commission for Russia." Hoover not only made it clear that this offer did not constitute recognition, but he also attached several severe conditions to his original food-relief plan for Russia. They included the unilateral cessation by the Bolsheviks of "all militant action across certain defined boundaries" and of their "subsidizing of disturbances abroad" in order to "test out whether this is a militant force engrossed upon world domination." In April he drafted another version of this plan and included an additional requirement: control of the entire Russian transportation system by the neutral relief commission. The timing of both proposals completely undermined a much more lenient and less anti-Communist truce that William C. Bullitt, an emissary for the State Department, had worked out with the Bolsheviks. Although Hoover's suggestions, under the name of the Nansen Plan, were approved in Paris on April 9, 1919, by the Council of Four, they never went into effect, and he had to wait until he became Secretary of Commerce to coordinate an independent U.S. effort to send food supplies to destitute Russians—primarily children and the sick "without regard to race religion or political status."[9]

9. For varying accounts of Hoover's Russian relief activities, see Herbert Hoover's *Memoirs*, Vol. 1, *Years of Adventure*, pp. 411–20; Hoover to Wilson, March 28, 1919, HHPC; Lewis L. Straus, *Men and Decisions*, pp. 31–37; Radosh, *Labor and Foreign Policy*, pp. 253–61; Hoover to Hughes, December 6, 1921, *FRP: 1921*, 2: 788–89; William Appleman Williams, *American-Russian Relations, 1781–1947*, pp. 200–201; Levin, *Wilson and World Politics*, pp. 217–20; Peter G. Filene, *Americans and the Soviet Experiment, 1917–1933*, pp. 76–82, 135–38; Herbert Hoover, address to International Chamber of Commerce, May 15, 1922, 227-HHPS; Robert James Maddox, *William E. Borah*

All of Hoover's relief proposals for Russia caused much consternation among liberals and radicals in the United States, who correctly suspected that he had, on occasion, utilized food relief to aid foreign counter-revolutionary groups in Eastern Europe during the Armistice period. Indeed, after converting the ARA from an official government agency into a pseudo-private relief organization in April 1919, he proceeded to conclude an agreement with a representative of the White forces, which were fighting the Bolsheviks. Although Hoover had remained steadfastly against military intervention into the Russian Civil War, at no time did he oppose giving material assistance to counter-revolutionary groups. Moreover, by attaching conditions to the aid, such as release of all American prisoners, and restricting the activities of other relief agencies more favorably disposed toward the Bolsheviks, his relief work in Russia did not contradict his ideological opposition to communism. Relief was at best a temporary expedient to aid the Russian people until bolshevism disappeared and, like trade, was no substitute for restored production "based upon sound economics." Above all else, relief was not a prelude to recognition.[10]

In the long run, Hoover hoped that Russian relief would contribute to the downfall of the Bolshevik regime either by directly modifying economic policies under the NEP or at

and American Foreign Policy, p. 45; John M. Thompson, Russia, Bolshevism, and the Versailles Peace, pp. 232–33, 238, 247–60; The Bullitt Mission to Russia: Testimony before the Committee on Foreign Relations, United States Senate, of William C. Bullitt, pp. 39–43, 75–79; Weissman, "ARA in Russia," passim; "Agreement Between the American Relief Administration and the Russian Socialist Federative Soviet Republic (Riga Agreement)," August, 1921, Hoover to Walter Lyman Brown, August 9, 1921, transmitted by Hoover to Richard M. Nixon, December 27, 1956, Nixon Correspondence: 1950–1959, Herbert Hoover Post-Presidential Papers (hereafter cited as HHPPP), Herbert Hoover Presidential Library.

10. George W. Hopkins, "The Politics of Food: United States and Soviet Hungary, March–August, 1919," Mid-America 55 (October 1973): 245–70; "Special Agreement between the American Relief Administration and the Provisional Government of Russia," July 16, 1919, FRP: 1919, pp. 693–96; Weissman, "ARA in Russia," pp. 36–37, 51–56, 75–76, 107–9, 138–39, 180–81, 208–9, 263–64, 341–49, 354.

least by leaving a "lasting impression" of good will and efficiency; thus, it would lay the groundwork for future U.S.
leadership in the reconstruction of the Russian economy. In
the short run, he thought, Russian relief would effect the
return of American political prisoners and help to alleviate
the postwar agricultural depression in the United States. Both
sets of goals could be accomplished, according to Hoover,
without requiring the establishment of normal relations until
Soviet leaders brought their policies in line with acceptable
Western thought, as epitomized in his own version of corporate liberalism based on associational activity. In actuality
the experiment in Russian relief accomplished none of these
objectives, except the return of U.S. citizens held by Soviet
authorities. If anything, contrary to Hoover's arguments to
other members of Harding's Cabinet and to Congress, the
ARA served instead as a "factor in the reversal of the disas-
trous course of the Soviet economy in 1921–22 and in the
stabilization of Bolshevik rule."[11]

Nonetheless, the activities of the ARA in Russia are significant for what they reveal about Hoover's ability to enhance
unilaterally his own reputation and bureaucratic functions at
the expense of Congress and other branches of the Government, most notably the departments of State and the Treasury. As a result, a variety of interdepartmental struggles
ensued, making a coherent Russian policy difficult, if not
impossible, to formulate in the early 1920s. They also reveal
how Hoover was able, in this instance, to temper his ideological opposition to bolshevism and to use federal power and
appropriations to alleviate depressed farm prices and to carry
on humanitarian work inside Russia, even though the latter
called for direct negotiations, compromise, and contact with
the Soviets on a day-to-day basis. Without Hoover there
would have been no ARA functioning in Russia, and probably no other public figure of the period could have succeeded
as well in temporarily uniting such disparate groups across
the country behind what was simultaneously a self-aggrandiz-
ing, humanitarian, anti-Communist, anti-depression effort.

11. Weissman, "ARA in Russia," pp. 102–3, 109, 236–42, 414–
15, 450–52. Hoover himself later admitted that his relief activities
had contributed to "saving" bolshevism. See "Interview with
Henry C. Wolfe," in Herbert Hoover Oral History Program, p. 11.

That these groups were as far apart ideologically as the ultra-conservative National Civic Federation and the Communist front group, Friends of Soviet Russia (FSR), is a tribute to his organizational abilities, his public-relations techniques, and his curiously impersonal brand of humanitarian charisma. At the same time, his dealings with both of these organizations reveal the ways in which interest groups, even small and normally uninfluential ones like the FSR, exercised substantial influence on Hoover as he tried to phase out the ARA in 1923 because he was so concerned about keeping controversial ARA publicity in the United States to a minimum.[12]

Most members of the ARA staff, including Hoover, did not change their minds about recognition, and those few who did —like Col. William N. Haskell, Director of the ARA in Russia—were discouraged by him from making their prorecognition views known. Yet a number of those former ARA members who continued to oppose recognition were later employed by companies interested in renewing trade relations with the USSR—an early indication within the business community of a separation between economic and political foreign policy where the Soviet Union was concerned. This separation is even reflected in the slight modification that took place in Hoover's hostility toward commercial relations with the Soviets as a result of his Soviet food-relief experience.[13]

Initially, his ideological opposition to the Soviet system was so strong that he sometimes suspected all commercial propositions from Russia of being nothing more than propaganda tactics aimed at obtaining recognition. When Hoover first became Secretary of Commerce, for example, he characterized those U.S. businessmen who wanted to obtain concessions in Russia as "would-be exploiters" of the Russian people. During the second year of ARA operations, however, he recommended to Secretary of State Hughes that the

12. For details, see Weissman, "ARA in Russia," pp. 26, 79–82, 109, 161–70, 179–80, 234–44, 248–57, 263–64, 337–49, 415, 434–38. Joan Hoff Wilson, *Herbert Clark Hoover: Forgotten Progressive*, chaps. 2, 4; Craig Lloyd, "Aggressive Introvert: A Study of Herbert Hoover and Public Relations Management, 1912–1932" (Ph.D. dissertation, University of Iowa, 1970), *passim*.

13. Weissman, "ARA in Russia," pp. 96–97, 311, 340, 410–18.

United States admit a trade representative into the country and issued a press release containing a highly qualified statement about opening up trade relations with the Soviets. He further modified his original opposition to trade in the course of the decade but recalled in his memoirs that he continued to consider the Soviet Union a "wicked and disgraceful neighbor."[14]

As Secretary of Commerce and later as President, Hoover consistently asserted and defended an ideological U.S. foreign policy, but his rhetoric became so exaggerated in the case of the USSR that it appeared to contradict his general goal of controlled trade expansion for the United States. In 1926, for example, he announced that the country was further away from recognizing Russia than ever before, despite the improvement in trade relations. His books, his campaign statements in 1928 and 1932, and his press releases immediately following recognition in 1933 and still later after World War II, if taken at their face value, seem to indicate no change in his original anti-Communist sentiments.[15] In fact, however, as

14. Hoover, address to International Chamber of Commerce, May 15, 1922, 227-HHPS; E. Dana Durand (chief, Eastern European Division, BFDC) to editor of *New Republic*, June 5, 1922, Hoover to Senator Joseph S. Frelinghuysen, June 17, 1922, Russian File, HHCD; Weissman, "ARA in Russia," pp. 96–97, 311–12, 340; Herbert Hoover, *Memoirs,* Vol. 2, *The Cabinet and the Presidency, 1920–1933,* pp. 27, 182; Hoover, *Memoirs,* Vol. 3, *The Great Depression, 1929–1941,* pp. 360–61.

15. Joseph Brandes, *Herbert Hoover and Economic Diplomacy: Department of Commerce Policy, 1921–1928,* p. 180; Williams, *American-Russian Relations,* p. 181; Herbert Hoover, press conference, June 19, 1926, Russian File, HHCD; William R. Castle, Jr. (Under-Secretary of State) to Hoover, August 17, 1932 (with suggested press release), Hoover to Castle, November 15, 1933 (including undated press release), Castle Papers; Hoover, *American Individualism,* pp. 1–13; Hoover, *The Challenge to Liberty,* pp. 1–22, 49–75; Hoover, *The New Day: Campaign Speeches of Herbert Hoover, 1928,* pp. 41–42, 84, 154, 167; Hoover, *Campaign Speeches of 1932,* pp. 167–74; Hoover, *A Cause to Win: Five Speeches on American Foreign Policy in Relation to Soviet Russia.* For details of Hoover's views on U.S. economic expansion, his role as an ideologue, and his evolving views on communism after 1933, see Joan Hoff Wilson, *American Business and Foreign Policy, 1920–1933,* pp. 87–122, 162–67, 171–218; Wilson, *Hoover,* chaps. 2 and 8.

the economic viability of the USSR became an indisputable fact between 1923 and 1933, Hoover's many public statements against recognition and communism itself, if analyzed closely in terms of both language and action recommended or taken, often exhibited an excessive rhetorical commitment to an ideological position, rather than practical or effective guides to action. Moreover, close analysis of the language reveals not only a great discrepancy at times between public thought and private action, but also a significant modification of his antitrade position.

Nonetheless, Hoover's exaggerated ideological opposition to the Soviets did affect the formulation of foreign policy. Probably the most debilitating feature of such rhetoric was its tendency to seem more credible in times of crisis and to limit both his diplomatic and domestic options in such confused times as the first years of the Depression of 1929. His role as an ideologue also negatively affected Hoover's usually efficient and pragmatic approach to economic foreign policy where the USSR was concerned. Finally, given the influential positions that he occupied in the Government from 1918 to 1933, Hoover was often able to impose his own ideological point of view on other Washington officials.

One of the first manifestations of Hoover's early dominance over Russian policy can be found in the statements made by Secretary of State Hughes on March 25 and April 5, 1921. They simply echoed the strong economic and ideological objections to the Soviet regime that Hoover had stated in his March 21 press release. Clearly, the Secretary of Commerce had co-opted the role of spokesman for official United States policy on Russian relations. With minor objections from the Secretary of State, this situation was to continue through 1923, when ARA operations in Russia ended.[16] Accordingly,

16. Hoover apparently released his statement somewhat precipitously because he wrote to Hughes on March 23, 1921, apologizing for the press's assumption that he was proclaiming the official position of the Government. Hoover did note that the press release was in accordance with an "earlier conversation" that he and Hughes had had, and he surmised that reporters had simply overemphasized what he had said because of the "strain to forecast government attitude." After making his own statement to the press on March 25, Hughes assured Hoover that the Commerce Secretary's original statement "did not cause any em-

Hughes told the Soviets in March that trade could not be considered until "fundamental changes" had been made in Russia "involving due regard for the protection of persons and property and the establishment of conditions essential to the maintenance of commerce." Later, in July, he wrote to Samuel Gompers, describing Russia, which was experiencing a virtual paralysis of industry and transportation, as a "gigantic economic vacuum." He emphasized that the situation would not improve as long as the "present economic and political system" continued, and concluded that the United States wanted to establish commercial relations with Russia but that such ties were not possible until "readjustments" had been made. Hughes, like Hoover, favored providing "adequate relief" as long as such operations were "of a distinctly humanitarian character," and he was similarly trying to counter the ideological threat of bolshevism by prohibiting commercial, as well as diplomatic, relations until Soviet political and economic thought conformed more with Western views.[17]

If anything, Hughes, a lawyer, was even more convinced of the ideological evils of bolshevism than was Hoover. Hughes viewed recognition as an "invitation to intercourse" resting on the sanctity of international obligations. Since the Bolsheviks had nationalized the property of foreigners and refused to honor the debts of the tsar, Hughes tried to discipline them by not recognizing their regime and by not attending the Genoa or Hague conferences in 1922 to discuss economic matters with them. This attempt to punish the Russian leaders and bring them to their senses was made most clear in Hughes's curt refusal to consider a request for diplomatic talks from Soviet Commissar of Foreign Affairs Georgi Chi-

barrassment." See U.S. Department of State, General Records, Record Group 59, File 661.1115/274. For details of the jurisdictional relationship between Hughes and Hoover during the administration of ARA relief in Russia, see Weissman, "ARA in Russia," pp. 57, 60, 108–9, 150, 178, 304, 318.

17. Charles Evans Hughes to U.S. consul at Reval (for transmission to Litvinov), March 25, 1921, U.S. Department of State, General Records, Record Group 59, File 661.1115/275A; Hughes to Samuel Gompers, April 5, 1921, July 21, 1923, Box 26, Charles Evans Hughes Papers, Library of Congress; Hughes to American Embassy, London, August 25, 1921, Nixon Correspondence: 1950–1959, HHPPP.

cherin in December 1923. In a brief telegram, Hughes told Chicherin that "there would seem to be at this time no reason for negotiations" because of certain offensive economic and political practices of the Soviet authorities. In particular, Hughes singled out the Communists' issuing propaganda that was intended to encourage overthrowing the institutions of the United States as the most obnoxious of all Soviet actions. Before leaving office in 1925 he compiled a 100-page report summarizing all the reasons that normal relations could not be established with the Soviet regime.[18]

By extending the ideological assumptions of the Colby Note and publicly discouraging commercial relations, Hoover and Hughes, in the administrations of Presidents Harding and Coolidge, forged a political and economic policy toward Russia that soon became a bundle of contradictions. Since Hoover and Hughes were convinced that the United States should increase its world trade, they found it difficult to decide whether to take advantage of what Russian market there was or to use economic pressure against the Soviets. Although they denied they were subordinating practical economic to abstract ideological considerations about the Soviet system, they allowed the public to assume that the United States' poli-

18. Charles Evans Hughes, *The Pathway of Peace: Representative Addresses Delivered during His Term as Secretary of State, 1921–1925*, pp. 62–64; Hughes to Gompers, July 21, 1923, Box 26, Hughes Papers, Library of Congress; Hughes to Commissar Chicherin, December 18, 1923, *FRP:1923*, 2: 788; Hughes to Hoover, February 28, 1925, Personal File, Herbert Hoover Presidential Papers (hereafter cited as HHPPF), Herbert Hoover Presidential Library; Floyd James Fithian, "Soviet-American Economic Relations, 1918–1933: American Business in Russia during the Period of Nonrecognition" (Ph.D. dissertation, University of Nebraska, 1964), pp. 60, 79–80, 85, 89–90, 351. Fithian and others have pointed out that Harding was not as ideologically opposed to the Soviet Union as were secretaries Hughes and Hoover. The same was true of Coolidge; see Robert James Maddox, "Keeping Cool with Coolidge," *Journal of American History* 53 (March 1967): 774–77; Howard H. Quint and Robert H. Ferrell, eds., *The Talkative President: The Off-the-Record Press Conferences of Calvin Coolidge*, pp. 255–57, 259–61, 265; Robert K. Murray, *The Harding Era: Warren G. Harding and His Administration*, pp. 353–54; Weissman, "ARA in Russia," pp. 79–80.

cy of nonrecognition constituted a "moral boycott."[19] They insisted, moreover, that recognition would not in any way improve commercial exchanges between the two countries, even when it could be demonstrated that the credit problem the Soviet Union experienced in this country before the Depression of 1929 was directly related to the absence of normal diplomatic relations. They also maintained, regardless of facts to the contrary, that there were no official restrictions on Russian trade after 1920.

To further complicate matters, despite Hughes's and Hoover's common ideological opposition to the USSR, their respective departments did not always agree when it came to regulating economic relations with the new Soviet regime. This disagreement represented only a small portion of a much larger and important jurisdictional dispute between the two men about whether the State Department or the Commerce Department should direct the economic foreign policy of the United States. Hoover had entered Harding's Cabinet determined to expand the functions of his department over foreign, as well as domestic, economic matters; thus, there was an immediate clash over control of commercial personnel abroad. Hoover won the first round when ARA agents in Russia assumed all the duties normally performed by consular officers.[20] When Hoover insisted on this same control in other areas of the world, the State Department countered with the Rogers bill of 1921, which not only combined the diplomatic and consular services and made merit, rather than politics, the basis of appointment and promotion in both, but also

19. Filene, *Americans and the Soviet Experiment*, pp. 89–92; Lasch, *American Liberals*, p. 217. Both Filene and Lasch note that even the proponents of recognition backed themselves into an ideological corner on the question of Russian recognition. Instead of admitting that the country was governed by a "revolutionary class dictatorship" that deserved recognition simply as an established power, they underplayed the less-desirable features of the Soviet system and often advocated the ideological and economic conditions for recognition set up by their opponents: Russia would have to pay her debts, renounce international revolution, and behave generally like a "civilized" nation. Thus, those in favor of recognition were hopelessly on the defensive in the 1920s. See *The New York Times*, August 17, 1929, p. 11.

20. Weissman, "ARA in Russia," pp. 104–5, 150, 219–33, 304.

gave the Department of State complete control over all federal personnel serving in foreign countries. Hoover's opposition helped to prevent a watered-down version of the original Rogers bill from becoming law until July 1, 1924. In the meantime he had also completely reorganized and greatly expanded his own department, especially the Bureau of Foreign and Domestic Commerce (BFDC), and had obtained from President Coolidge in April an Executive Order that assigned to representatives of the Department of Commerce "prime responsibility in economic matters and provided for the cooperative exchange of information among all American agents abroad."[21]

In 1925 Hughes unofficially endorsed a book, *The Foreign Service of the United States*, published by Consul General Tracy H. Lay. It contained a strong defense of the State Department's foreign-service personnel, at the expense of those of the Commerce Department, and was widely distributed to opponents of Hoover's departmental aggrandizement. Nevertheless, the Secretary of Commerce continued to expand his overseas foreign operations through congressional appropriations. By the end of the decade he had convinced most U.S. businessmen that his department was best equipped to serve their interests at home and abroad. Hoover was never able, even after Hughes's resignation in 1925, to obtain primary responsibility for the loan, oil, and reparations policies of the United States as he desired. Under his leadership, however, the Department of Commerce "was acting as the Administration's official spokesman on economic foreign policy" by the end of 1927.[22]

21. Brandes, *Hoover and Economic Diplomacy*, pp. 4–6, 41–42, 50; Graham H. Stuart, *American Diplomatic and Consular Practice*, pp. 99–103; Wilson, *Hoover*, chap. 4. The BFDC expanded more than any other single division after Hoover reorganized it along the same seventeen commodity lines used by U.S. companies trading abroad, and placed Dr. Julius Klein in charge as director. BFDC expenditures rose from $860,000 in 1921 to $5,000,000 in 1928, while its personnel increased fivefold. During the same time the number of BFDC foreign offices doubled from 27 to 57, and its domestic offices expanded from 9 to 23. In 1939 it was greatly weakened when its foreign personnel was transferred to the Foreign Service of the State Department.

22. Brandes, *Hoover and Economic Diplomacy*, pp. 55–60;

Thus, except for the brief period during which the ARA operated in Russia, this perennial jurisdictional dispute between Hughes and Hoover over control of economic foreign policy and the subsequent reorganization of their respective departments did not produce a conclusive winner, but it did prevent efficient coordination of economic and political foreign policies. Generally speaking, the Department of Commerce, with its highly informed Slavic Section of the European Division of the BFDC, was privately more willing to encourage U.S. businessmen to take advantage of Russian trade opportunities than was the State Department, Hoover's public statements notwithstanding. At least this was true until 1929, when the Depression made President Hoover and officials in his former department privately, as well as publicly, more ideologically defensive about promoting trade with the Soviets. Therefore, the most cursory review of the economic restrictions placed on transactions with Russia reveals clear areas of jurisdictional disagreement and organizational competition between the departments of State and Commerce, which compounded the already existing contradictions in the ideological and economic components of the Hoover-Hughes policy toward the USSR.

After the 1917 November Revolution, the Allies included all Russian territory in the general blockade then being conducted against the Central Powers. Soon after the Treaty of Brest-Litovsk in the spring of 1918, Russia was officially categorized as a "neutral territory from which the enemy might draw sustenance," and the blockade was continued. This classification did not end after the Armistice had been signed with Germany, because by that time the Allies and the United States had intervened militarily in Russia and wanted to prevent the Bolsheviks from obtaining supplies and food. As late as October 1919, the Supreme Council attempted to obtain the support of neutral nations for the Soviet blockade.

Hoover, *Memoirs*, Vol. 2, *Cabinet and Presidency*, pp. 40, 44; Wilson, *Hoover*, chap. 4. By broadly interpreting the provisions of the enabling act that created the Department of Commerce, Hoover increased the number of Commerce employees from 13,000 in 1921 to 15,850 in 1928. Appropriations from the very economy-minded Congress of the 1920s increased from $24,500,000 to $37,600,000.

Such support was not obtained, but the Allied blockade continued until January 16, 1920. While the United States Government condoned this extended blockade in spite of sporadic criticism from businessmen, it never assigned war vessels to help enforce it. However, since November 1917 it had been enforcing a stringent domestic embargo on trade with Russia.[23]

At the same time, the departments of Commerce and State were competing for bureaucratic control over future Russian trade. During Wilson's administration, Secretary of Commerce William C. Redfield suggested sending a special Government commission to Russia to organize trade in areas the Soviets did not yet control. In the summer of 1918 Wilson rejected Redfield's idea in favor of a commission composed of businessmen under the auspices of such private organizations as the American-Russian Chamber of Commerce, the Red Cross, or the YMCA. Redfield argued that such an arrangement might result in economic exploitation by a few firms, but Secretary of State Robert Lansing and Colonel House supported Wilson, and Hoover expressed a willingness to head such a group. For the moment it appeared that the United States might try to substitute private economic intervention for military intervention in order to strengthen Russian resistance to both the Bolsheviks and the Germans. This was the course preferred by the majority of U.S. companies who were then operating in Russia. Some businessmen were even considering the possibility of establishing a barter system within the destitute areas of Russia. But in July, Wilson, satisfying his own ideological anti-Bolshevik sentiments and those of most of his advisers, succumbed to Allied pressure for military intervention; the domestic embargo on Rus-

23. State Department memorandum, March 1920, U.S. Department of State, General Records, Record Group 59, File 661.115/40; Edward Hallett Carr, *The Bolshevik Revolution, 1917–1923*, 3: 149, 155–56; Frederick Lewis Schuman, *American Policy toward Russia since 1917*, pp. 148–49. For business criticism, see *Bradstreet's* 47 (April 26, 1919): 168; 48 (January 24, 1920): 64. Also see Hoover to Wilson, January 1, 1919, Hoover–Woodrow Wilson Correspondence, 1914–1919, Folder 2, Hoover Papers, Stanford University; Winton U. Solberg, "The Impact of Soviet Russia on American Life and Thought, 1917–1933" (Ph.D. dissertation, Harvard University, 1952), pp. 187, 211–12.

sia continued. By the end of 1919 the State Department, acting through the Russian Corporation of the War Trade Board (WTB), was refusing all requests for export licenses that involved Russia, except those portions of Siberia not controlled by the Bolsheviks.[24]

The WTB presented a structural problem that confused the formulation of Soviet policy by U.S. decision makers before Hoover and Hughes began their conflict. It was a "particularly good example of uncontrolled bureaucratic growth"; its officials were still working out the details of its organization only scant months before the Armistice. According to one WTB division chief, "Unfortunately, as yet the machinery for carrying into orderly operation foreign service for the War Trade Board has not been set up and turned to its job." Yet this was the body that officially became a section of the Department of State and that for the entire decade of the 1920s continued to enforce certain licensing, commercial, and financial restrictions on those Americans trying to do business with the Soviets, despite an official pronouncement by Washington that technically ended such wartime prohibitions and despite periodic recommendations from WTB members in favor of unencumbered trade with the USSR.[25]

24. Williams, *American-Russian Relations*, pp. 149–50; Fithian, "Soviet-American Economic Relations," pp. 41–51; Levin, *Wilson and World Politics*, pp. 90, 98, 107; Schuman, *American Policy*, pp. 148–49; Alfred L. P. Dennis, *The Foreign Policies of Soviet Russia*, pp. 458–59; M. A. Oudin (vice-president, International General Electric Company) to William C. Redfield, June 3, 1918, U.S. Department of Commerce, General Records, Record Group 40, File 77295. According to Oudin's letter, twenty companies with interests in Russia favored economic assistance over military intervention; these companies included the New York Life Insurance Company, the Chase National Bank, International Harvester, Vacuum Oil, Singer, and Baldwin Locomotive. For references to bartering with the Russians, see *The Annalist* 13 (April 28, 1919): 429; Philadelphia Board of Trade, *Proceedings*, January 26, 1920, p. 54; *Iron Age* 106 (July 22, 1920): 197. For the anti-Bolshevik overtones of U.S. military intervention in Russia, see William Appleman Williams, "American Intervention in Russia, 1917–1920," *Studies on the Left* 3 (Fall 1963): 24–48 and 4 (Winter 1964): 39–57.

25. Joseph S. Tulchin, *The Aftermath of War: World War I and U.S. Policy toward Latin America*, pp. 16–17; Anthony C.

After the Supreme Council ended the Soviet blockade at the beginning of 1920, increased business pressure was brought to bear upon the State Department to end this U.S. embargo.[26] Partially in response to this pressure and because the embargo policy was no longer militarily defensible once the last U.S. troops left Russia in April, the Government appeared to capitulate. In accord with recommendations from President Wilson and Norman Davis, the State Department issued a statement on July 7, 1920, declaring that the wartime trading restrictions were removed, with the exception "of material susceptible of immediate use for war purposes." The department carefully stressed that no political recognition of the Soviet regime was implied in the lifting of the embargo and that U.S. businessmen, while free to trade with the Bolsheviks, did so at their own risk and could expect no diplomatic or consular aid if trouble developed. From this date the Government publicly maintained that all trade restrictions had been removed. Business groups generally acclaimed what appeared to be a "hands-off" policy. However, most of them in the summer of 1920 and during the next several years considered immediate trade possibilities with Russia to be negligible.[27] In truth, many obstacles remained to hamper commercial relations between the two countries.

Sutton, *Western Technology and Soviet Economic Development*, Vol. 1, *1917 to 1933*, p. 296.

26. *The Magazine of Wall Street* 25 (May 1, 1920): 976–78; 25 (May 29, 1920): 84. *Nation's Business* 8 (June 1920): 34. *Iron Age* 105 (April 8, 1920): 1033–34; 106 (July 15, 1920): 139, 150. League of Free Nations to George Foster Peabody, February 14, 1920, Box 75, Peabody Papers. For representative samples of the letters by businessmen and such economic interest groups as the American Manufacturers Export Association (AMEA), the American-Russian Chamber of Commerce, and the National Foreign Trade Council, who were interested in lifting the trade restrictions, see U.S. Department of State, General Records, Record Group 59, File 661.1115/11–92, and U.S. Department of Commerce, General Records, Record Group 40, File 77295.

27. Woodrow Wilson to Norman H. Davis, June 23, 1920, U.S. Department of State, General Records, Record Group 59, File 661.1115/308; Davis to Bainbridge Colby, June 25, 1920, Box 8, Davis Papers; State Department, press release, July 7, 1920, *FRP: 1920*, 3: 717; AMEA to Robert Lansing, February 13,

The July 7, 1920, statement had itself included a few of these debilitating restrictions. It stated that no passports were to be issued for travel between the United States and Soviet Russia, no change was to be made in existing visa regulations, and no mail service was to be instituted. In addition, exporters were explicitly told that "they could expect no assistance from consuls or aid in facilitating credit arrangements." Also, the Federal Reserve Board, before July 7, had warned U.S. banks against honoring Estonian bank drafts, which the Soviet Government had intended to use in payment for U.S. goods. And finally even after the United States Government had admitted the "potential of Russia as a market," it continued throughout the decade to restrict, by direct and indirect means, long-term financial and commercial credit in several ways.[28]

For example, the State Department instituted a virtual loan embargo against the USSR by prohibiting the public sale of Soviet securities in retaliation for the Bolsheviks' repudiation of debts and their confiscation of property. Although long-term commercial credit was not officially forbidden by the Department of Commerce, its public and private statements did not usually encourage such transactions. Instead, the Commerce Department urged manufacturers to exercise unusual care when extending credit to the Soviets, and most firms dealing with Russia followed the department's formula of not granting credit for any sale in excess of the anticipated

---

1920, American-Russian Chamber of Commerce to Charles Evans Hughes, January 13, 1922, U.S. Department of State, General Records, Record Group 59, Files 661.1116/25, 661.1115/362; Hoover, address to International Chamber of Commerce, May 15, 1922, 227-HHPS. *Bradstreet's* 48 (April 3, 1920): 224; 48 (July 10, 1920): 448; 48 (July 24, 1920): 480; 48 (December 25, 1920): 832; 49 (January 29, 1921): 85; 50 (April 1, 1922): 223. *Iron Age* 101 (May 16, 1918): 1266–67; *The Magazine of Wall Street* 25 (May 1, 1920): 976–78; *Journal of the American Bankers Association* 25 (September 1922): 126–28; *Nation's Business* 8 (June 1920): 34; Sutton, *Western Technology*, Vol. 1, *1917 to 1933*, p. 296.

28. *Iron Age* 106 (July 15, 1920): 139, 150; *Bradstreet's* 48 (July 10, 1920): 448; *The Wall Street Journal*, November 6, 1920, p. 10; Schuman, *American Policy*, p. 195; Acting Secretary (Davis) to French Ambassador (Wallace), July 7, 1920, *FRP: 1920*, 3: 717.

gross profit. In addition, the department cautioned U.S. businessmen to collect 50 per cent in cash before their goods left the country and the rest in six to nine months. By 1927 the department was privately admitting that its advice was probably responsible for the harsh credit terms Soviet purchasing agents had to face.[29] Because credit relations between countries are often dependent upon the attitudes of the governments involved, it is no wonder that the USSR was unable to obtain direct long-term financial or commercial credit from the United States in the 1920s.

Even indirect long-term credit to the Soviets by means of U.S. loans to German export and manufacturing firms was opposed by the State Department in 1926 when first W. Averell Harriman and Company and later the New York Trust Company attempted to extend it. In March 1926 the law firm of Davis, Polk, Wardwell, Gardiner, and Reed wrote the State Department asking what its attitude would be toward a $25,000,000 to $35,000,000 loan by W. A. Harriman and Company to a German export firm. The firm made it clear that the proceeds from the loan would be used to extend credit to German industrialists in order to enable them to grant credit to Russia so the Soviets could purchase German goods (presumably through the export firm). The State Department's reply of April 2 said that the proposal could not be approved because the loan would amount to indirect Russian financing. Harriman did not, however, let the matter drop, and as late as June 17 the U.S. embassy in Berlin informed the

---

29. E. Dana Durand, confidential circular, "Trade with Russia," April 9, 1923, Hoover to Chester Gray, November 18, 1926 (a handwritten note by Director of the BFDC Julius Klein attached to this letter contained the standard credit terms recommended by the department), Russian File, HHCD; E. C. Ropes (chief, Slavic Section, European Division, BFDC) to Des Moines district office, December 13, 1927, U.S. Department of Commerce, Records of the Bureau of Foreign and Domestic Commerce, Record Group 151, File 488-U.S.; Fithian, "Soviet-American Economic Relations," pp. 133, 139–40, 142–43; Louis Fischer, *The Soviets in World Affairs*, 2: 806–8; Brandes, *Hoover and Economic Diplomacy*, p. 179; Frank B. Kellogg to the law firm of Davis, Polk, Wardwell, Gardiner, and Reed, March 17, 1926, *FRP: 1926*, 2: 907; Under-Secretary of State (Olds) to vice-president of American Locomotive Sales Corporation (Muchnic), November 28, 1927, *FRP: 1927*, 3: 653–54.

State Department that German businessmen still hoped that the loan would materialize. The deal ultimately fell through because of the Government's disapproval, as did similar proposals from the New York Trust Company and from Percival Farquhar, a U.S. financier.[30]

A State Department memorandum written in October 1927 by Robert F. Kelley, chief of the Eastern European Division, stated that in each of the above cases the department's position had been dictated "by the consideration that the transaction in question involved an advance of money to a regime which had repudiated Russia's obligations to the United States and its citizens, rather than by the consideration that American money was to be used to facilitate the purchase of German commodities by the Soviets." He reiterated that the department had no objection to short-term banking credit when it was "considered as incidental to ordinary commercial intercourse"; indeed the Chase National Bank had granted such credit to the All Russian Textile Syndicate in 1925. Then Kelley explained:

> The object of the State Department's policy is to exercise pressure on the Soviet regime to the end that this regime may eventually come to realize the necessity of abandoning its interference in the domestic affairs of the United States and of recognizing the international obligations devolving upon it with respect to the indebtedness of Russia to the United States and its citizens, and with respect to the property of American citizens in Russia.

For these reasons, the memorandum concluded, the department felt obliged to "view with disfavor all financial arrangements whether in the form of bond issues or long-term bank credits and whether designed to facilitate American exports

30. For the following details from the correspondence between lawyers for Harriman, the New York Trust Company, and the State Department, see U.S. Department of State, Records Relating to Internal Affairs of Russia and the Soviet Union, Record Group 59, Files 861.51/2010–14, 861.51/2017–22, 861.51/2037–68; Robert F. Kelley, memorandum, October 28, 1927, ibid., File F. W. 861.51Am3; Gould and Eberhardt to Commerce Department, January 20, 1933, Barnes Drill Company to Commerce Department, January 12, 1932, U.S. Department of Commerce, Records of the Bureau of Foreign and Domestic Commerce, Record Group 151, File 221-Russia; Percival Farquhar USSR Papers.

to Russia or to serve other purposes which would result in making financial resources available to the Soviet government." Thus, as of the end of 1927 the State Department, on the advice of Kelley and the Eastern European Division, disapproved of all Russian financing "for whatever purpose and under whatever form," except that involved in "ordinary current commercial intercourse."[31]

In contrast to the State Department, however, both the Commerce and Treasury departments initially indicated they had no objection to the proposed extension of credit by Harriman. Some Commerce officials said it was "an important forward step . . . in the economic rehabilitation of Russia"; however, although Treasurer Andrew Mellon did not agree, Hoover overruled them and supported the State Department's view that such loans to foreign export firms would violate the established policy of the Government. Hoover wrote his final objections to this means of providing the Soviets with credit on the back of a memorandum he had received from two division chiefs in the Bureau of Foreign and Domestic Commerce, both of whom had tentatively approved of the Harriman proposal. His handwritten conclusion was that the action should be discouraged because "it is only indirect financing of a debtor who refused to fund. It is my impression [that the loan is] being offered in the United States because of British refusal."[32]

However, none of the departmental debate or detailed reasoning behind the State Department's negative decision was ever communicated in writing to Harriman, Farquhar, or others who made inquiries about loans that would have resulted in Soviet purchases of German products. In the case of a request made by Charles M. Muchnic, vice-president of the American Locomotive Sales Corporation, to grant long-term credit to the Soviets for the purchase of U.S. railroad equipment, the initial unfavorable decision of the State De-

---

31. Robert F. Kelley, memorandum, October 28, 1927, U.S. Department of State, Records Relating to Internal Affairs of Russia and the Soviet Union, Record Group 59, File F.W. 861.51Am3.

32. E. C. Ropes and Grosvenor Jones, memorandum to Paul S. Clapp (Hoover's personal assistant), July 1926, World War Debt Commission File, HHCD.

partment was explained over the telephone and then over-ruled by President Coolidge after he consulted Hoover and Secretary of the Treasury Andrew Mellon. This verbal means of communication was recommended by the major architect of Soviet policy in the Department of State, Robert F. Kelley. According to an October 1927 memorandum, Kelley recommended that details of the department's decisions on economic foreign policy should not be committed to writing because future requests or circumstances might require a modification of the Government's position. This was exactly what happened in the case of the Locomotive Sales Corporation—a classic example of interdepartmental disagreement—a victory of Hoover and Mellon over Kelley's policy. It also was an indication that direct long-term credit to the Soviets for the purchase of U.S. products, as opposed to indirect credit for Soviet purchases from foreign countries, was more acceptable to the Secretary of Commerce than to the Secretary of State.[33]

Business reaction to this policy against indirect long-term credit was mixed. Those firms interested in providing such financing obviously were not happy with it. Hence, George Murnane, president of the New York Trust Company, publicly acquiesced to the position but privately complained to the State Department about its short-sightedness. Murnane was convinced that at some time in the future, his firm would provide to German banks an "equivalent amount of funds" that would have "no Russian flavor" but that would, nonetheless, be used to provide credit for the Soviets.[34] By 1933 this covert practice on the part of financiers made headlines in business journals and incurred the wrath of those U.S. businessmen who resented the use of U.S. money to finance German-Russian trade when they could not tap similar sources of credit at home.

33. Robert F. Kelley, memorandum, October 28, 1927, U.S. Department of State, Records Relating to Internal Affairs of Russia and the Soviet Union, Record Group 59, File F.W. 861.51Am3; Sutton, *Western Technology*, Vol. 1, *1917 to 1930*, pp. 90, 297–98.

34. New York Trust Company to State Department, July 19, 1926, U.S. Department of State, Records Relating to Internal Affairs of Russia and the Soviet Union, Record Group 59, File 861.51/2059.

Another indirect attempt to extend long-term credit to the USSR occurred in 1928 when four U.S. banks announced that the Soviet State Bank was offering railway bonds for sale and that they were going to pay the interest coupons on that portion of the issue exported from the USSR. In this case the Chase National Bank and the Amalgamated Bank of New York, the Amalgamated Trust and Savings Bank of Chicago, and the Bank of Italy of San Francisco did not attempt to sell these bonds in the United States because they were well aware of the Government's opposition to that form of direct Soviet financing. Instead, they argued that they were simply providing a standard service for their customers "with regard to the payment of coupons of domestic or foreign bonds." The funds were to come out of credit deposits placed in these banks by the Soviet State Bank.

The State Department opposed this financial arrangement after receiving protests from the National Tin Corporation, the Allied Patriotic Societies, the National Civic Federation, individual red-baiters, such anti-Soviet newspapers as *The Wall Street Journal*, and most importantly, the New York Life Insurance Company. New York Life had lost approximately $20,000,000 in Russian railway bonds at the time of nationalization, and spokesmen for New York Life argued that this issue of railway bonds was a blatant "attempt by those now in power in Russia to realize on the credit of the Russian railways, while at the same time repudiating the earlier obligations of the same railways." The State Department concurred, and the proposed transaction by the four U.S. banks was stopped.[35]

While the Government was interfering with long-term credit arrangements for the Soviet Union, it was also preventing the U.S. Mints and the Assay Office from accepting gold of Russian origin in payment for purchases. Hoover opposed this gold ban when he came into office in 1921 because he feared that U.S. businessmen would not be able to compete successfully for Russian trade with their British counterparts, whose government was accepting Soviet gold. Hoover argued

35. For the correspondence between the State Department and those who opposed or supported the railway-bond transaction, see U.S. Department of State, General Records, Record Group 59, File 861.51 State Bank/1–38.

in a letter to Hughes that since the State Department officially allowed "trade with Bolshevik Russia at the risk of the trader," it was unfair not to permit U.S. businesses the right to take that risk. Gold was the only commodity the Russians had to exchange for goods at the beginning of the decade, and in 1922 Hoover successfully manipulated the transfer of Soviet gold for grain purchases from the ARA. But the State and Treasury departments stubbornly continued to adhere to the policy established during the last year of the Wilson administration on all other proposals for acceptance of Soviet gold, even though major European nations soon lifted their bans on it. The U.S. gold ban was reaffirmed as late as February 1928 in an incident involving an attempt by the Soviet State Bank to increase its bank deposits in the United States by transferring $5,000,000 in gold bars to the Chase National Bank.[36]

Within the decade Hoover's opposition to the gold ban was vindicated. The ban quickly became simply a token gesture on the part of the U.S. Government as untold amounts of "tainted" Soviet gold entered the country via foreign sources, namely, Sweden, Switzerland, France, and Germany. These European nations and others readily accepted gold from the Communists, melted it down, and re-issued it as their own. In this fashion, according to an American who was doing business in Russia, Armand Hammer, over $350,000,000 entered the United States from 1920 to 1922 alone, and "everyone concerned," including those at the Treasury and the Assay Office, was aware of the process. Thus, it was only with respect to direct importations of Soviet gold that the State Department felt obliged to enforce what appeared to be a complete embargo but what in practice affected only a very

36. Hoover to Hughes, March 16, 1921, *FRP: 1921*, 2: 762; Fischer, *Soviets*, 2: 810; Assistant Secretary of State (Castle) to Under-Secretary of Treasury (Mills), February 17, 1928, Under-Secretary of State (Olds) to Mills, February 24, 1928, *FRP: 1928*, 3: 829; Weissman, "ARA in Russia," pp. 244–47. The second note of the Under-Secretary cited here does indicate a slight change in the attitude of the State Department, for it denied "that the purchase of Soviet gold could be regarded as a recognition of the Soviet regime." Nonetheless, the Treasury Department continued to oppose the direct purchase of gold until recognition was actually accorded.

small portion of the Soviet gold entering by other means.[37] However, the ban did make it impossible for the Soviets to increase their credit in the United States through direct bank deposits.

Hughes and Hoover also disagreed about the advisability of permitting the use of German middlemen to facilitate Russian-U.S. trade. They had been used before the war, but Hoover was adamantly opposed to the continuation of this practice while Hughes expressed approval of it. Hoover, who wanted to preserve the future Russian market for U.S. domination, argued that inroads had been made during the war and that U.S. relief operations had fostered greater rapport among the citizens of the two countries than had ever existed before. Hoover viewed Russia as he did other foreign markets; it was an area in which direct U.S. investment and participation in trade was the best long-term policy. In this particular dispute the Commerce Department carried the day, and the Government opposed attempts to finance Russian trade through German or other foreign intermediaries on the basis of the Commerce Department's urging the establishment of "direct trade with the Russians when that country opens up."[38]

Those members of the business community interested in promoting U.S.-Russian trade became increasingly impatient with the gold ban, the policy restricting the use of German middlemen, and the opposition to extending the Soviets indirect long-term credit by loans to Germany. It was evident to them by the middle of the decade that none of these restrictions could be strictly enforced or could bring about a change in Soviet economic or political practices. Since all of the other

37. Saul G. Bron, *Soviet Economic Development and American Business*, p. 95; Armand Hammer, *The Quest for the Romanoff Treasure*, p. 99.

38. Hughes to Hoover, December 1, 1921, Hoover to Hughes, December 6, 1921, *FRP: 1921*, 2: 785–88; Norman Meese (chief of district offices, BFDC) to A. Barnaud (New York BFDC district manager), April 4, 1922, Alan G. Goldsmith (chief, Western European Division, BFDC) to H. C. MacLean (commercial attaché, Rome), April 1, 1922, U.S. Department of Commerce, Records of the Bureau of Foreign and Domestic Commerce, Record Group 151, File 448-U.S.

restrictions had been violated periodically through indirect means, the only justification for them in the long run was that they were in keeping with the Government's ambivalent desire to allow trade in theory but to make it somewhat difficult in practice in order to bring economic pressure to bear on the Soviet regime for ideological reasons.

The two secretaries did not always disagree in their attempt to devise a cohesive economic foreign policy that served ideological ends. Even when they agreed, however, their implementation was hindered by the interdepartmental and reorganizational rivalries discussed above. Hughes was generally more pessimistic about the possibilities of resuming direct business contacts with the Russians than was Hoover, but in 1922, as the ARA was being phased out, they agreed that the best way to try to improve relations between the two countries was not through conferences like those at Genoa and the Hague, but through relief measures and by sending a technical mission to Russia for an "expert study of conditions." In 1917 several commissions visited Russia while the Provisional Government was in power, but the 1922 commission failed to materialize because the Soviets requested permission to send a similar group to the United States, and this Hoover and Hughes refused to permit. Although the State and Commerce departments consistently supported the nonrecognition policy and discouraged Government officials from traveling to the USSR in the 1920s, the idea of an unofficial commission of experts to study conditions under communism remained a popular one with Government officials and businessmen. They wanted information about the Soviet Union that could be helpful if normal relations were resumed. They also naïvely hoped that Russian leaders would accept the U.S. experts' practical advice about modifying their system. Much to the chagrin of conservative businessmen, labor leaders, and the Government, many members of the private groups that went to the USSR between 1922 and 1933, including a party of congressmen in 1923 and another of prominent businessmen and editors in 1929, came back so impressed with certain aspects of the Soviet experiment that they became staunch advocates of trade and, in some cases, recognition.[39]

39. Hughes to Hoover, March 22, 1922, E. Dana Durand to Christian A. Herter (Hoover's personal secretary), April 1, 1922,

Despite the confused picture presented by these two competing departments, most businessmen thought that the Commerce Department was doing more than the State Department to promote trade with the USSR. This judgment was generally true for Wilson's last administration, as well as those of Harding and Coolidge. The Commerce Department had, of course, many opportunities in private communications with businessmen to advise about commercial opportunities in Russia, whereas the State Department was limited often to prohibiting certain commercial, financial, and political activities in relation to the Soviet Union. Therefore, Hughes, rather than Hoover, was more often found to be forcing compliance with the government's ideological opposition to the USSR.

There is some evidence, however, to indicate that before 1925, some of Hoover's subordinates within the department were more eagerly encouraging the development of U.S.-Russian trade than was the Secretary himself. It is true that as early as July 1921, Dr. Julius Klein, director of the Bureau of Foreign and Domestic Commerce, answered an inquiry from shoe manufacturers in Boston by saying that "the chief [Hoover] has not the slightest objection to shoes being shipped to Russia." Klein had been further instructed by Hoover's secretary to tell these manufacturers that the department was glad to see the transaction and generally "very interested in any trade relations with Russia." On occasion, however, Hoover forbade the dissemination of favorable information about commercial possibilities for U.S. business.

Russian File, HHCD; William R. Castle, Jr. (Under-Secretary of State) to Hoover, June 28, 1927, Tariff File, HHCD; Hoover to Hughes, July 14, 1922, *FRP: 1922*, 2: 825–26. For all State Department correspondence about the technical mission, see U.S. Department of State, Records Relating to Internal Affairs of Russia and the Soviet Union, Record Group 59, File 861.50Am3/1-20; Weissman, "ARA in Russia," pp. 316–18. Reaction of the various groups visiting Russia can be found in New York State Chamber of Commerce, *Monthly Bulletin* (November 1926): 51–67; Lewis S. Feuer, "American Travelers to the Soviet Union, 1917–1932: The Formation of a Component of New Deal Ideology," *American Quarterly* 14 (Summer 1962): 122–36; Filene, *Americans and the Soviet Experiment*, pp. 74, 198–200. *The New York Times*, July 16, 1929, p. 5; August 17, 1929, p. 11.

In one instance Gordon Lee, chief of the Automotive Division of the Commerce Department, excited by the possibility of obtaining Soviet orders for U.S. trucks, requested that a circular be distributed to automotive manufacturers and reported to the assistant director of the BFDC that "if there is any business to be gotten for American motor truck manufacturers, we want to help them if they are to be sold to the polar bears." Hoover, however, informed the bureau that it "had better go easy on this business for the present," and no public or private announcement was made about the prospects in Russia for automobile producers. At times Hoover also wrote very discouraging answers to inquiries about economic opportunities in Soviet Russia, saying that no Government protection could be expected because the Soviet regime had not been recognized and that those U.S. businessmen who were endeavoring to do business there were not having any great success.[40]

In this manner Hoover privately exercised a certain amount of restraint in the early 1920s, and of course the department under his direction consistently warned businessmen against making any long-term commercial credit available to Soviet purchasing agents. Nonetheless, most division chiefs with the BFDC by the end of 1921 were sending confidential information to all businessmen who inquired about conditions in Russia, and many of them, like Lee, strongly promoted commercial transactions with that country. Also, by 1922 Russian trade figures began appearing regularly in *Commerce Reports*

40. Christian A. Herter to Klein, July 22, 1921, BFDC File, HHCD; Hoover to Knox Taylor (president of Taylor-Wharton Iron and Steel Company), March 2, 1922, E. Dana Durand, memorandum to Hoover, June 5, 1922, Richard Emmett (Hoover's personal assistant) to Durand, June 14, 1922, Leonard J. Lewery (assistant chief, Eastern European Division, BFDC) to Harold P. Stokes (Hoover's personal assistant), December 23, 1924, Stokes to Durand, March 9, 1925, Russian File, HHCD; Gordon Lee to Thomas Taylor (assistant director, BFDC), May 1, 1922 (an attached note from Emmett to Taylor carried Hoover's negative reply), Klein to Boston district BFDC office, July 25, 1921, U.S. Department of Commerce, Records of the Bureau of Foreign and Domestic Commerce, Record Group 151, File 488–U.S.

and *Supplements,* and inquiries became so frequent by 1923 that Klein had a confidential circular prepared.

The circular was limited to very general information about the Soviet monopoly on foreign commerce and the kinds of trading organizations that were permitted, because as the head of the Eastern European Division explained to Hoover's secretary, "We have avoided saying anything which would be embarrassing if it should become public." The circular was sent out only upon request, but all inquiries for more specific details were sent directly to the Slavic Section of the Eastern European Division of the BFDC for individual consideration. In 1924 the department prepared another confidential circular, one on the rights of foreigners in Soviet Russia, and by 1925 the various commodity divisions of the department were referring interested exporters and importers to the Amtorg Trading Corporation, a Soviet purchasing agency in New York, and to the Allied American Corporation, Armand Hammer's trading concern, which was operating under a special license from the Soviet Government.[41] Obviously these actions of the Commerce Department appeared to businessmen to be more lenient and helpful than those of the State Department in economic matters. Given the Government's opposition to recognition, however, the Commerce Department did not promote and encourage trade with Russia to the extent that it did with other countries.

Hoover was never able to solve the dilemma that ideological opposition to the Soviet Union posed for him and his department. In a letter to the editor of *Export Trade* in 1923 he lamely tried to explain that because Soviet foreign trade was conducted as a government monopoly and because there were "numerous claimants against the Soviet government in

---

41. E. Dana Durand to Christian Herter, March 31, 1923, Klein to BFDC district offices, April 13, 1923, H. W. Gruber (acting chief, Commercial Intelligence Division, BFDC) to Frick Company, August 16, 1924, T. L. Gaukel (St. Louis district manager, BFDC) to Harold Dotterer (chief of district offices), February 21, 1925, Dotterer to Gaukel, February 26, 1925, U.S. Department of Commerce, Records of the Bureau of Foreign and Domestic Commerce, Record Group 151, File 488-U.S.; L. J. Lewery to Julius Klein, September 22, 1924, Harold Stokes to E. C. Ropes, July 13, 1925, Russian File, HHCD.

this country," it was impossible for normal banking channels to be used to finance Russian-U.S. commerce. He then referred to "certain circumscribed methods" that were available but flatly denied that the Federal Government had anything to do with financial restrictions or the curtailment of credit. Hughes also wrote to *Export Trade*, agreeing with Hoover and stressing the now-familiar cliché that anyone could trade with Russia at his own risk. Under the influence of his friend and Under-Secretary of State William R. Castle, Jr., Hoover approved a press release on the attitude of the Government on Russian trade and recognition in the event that FDR raised the issues during the campaign of 1932. This proved an unnecessary precaution, but significantly the statement underplayed the issues of Soviet propaganda and the debt question as reasons behind nonrecognition. Most important, it stated that "trade with Russia is not a matter of recognition, but of credit" and denied that the U.S. Government opposed commerce with the Soviets, asserting instead that it had "encouraged the fullest informal trade relations and has removed, wherever possible, hindrances to trade." [42]

As ideological fears prevailed over honesty and immediate economic self-interest, commercial and financial restrictions affecting relations with the Soviet Union were publicly denied but privately enforced by the United States Government.

42. Hoover to editor of *Export Trade*, April 13, 1923, Hughes to editor of *Export Trade* (undated, but written during the spring of 1923), U.S. Department of Commerce, Records of the Bureau of Foreign and Domestic Commerce, Record Group 151, File 488–U.S.; William R. Castle, Jr. (Under-Secretary of State) to Hoover, August 17, 1932 (with suggested press release), Castle Papers.

III

DISHARMONY: MINORITY
AND MAJORITY VIEWS
WITHIN THE BUSINESS COMMUNITY

The removal of these commercial and financial restrictions, which had been officially denied, proved a very difficult and gradual process. Many remained in effect until 1934, despite Government protestations to the contrary.[1] Between July 1920 and May 1925 only three significant modifications were made in the Government's trade policy toward Russia. Each can be attributed to pressure from a minority within the business community. First, on December 19, 1920, the Treasury Department removed all restrictions on currency transactions with Russia, except the most important one on Soviet gold.[2] This removal was a somewhat delayed reaction

1. Charles Evans Hughes to American Traders Corporation, April 5, 1921, Hughes to Compton and Delaney, April 18, 1924, U.S. Department of State, General Records, Record Group 59, Files 661.1115/278, 661.1115/450; Hughes and Herbert Hoover to Samuel Gompers, June 23, 1922, Russian File, HHCD; Robert E. Olds (Under-Secretary of State) to Charles A. Muchnic (vice-president of American Locomotive Sales Corporation), November 28, 1928, *FRP: 1928*, 3: 653–54; Frank B. Kellogg to chairman of Republican National Committee, February 23, 1928, *FRP: 1928*, 3: 824; E. C. Ropes (chief, Slavic Section, European Division, BFDC) to Memphis district office, December 30, 1927, Robert P. Lamont (Secretary of Commerce) to Allen Wardwell, November 19, 1930, Lamont to Col. Hugh L. Cooper, January 20, 1931, Frederick M. Feiker (director, BFDC) to Farm Tools, Inc., August 23, 1931, U.S. Department of Commerce, Records of the Bureau of Foreign and Domestic Commerce, Record Group 151, File 448-U.S.

2. Treasury Department, press release, December 20, 1920, *FRP: 1920*, 3: 724; Frederick Lewis Schuman, *American Policy toward Russia since 1917*, pp. 195–96.

to the official end of the wartime embargo announced by the State Department in July. The major assertion used by Government officials to justify this action was the one that established business groups had been employing since the end of the war in their arguments against both the Allied blockade and the embargo on Russian trade. They maintained that the removal of commercial and financial restrictions would undermine a powerful Bolshevik shibboleth, namely, that Russia's internal economic chaos resulted from unreasonable foreign restrictions on trade and currency exchange. Such an argument was convincing to Government officials and the vast majority of businessmen immediately following the war because they believed that Bolshevik opposition to free enterprise had placed the Russian nation temporarily outside the realm of profitable foreign penetration. So, it was thought, the removal of U.S. restrictions upon commercial relations would not improve Russia's trade and investments, and thus the Soviet leaders would be trapped by their own propaganda and forced to compromise at home and abroad.[3]

This estimation of the insignificance of future economic contact between Russia and the United States was not based simply on anti-Bolshevik sentiment of Government officials

3. Alonzo E. Taylor to Robert Lansing, June 2, 1920, Hughes to consul at Reval, March 25, 1921, U.S. Department of State, General Records, Record Group 59, Files 661.1115/71, 661.1115/275A; Hughes to Samuel Gompers, July 21, 1923, Box 26, Hughes Papers. *Nation's Business* 7 (November 1919): 11–12, 44; 7 (June 1920): 34. *The Wall Street Journal*, March 22, 1921, p. 3. *The Annalist* 17 (March 28, 1921): 372; 20 (December 4, 1922): 594. *The Magazine of Wall Street* 25 (May 1, 1920): 976–78; 26 (July 19, 1920): 312. *Bradstreet's* 48 (December 25, 1920): 932; *Journal of the American Bankers Association* 25 (September 1922): 126–28; Philadelphia Board of Trade, *Proceedings*, January 23, 1922, pp. 14–15; George S. Moyer, *Attitude of the United States toward Recognition of Soviet Russia*, pp. 239–83; Herbert Hoover, address to American Institute of Mining Engineering (AIME), September 16, 1919, and statement to Newspaper Enterprise Association, June 3, 1920, Speeches and Addresses, 1915–1923, Hoover Papers, Stanford University; Hoover, *American Individualism*, pp. 32–47; Joseph Dorfman, *The Economic Mind in American Civilization*, 4: 65; William Starr Myers, *The Foreign Policies of Herbert Hoover, 1929–1933*, p. 11; Schuman, *American Policy*, pp. 196, 201; Louis Fischer, *The Soviets in World Affairs*, 1: 315.

and businessmen. Statistics about U.S. trade with Russia before World War I were also taken into consideration. Such figures showed that before the war, private U.S. investment in Russia had amounted to only about 5 per cent of all private foreign investments abroad, and trade with the tsarist empire amounted to less than 1.5 per cent of the total trade of the United States. The amount of U.S. capital in prewar Russia was considered negligible in comparison with that supplied by European nations, and most of it had been invested by seven large companies in enterprises that had been made state monopolies after the November Revolution. Thus, businessmen and Government officials concluded that postwar economic contact would be even less significant under the Bolsheviks.[4]

This judgment seemed to be confirmed between 1918 and 1922 because the internal disorder and civil war totally disrupted Russia's trade relations with the rest of the world. Until 1923, when Commerce Department reports showed increased trade with the Soviet Union, nothing undermined this original assumption. Even so, Hoover and other Department of Commerce officials continued until the middle of the 1920s to point out the insignificance of U.S. trade with Russia in relation to that with other countries and to note that relief shipments, not commercial orders, made up over half of the total U.S. exports to Russia between 1921 and 1923.[5] It was natural, therefore, that in 1920, doubts about the revival of Russian trade, based on both prewar statistics and postwar ideological opposition to communism, were used to justify

4. U.S. Department of Commerce, Bureau of Foreign and Domestic Commerce, *Foreign Capital Investments in Russian Industries and Commerce,* by Leonard J. Lewery, Department of Commerce Miscellaneous Series no. 124, pp. 27–28; American-Russian Chamber of Commerce, *Handbook of the Soviet Union,* pp. 352–53.

5. Hoover to Hughes, May 3, 1923, E. Dana Durand (chief, Eastern European Division, BFDC) to Evan E. Young (chief, East European Division, State Department), November 2, 1923, U.S. Department of Commerce, Records of the Bureau of Foreign and Domestic Commerce, Record Group 151, File 448-U.S.; Leonard J. Lewery (assistant chief, Eastern European Division, BFDC) to Hoover, September 22, 1924, Russian File, HHCD; Hoover, address to International Chamber of Commerce, May 15, 1922, 227-HHPS.

the Treasury Department's decision not to remove the ban on Russian gold.

The postwar depression of 1920–1921 and the establishment of the New Economic Policy in Soviet Russia prompted a small group of labor leaders and businessmen to request further modifications of the remaining commercial and financial restrictions. Although a Senate hearing on January 26, 1921, failed to produce any specific recommendations, in May the Government restored postal service between the two countries. Then several of the Russian trading organizations that formed during the first years of the NEP began to petition the State Department for a more liberal visa policy. Finally in May 1925, visas were authorized for Russian nationals to enter the United States, "provided the bonafide purpose of the visit involve[d] solely trade or commerce."[6] None of these modifications between 1920 and 1925 represented any basic change in the Government's ideological attitude toward the Soviet Union.

In the first half of the decade, only one business group advocated a total re-evaluation of economic relations with Russia. It was the American Commercial Association to Promote Trade with Russia, which represented approximately 100 small business firms. It had been organized in December 1919 by Emerson P. Jennings, president of the Lehigh Machine Company of Lehighton, Pennsylvania. In the fall of 1919, Jennings's company had been offered a printing press contract for $4,500,000 by Ludvig C. A. K. Martens, a German engineer who headed the Soviet Commercial Bureau and who had been appointed diplomatic and commercial representative by the People's Commissar of Foreign Affairs for the new Soviet Government, Georgi Chicherin. With such a large contract in the offing, Jennings naturally was eager to obtain an export license for his merchandise, and in October he began to bombard State Department officials

<hr>

6. U.S. Congress, Senate, Committee on Foreign Relations, *Relations with Russia: Hearings on S.J.R. 164 for Re-establishment of Trade Relations*, 66th Cong., 3d sess., January 26, 1921, pp. 1–112; Schuman, *American Policy*, p. 203; Hoover to Hughes, March 23, 1921, U.S. Department of State, General Records, Record Group 59, File 661.1115/274; Hughes to consul general at Paris, May 19, 1925, *FRP: 1925*, 2: 703.

with a series of letters, telegrams, and requests for personal interviews. Apparently in an attempt to bring organized pressure upon the State Department, which controlled the Russian licensing policy through the War Trade Board, Jennings formed the American Commercial Association. It was composed of a number of small export and manufacturing companies, all of whom Martens had offered sizable orders from the Soviet Government.[7]

Subsequently Jennings's organization, its relationship to the Soviet Bureau, and Martens were investigated by the Government. A subcommittee of the Senate Foreign Relations Committee concluded the following about Martens and his contracts:

> These proffers . . . proved to be wholly tentative; the form of contract . . . was wholly in the lateral; the burden of securing shipment to Soviet Russia was placed entirely upon the producer; no earnest money was ever deposited; . . . while the American contractor by one means or another was led to bring pressure upon the Government of the United States for the purpose of forcing either a *modus vivendi* with or an actual recognition of the Russian Soviet Government. To the committee, therefore, the conclusion is inescapable that the entire fabric of trade negotiations which Martens unrolled was part of an ingenious scheme of propaganda to create sympathy, based upon cupidity, for the Russian Soviets, and to produce by indirect means the admission of the Soviet Russia into the companionship of international relations which other means had failed to secure.[8]

Influenced by this Senate appraisal of Marten's operations, the Division of Russian Affairs of the State Department, conducting its own investigation, concluded that "the

7. American Commercial Association to Robert Lansing, January 27, 1920, memorandum and membership list of American Commercial Association, Division of Russian Affairs (Cole), memorandum, May 11, 1920, U.S. Department of State, General Records, Record Group 59, Files 661.1115/11, 661.1115/20–21, 661.1115/68. Most of the companies represented by the American Commercial Association were from New York State.

8. Cole, memorandum, May 11, 1920, U.S. Department of State, General Records, Record Group 59, File 661.1115/68; U.S. Congress, Senate, Subcommittee of the Committee on Foreign Relations, *Russian Propaganda*, Senate Report 526, 66th Cong., 2d sess., April 14, 1920, p. 4.

chief and most willing instrument of this [Soviet] propaganda [in the United States] was Mr. Jennings' American Commercial Association." It further noted that the large, established U.S. firms interested in Russian trade had either criticized the association or had remained indifferent to its activities and that "no bank or large financial interests having investments or capital tied up in Russia have evinced the slightest inclination to press for trade with Russia at this time." The division summarily dismissed the activities and demands of the American Commercial Association with the statement, "Mr. Jennings' company is a small organization which had probably never dreamed even of a $4,500,000 order to be paid for in gold on delivery. When stripped of the trapping of talk about 'rights,' 'British duplicity,' 'Soviet Friendship for America,' et cetera, the dominant motive of all the Association's pleas is greed, pure and simple."[9]

The activities of the Soviet Bureau and the American Commercial Association coincided almost precisely with the hysteria of the Red Scare, which may well have affected their reception by the various branches of the Government. Regardless of the precise relationship between the two groups, their actions were legal. Nonetheless, not only were Martens's credentials as the representative of the People's Commissariat of Foreign Affairs rejected by the State Department and his affairs investigated by the Senate, but his New York offices were raided at the instigation of the Lusk Committee, an antiradical investigating committee of the New York State Assembly. Finally, on December 15, 1920, Secretary of Labor William B. Wilson recommended that Martens be taken into

9. Cole, memorandum, May 11, 1920, and report about March 4, 1920, meeting of six delegates of the American Commercial Association with Breckenridge Long of the Division of Russian Affairs, U.S. Department of State, General Records, Record Group 59, Files 661.1115/68, 661.1115/40. This opinion of State Department officials is corroborated by *Bradstreet's* 48 (February 21, 1920): 131; *Iron Age* 105 (April 8, 1920): 1033; George F. Kennan, *The Decision to Intervene*, p. 324. Both *Iron Age* and Kennan also confirm that associations like the American-Russian Chamber of Commerce and the Chamber of Commerce of the United States were not pressing for establishment of greater trade relations in 1920.

custody and deported from the country. On January 22, 1921, after receiving instructions from Chicherin, he cancelled all commercial orders he had made and left the United States on his own volition. Such treatment can be explained, but certainly not justified, in terms of "the reaction against the Soviets which had been developing since the November Revolution" and which climaxed in the Red Scare in 1919 and 1920.[10]

Jennings and his associates were not harassed in the same manner and were, of course, permitted to carry on limited trade with Russia after the declarations of July 7 and December 20, 1920. However, most of the demands presented by the American Commercial Association in a memorandum to the State Department on February 18, 1920, went unfulfilled for an entire decade. In addition to export and import licenses, this memorandum specifically requested "full shipping rights under the protection of our Government"; mail, telegraph, and wireless communication with Russia; and facilities for establishing business credits based on Soviet gold shipments. (Small business firms, such as those represented by the American Commercial Association, remained at a disadvantage in terms of commercial credit throughout the decade because only such mammoth U.S. companies as General Electric, General Motors, Standard Oil, International Harvester, and the Ford Motor Company could inde-

10. Schuman, *American Policy*, pp. 185–94; Winton U. Solberg, "The Impact of Soviet Russia on American Life and Thought, 1917–1933" (Ph.D. dissertation, Harvard University, 1952), p. 352; Robert Paul Browder, *The Origins of Soviet-American Diplomacy*, pp. 13–15. Another reason for the Government's cool treatment of Martens was the embarrassment that his presence caused the Wilson administration, which was still providing large amounts of money to the defunct Provisional Government through Boris Bakhmetev, the officially recognized Russian ambassador. See Robert James Maddox, *William E. Borah and American Foreign Policy*, pp. 46–49, 193–96, and Robert James Maddox, "Woodrow Wilson, the Russian Embassy and Siberian Intervention," *Pacific Historical Review* 26 (November 1967): 435–48. For approval of the harsh judgment and treatment of Jennings and Martens, see Anthony C. Sutton, *Western Technology and Soviet Development*, Vol. 1, *1917–1930*, pp. 287–88.

pendently finance trade contracts with the Soviets or arrange "unlimited long-term credits with large American banks."[11] Finally, the American Commercial Association requested that a Government-sponsored committee of businessmen visit Russia "in the interest of American trade." With the exception of the request for licenses and the provision of certain communication facilities, these demands were not met by Washington officials until after the United States recognized the USSR in 1933.

Commercial arrangements constituted only one area in which the Government thwarted this newly established group of small companies. Members of the association were so convinced in 1920 and 1921 of the enormous immediate and future trade possibilities of Soviet Russia, and they were so fearful that U.S. business would fail to capitalize on such trade, as England and Germany apparently were after negotiating commercial agreements with the Soviets, that they tended to accept the Bolshevik Government as "a government of fact." For different reasons they believed—as did many liberal intellectuals of the period—that the Bolsheviks were in to stay and could not be ignored or wished away.[12]

The possibility that the United States was trying to dictate the form of the Russian Government or that this country was indeed poorly informed about conditions in the Soviet-held territories was not generally raised by U.S. businessmen. When the American Commercial Association bluntly expressed these ideas, they were not well received by the Com-

11. Fischer, *Soviets*, 2: 765; Maddox, *Borah and Foreign Policy*, p. 209. Hence, these large firms remained relatively indifferent to the entire question of recognition throughout the decade. For details of their activities and attitudes, see Chapter IV and Appendixes C and D.

12. Jennings to Colby, April 3, 1920, Eugene Schoen (chairman of executive committee of American Commercial Association), statement, February 21, 1921, U.S. Department of State, General Records, Record Group 59, Files 661.1115/44, 661.1115/21; James P. Goodrich, memorandum to President Harding, June 1923, in Anne Vincent Meiburger, *Efforts of Raymond Robins toward the Recognition of Soviet Russia and the Outlawry of War, 1917–1933*, p. 206; Christopher Lasch, *The American Liberals and the Russian Revolution*, p. 105; *Iron Age* 105 (April 8, 1920): 1033.

merce or State departments because such statements obviously implied a demand for re-evaluation of the official ideological, as well as commercial, attitude toward the Bolsheviks.
Only a dozen years later did the attitudes and policies toward
trade and recognition that had formed in this early period of
emotions and misinformation begin to be reconsidered in
Washington. The American Commercial Association may
well have been a greedy organization, but its immediate self-
interest did lead it to a temporary acceptance of the existing
and probable future conditions in Soviet Russia—a realistic
acceptance that was sorely lacking among Government officials and most business organizations and representatives of
the early 1920s.

The optimism of the American Commercial Association
did not last beyond the fall of 1921. After spending six months
in Russia (from December 10, 1920, to June 30, 1921), Jennings returned to the United States and reported to his organization that the Soviets and Martens were a "bunch of
pikers, fakers and crooks" and that unless the Communists
undertook "to carry out the contracts and agreements they
have made with us we can see no possible excuse for their
being trusted by American manufacturers or businessmen
with one cent of credit." Jennings asserted that he and other
members of his group had been "deceived, humbugged and
flimflammed" into thinking that they had definite contracts
with the Soviets. He was unable to get any of these contracts
honored after six months in Russia. Obviously the Soviets
had wanted the goods on credit, and the small companies
who composed the association were either unwilling or,
more likely, unable to meet the terms. Far from financing the
activities of the Soviet Bureau, as has been charged, Jennings's association could not even finance its own credit.
When he met with both Hughes and Hoover in October, Jennings continued to recommend ways to end the postwar depression and to ask the United States Government to advance
credit to the USSR, but his personal enthusiasm about Russian trade died in the fall of 1921.[13]

13. Jennings, report to American Commercial Association,
August 31, 1921, U.S. Department of State, Records Relating to
Internal Affairs of Russia and the Soviet Union, Record Group

The Jennings affair confirmed the Government's opinion of the economic bankruptcy of the Soviet experiment and hardened resistance to any drastic modification of official Russian policy. Formal organizations within the U.S. business community, except the American Commercial Association, offered no significant opposition to the commercial aspects of the policy once the wartime embargo was lifted. As noted above, the majority of businessmen supported Russian trade *in theory* but did not believe that it would materialize *in practice* because they viewed communism as economically, politically, and morally unsound. Simultaneously, therefore, most members of the business community apparently supported lifting trade restrictions but opposed resuming commercial or diplomatic relations.

An official of the American-Russian Chamber of Commerce reflected this thinking when he wrote to Secretary Colby in 1920:

> ... vital as is the matter of resumption of trade with Russia, such trade is practically impossible under the Soviet government. This Government is the fundamental obstacle, both economic and moral, that stands in the way of European reconstruction. It rests upon terror, both political and physical, and denies to the people of Russia, not only political representation, but the primary rights of personal safety and liberty. To recognize it now would be a criminal act, since it would only tend to lengthen its existence and prolong the agony of the Russian people, and such recognition would at the same time be a repudiation of all the moral principles for which we fought in the war.[14]

Following the lead of the Government, the best organized and usually the most internationally oriented segments of the business community went beyond the initial economic argument that Socialist or Communist systems inevitably retarded industrial and agricultural production and therefore destroyed trade possibilities. These groups of banking,

---

59, File 861.50/235; Jennings, "Open Letter to Congress," October 1921, Jennings to Hoover, October 26, 1921, BFDC File, HHCD; Sutton, *Western Technology*, Vol. 1, *1917–1930*, p. 288.

14. Jerome Landfield (executive vice-president, American-Russian Chamber of Commerce) to Bainbridge Colby, April 12, 1920, U.S. Department of State, General Records, Record Group 59, File 661.1115/268.

financial, and established import-export interests ended up assuming an ideological position by maintaining that until the Russian political and socioeconomic structure was altered, the United States should refuse to recognize or do business with that country. Under their leadership, the business community in general supported the economic and ideological features of the Government's Russian policy during the first half of the decade. In addition, strong support came from lumber and mining industries, whose members feared that recognition would result in the resumption of trade detrimental to their own already declining domestic sales.[15]

The basic leadership provided by these internationalist business groups in opposing trade and recognition is somewhat surprising. They were normally the most concerned with expanding their operations abroad throughout the period from 1918 to 1933, and theoretically the least likely to support Government policies that might have limited their economic activities. At the same time, the more nationalistic and broadly representative elements within the business community, represented in such publications as *American Industries* and *Nation's Business*, devoted less time and energy to upholding the Government's policy than might be expected.[16] In other words, on the question of political and economic relations with the Soviets, business concerns generally agreed, but the internationally oriented enterprises were most actively determined to preserve this unanimity because their business activities were more threatened by what they deemed the economic irresponsibility of the Bolsheviks than were those of average businessmen. They also appeared more organized in both centralized leadership and coordinated propaganda efforts than any of the more domestically based groups who followed their lead.

Banking groups in particular were tightly knit structural units that remained hostile to the Soviet Union long after

15. William Appleman Williams, *American-Russian Relations, 1781–1947*, p. 203.
16. There were many articles about bolshevism both during and after the Red Scare in *American Industries, Nation's Business*, and *Iron Age*, but none of these articles broached the issue of recognition before 1925.

the general business associations and individual manufacturing and import-export companies had begun to be commercially and diplomatically less suspicious of the Soviets. Their lingering opposition was encouraged by the activities of a powerful group of New York banks and life insurance companies. Two members of this group—the National City Bank and the New York Life Insurance Company—had tried unsuccessfully to obtain compensation for the losses they had incurred when their property was nationalized by the Bolsheviks.[17] In general, banking opposition was solidified by the Depression of 1929, which not only put most financiers on the defensive, but also made their organizations inordinately suspicious of any country that repudiated contractual obligations.

There were, nonetheless, a few bankers who privately expressed disapproval of certain aspects of the Government's policy between 1917 and 1933. Financiers Thomas Lamont, William Boyce Thompson, Dwight Morrow, Reeve Schley, and Frank A. Vanderlip, for example, publicly supported nonrecognition and at the same time urged development of "unofficial relations" and trade with the Soviets. Vanderlip, who was president of the National City Bank, had long been personally interested in establishing "direct commercial relations with Russia," rather than using British middlemen. Before the Bolshevik Revolution the State Department had supported his efforts. Although his company was a victim of Russian nationalization, he continued to think that strong commercial relations should be cultivated. Publicly, however, the respective financial institutions of such financiers as Vanderlip and others registered no complaint with the established policy.[18]

17. Fischer, *Soviets*, 2: 813; John Foster Dulles, brief for New York Life Insurance Company, June 3, 1926, Russian File, HHCD; Donald G. Bishop, *The Roosevelt-Litvinov Agreements: The American View*, pp. 142–43.

18. E. Dana Durand to Klein, November 8, 1923, U.S. Department of Commerce, Records of the Bureau of Foreign and Domestic Commerce, Record Group 151, File 448-U.S.; Thomas W. Lamont, *Across World Frontiers*, pp. 91–95; Hermann Hagedorn, *The Magnate: William Boyce Thompson and His Times*, p. 259; George F. Kennan, *Russia Leaves the War*, p. 247; Lasch, *American Liberals*, p. 105; Harold Nicolson, *Dwight Morrow*,

Trade and recognition were unequivocally opposed in the early 1920s by the American Manufacturers' Export Association, the American-Russian Chamber of Commerce, the Cleveland Chamber of Commerce, the Philadelphia Board of Trade, and the American Bankers Association. These groups received support from such publications as *The Wall Street Journal*, the *Coast Banker*, *The Annalist*, and *Bradstreet's*. The Investment Bankers' Association of Boston, the *Pacific Banker*, and the *Bankers Magazine* registered conditional opposition to recognition of Russia; they stipulated that Russia should be recognized only after the Bolsheviks agreed to honor past and future debts and other contractual obligations and to abandon propaganda activities encouraging the overthrow of traditional forms of government. Such prerequisites, however, were tantamount to a denial of recognition and trade, because Soviet leaders showed little inclination between 1920 and 1925 to meet the prescribed conditions.[19]

This publicly organized business opposition to official

---

p. 288; Frank A. Vanderlip to Col. V. O. J. Philipsen, March 27, 1920, Vanderlip to Acting Secretary of State (Polk), February 17, 1920, Vanderlip, fragment for *New York World* article about Russia, May 21, 1922, Vanderlip Papers; Carl Philip Parrini, "American Empire and Creating a Community of Interest: Economic Diplomacy, 1916–1922" (Ph.D. dissertation, University of Wisconsin, 1963), pp. 49–50.

19. American Manufacturers Export Association to Robert Lansing, February 13, 1920, American-Russian Chamber of Commerce to Bainbridge Colby, April 6, 1920, American Manufacturers Export Association to Colby, May 13, 1920, U.S. Department of State, General Records, Record Group 59, Files 661.1116/25, 661.1115/46, 611.613/185; Cleveland Chamber of Commerce, *Annual*, 1921, pp. 115–16; Philadelphia Board of Trade, *Proceedings*, January 24, 1921, pp. 9–10; Philadelphia Board of Trade, *90th Annual Report*, January 23, 1922, p. 16. *Journal of the American Bankers Association* 14 (March 1922): 631–32; 15 (May 1923): 703–6. *The Wall Street Journal*, January 5, 1918, p. 1; May 27, 1922, p. 1; September 14, 1922, p. 2; January 8, 1925, p. 1; April 3, 1925, p. 1. *Coast Banker* 25 (September 1920): 279; 25 (October 1920): 512; 28 (April 1922): 375; 29 (July 1922): 29–32. *The Annalist* 17 (March 7, 1921): 299; 19 (May 22, 1922): 555. *Bradstreet's* 48 (August 14, 1920): 529; 50 (May 6, 1922): 292. *Pacific Banker*, July 31, 1920, p. 1; *Bankers Magazine* 105 (August 1922): 300–303.

diplomatic and commercial relations with Russia was so pervasive during the first half of the 1920s that few individual businessmen urged recognition, not even most of those who were quite eager to trade or to establish informal contact with the Soviets. The most notable exceptions to this principle were Washington B. Vanderlip and Harry F. Sinclair, both of whom had been granted tempting concessions in Russia. In 1920 Lenin had deliberately made Vanderlip's Siberian and Kamchatka concessions and Sinclair's Sakhalin concession contingent upon U.S. recognition, and the two men attempted to use their personal connections within the Harding administration to re-establish diplomatic contact in the early 1920s. Both failed, and so did their concessions.[20] For the most part, however, U.S. businessmen who were interested in trade with Russia operated enterprises within this country and conformed to the prevalent antirecognition sentiment of the early postwar years. Even Jennings, who insisted that trade with Russia was a "matter of business" and not a "matter of politics," always refrained from taking a stand on the question of recognition.[21]

Thus, the vast majority of businessmen, who were not personally involved in commercial transactions with the Soviets and who were not members of those few, small groups that openly dared to pursue such trade, were not advocating recognition of the Soviet regime. Some prominent business spokesmen of the period—Herbert Hoover, Frank A. Vanderlip, John Hays Hammond, Jr., Norman H. Davis, Henry Ford, Fred I. Kent, Oscar S. Straus, Andrew Mellon, Henry Clay

20. Albert Parry, "Washington B. Vanderlip, the 'Khan of Kamchatka,'" *Pacific Historical Review* 17 (August 1948): 322–29; Louis Fischer, *Oil Imperialism: The International Struggle for Petroleum*, pp. 156–61; Louis Fischer, *The Life of Lenin*, pp. 424–28, 510; Simon Liberman, *Building Lenin's Russia*, pp. 150–51.

21. Jennings to American Manufacturers Export Association, February 25, 1920, U.S. Department of State, General Records, Record Group 59, File 661.1115/41. Jennings also made no mention of recognition in his letters to secretaries Lansing and Colby. See Jennings to Lansing, January 27, 1920, Jennings to Colby, March 29, April 3, 1920, U.S. Department of State, General Records, Record Group 59, Files 661.1115/11, 661.1115/41, 661.1115/44.

Frick, Otto Kahn, Bernard Baruch, and Elbert H. Gary—
publicly opposed recognition. Others did not directly speak
out against recognition but belonged to organizations that
did. One such organization was the Russian Information
Bureau, which included among its honorary advisers C. A.
Coffin, head of the General Electric Company; Darwin P.
Kingsley, president of the New York Life Insurance Com-
pany; Samuel McRoberts, executive manager of the National
City Bank; Charles H. Sabin, president of the Guaranty
Trust Company; and Jacob H. Schiff of Kuhn, Loeb, and
Company.[22] Then there were these powerful business lead-
ers who also remained in silent agreement on the topic: James
A. Farrell of the United States Steel Corporation; A. C. Bed-
ford of the Standard Oil Company; W. C. Durant of the
General Motors Company; E. M. Herr of the Westinghouse
Electric and Manufacturing Company; James K. Armsby of
the California Packing Company; F. A. Seiberling of the
Goodyear Tire and Rubber Company; and W. W. Nichols of
the Allis-Chalmers Manufacturing Company.[23]

The American-Russian Chamber of Commerce was another business group whose most prestigious members tacitly
supported its official policy against recognition. They included Maurice A. Oudin, president of the International
General Electric Company; Daniel G. Wing, president of the
First National Bank of Boston; W. F. Dixon, director of the
Russian Singer Company; W. H. Woodin, president of the
American Car and Foundry Company; Charles M. Muchnic,
vice-president of the American Locomotive Sales Corporation; and William Butterworth, president of Deere and Company.[24] Finally, one of the most vociferous antirecognition

22. The Russian Information Bureau was officially headed by
A. J. Sack but came under the direct influence of the Russian
Embassy and the Provisional Government's ambassador, Boris
Bakhmetev, who was accredited by the State Department until
the spring of 1922. Only the prominent businessmen advising the
bureau have been listed. See Kennan, *Decision to Intervene*, pp.
322–23.

23. These were the more prominent businessmen who were
the officers and directors of the American Manufacturers Export
Association.

24. These men were on the board of directors and were executive committee members of the American-Russian Chamber of

business organizations, the National Civic Federation, contained in its membership Henry P. Davison of J. P. Morgan and Company; T. Coleman Du Pont, chairman of the executive committee of the Equitable Office Building Corporation; Ogden L. Mills, director of the International Paper Company; Haley Fiske, president of the Metropolitan Life Insurance Company; George M. Reynolds, president of Continental and Commercial National Bank of Chicago; Harris Weinstock, president of Weinstock-Nichols Company, San Francisco; George B. Cortelyou, president of Consolidated Gas Company, New York; and George W. Perkins of J. P. Morgan and Company.[25] None of these men spoke out publicly against recognition, but their private opposition was well known. The active leadership of a handful and the indirect example of so many influential businessmen enabled a contemporary observer to write in 1924 that "very few favor recognition on business grounds or because they hope for concession and opportunity to trade."[26]

This dearth of organized business support for recognition was most apparent during the years 1918 to 1923, for basically five reasons. Like those men in the United States Government, most businessmen were convinced until approximately 1923 that very few chances for profitable trade or other economic opportunities existed in Russia for them.[27]

Commerce. This organization was closely associated with both the Russian Embassy and the Russian Information Bureau. Kennan, *Decision to Intervene*, pp. 323–24.

25. These were the members of the executive committee of the National Civic Federation, which was opposed to both recognition and trade with Russia throughout the 1920s and the early 1930s. See Williams, *American-Russian Relations*, pp. 137, 153, 181, 223, 238.

26. Alfred L. P. Dennis, *The Foreign Policies of Soviet Russia*, p. 454.

27. American Manufacturers Export Association to Lansing, February 13, 1920, American-Russian Chamber (Redfield) to Hughes, January 13, 1922, U.S. Department of State, General Records, Record Group 59, Files 661.1116/25, 661.1115/362; Norman H. Davis to John Spargo, August 12, 1920, Box 53, Davis Papers; Herbert Hoover, "Russia the Great Drawback in Europe," *The Wall Street Journal*, March 22, 1922, p. 3; *The Annalist* 20 (December 25, 1922), p. 691. *Journal of the American Bankers Association* 14 (March 1922), pp. 631–32; 15 (September 1922):

Also, it was not until 1923 and 1924 that Soviet officials modified and regularized their laws concerning concession and
trade so that foreign businessmen could begin to conduct affairs on a more secure and orderly basis. Then, prior to 1923
there was a distinct lack of communication between those
business houses interested in trade with the Soviets, and the
politicians and liberal intellectuals who, since the end of the
war, had been supporting recognition in the name of world
peace.[28] Further, members of all U.S. business circles believed that communism threatened the American way of
life, especially the concept of the sanctity of property rights.
Finally, U.S. businessmen adhered to the pervasive postwar
diplomatic view that economic and political relations between countries of opposing ideologies were difficult, if not
absolutely impossible.[29]

126–28. *Pacific Banker*, June 8, 1922, p. 1; *The Magazine of Wall
Street* 30 (October 28, 1922): 986–87, 1038. *The Wall Street
Journal*, November 6, 1920, p. 10; May 26, 1923, p. 3; October 2,
1924, p. 1; August 14, 1925, p. 13; January 29, 1926, p. 1. *American Industries* 21 (August 1920): 31–32; 22 (October 1921): 40.
Bradstreet's 48 (April 3, 1920): 224; 48 (July 24, 1920): 480;
48 (December 25, 1920): 832; 49 (January 29, 1921): 85; 49
(February 19, 1921): 133; 49 (April 2, 1921): 229; 50 (April
1, 1922): 223; 50 (August 26, 1922): 550; 50 (September 17,
1922): 612. *Coast Banker* 23 (August 1919): 159; 26 (June
1921): 689. *Iron Age* 106 (July 22, 1920): 197–98; 107 (March
31, 1921): 847; 112 (September 6, 1923): 619.

28. Williams, *American-Russian Relations*, pp. 178–79. Some
of the earliest and most vocal advocates of Russian recognition
were Senator William E. Borah, Raymond Robins, James P.
Goodrich, and Alexander Gumberg. Gumberg finally assumed the
all-important role of liaison between protrade business interests
and prorecognition groups. See Chapter IV.

29. For general support of Hoover's and Hughes's policy, see
The Annalist 17 (March 28, 1921): 371–72; 19 (January 23,
1922): 147–48; 19 (March 13, 1922): 315; 19 (May 22, 1922):
555. *Bankers Magazine* 102 (May 1921): 812. *Bradstreet's* 49
(February 19, 1921): 133; 49 (April 2, 1921): 229; 49 (April
23, 1921): 277; 49 (September 17, 1921): 612; 50 (April 1,
1922): 223; 50 (August 26, 1922): 550. Philadelphia Board of
Trade, *Proceedings*, January 23, 1922, pp. 14–15. *Pacific Banker*,
March 31, 1921, p. 1; May 19, 1921, p. 1. *The Wall Street Journal*, November 23, 1921, p. 1; September 6, 1922, p. 7; October
2, 1924, p. 1; August 14, 1925, p. 13. Philadelphia Board of Trade,
resolution approving his position to Hughes, April 23, 1921, Amer-

In addition to these general reasons, several other arguments were sometimes used by business spokesmen to support the Hoover-Hughes policy. The *Annalist* and the American-Russian Chamber of Commerce argued that by not supporting the Bolsheviks, the United States would ultimately gain the gratitude of the people and consequently have the "inside track in Russian trade."[30] At the same time, the Philadelphia Board of Trade was convinced that the policy represented the best way simultaneously "to protect our own Government from the undermining influences of radical agitators" and to encourage the democratic forces in Russia. Businessmen also readily admitted that nonrecognition, combined with the unstable political and economic conditions in Russia, prevented the Soviets from obtaining the confidence of U.S. bankers, which was a necessary basis for long-term financial credit.[31]

Hoover's and Hughes's acceptance of the basic policy established in the Colby Note stifled the development of any significant partisan opposition to nonrecognition during the decade. In fact, a leading representative of Democratic businessmen, Norman Davis, was probably more suspicious of the Soviets and of those who advocated trading with them than were most of the leading Republican businessmen who supported the Harding and Coolidge administrations.[32] If anything, the strongest business opposition to the official policy came from within Republican ranks, for the Republican party contained those most strongly against trade and recognition—Hamilton Fish and Elihu Root—and those most strongly for it—Raymond Robins and Senator William E. Borah.

---

ican-Russian Chamber of Commerce to Secretary Hughes, January 13, 1922, U.S. Department of State, General Records, Record Group 59, Files 661.1115/294, 661.1115/362.

30. *The Annalist* 17 (March 28, 1921): 371–72; American-Russian Chamber of Commerce to Hughes, January 13, 1923, U.S. Department of State, General Records, Record Group 59, File 661.1115/362.

31. Philadelphia Board of Trade to Hughes, April 23, 1921, reprinted in *Proceedings*, January 23, 1922, pp. 14–15. *The Wall Street Journal*, November 6, 1920, p. 10; November 18, 1925, p. 1.

32. *The Annalist* 17 (March 28, 1921): 371–72.

Businesses in different parts of the country varied in the degree of support they gave to the policy's restrictions on commerce. Banking publications and individual businessmen from the West Coast were less committed to the ideological reasons for severely limiting trade than were their Eastern and Midwestern counterparts.[33] West Coast businesses were closer to Siberian and Oriental markets, and like the American Commercial Association, businessmen in the Far West were quick to subordinate ideological considerations to apparent economic opportunity. Also, because Japanese exploitation of the markets in Manchuria and Siberia was a much more immediate threat after the war than was the possibility of German and English competition there, some West Coast enterprises naturally felt more threatened and thus more economically motivated to question the official policy of nonrecognition.

In summary, financial, banking, and established import-export groups from all over the country actively supported the Hoover-Hughes position on nonrecognition of, and little trade with, Soviet Russia in the early 1920s. They did so for the combination of reasons cited above. The broadly based manufacturing and general business organizations of the period commented much less frequently, if at all, on the official policy but implicitly supported it, nonetheless.

By 1925, however, individual engineering companies, exporters of heavy machinery, and producers of cotton, flour, automobiles, iron, and steel for foreign markets began to deal with the Bolsheviks when it became profitable to do

33. Between 1918 and 1922, most of the articles on Russian trade in the *Coast Banker* did not reflect ideological condemnation of the Soviets. The authors stressed the economic opportunities that the USSR offered, and when they did comment on the internal instability, their criticisms were pragmatic, rather than subjective. *Coast Banker* 23 (July 1919): 8; 23 (August 1919): 159; 23 (November 1919): 435, 452–53; 24 (May 1920): 647. The only exceptions to this nonideological approach in Western publications were signed articles by two bankers from New York. The *Pacific Banker* strayed so far from the ideological approach as to publish on two occasions articles suggesting that Russia be recognized pending certain conditions. See *Pacific Banker*, July 31, 1920, p. 1; March 31, 1921, p. 1. This sectionalism was not so apparent after 1925, when more firms across the country began to take an interest in Russian trade.

so.[34] The typical attitude of such highly specialized and often extremely competitive groups was summarized by one machine-tool manufacturer when he told a representative of the Commerce Department that he didn't care if the total amount of trade with Russia was insignificant. He explained:

> They are now in the market for $350,000 worth of machine tools. If we land this order it will keep several of our shops busy for four months. That is all the business we care to handle for that part of the world. From the standpoint of international trade statistics it may be very little business for a country like Russia, and your economic data are all very well in their place, but from the standpoint of individual manufacturing concerns, this is a whale of an order and we are going after it.[35]

Since leaders in these specialized industries had been critical of communism and conditions in Russia from 1918 to 1925, they all seem to have subscribed in theory to the ideological position of the Government. They simply were not as

34. Between 1918 and 1925 *Nation's Business*, the publication of the Chamber of Commerce of the United States, did not once comment on the Hoover-Hughes policy, although it carried many articles critical of the internal situation in Russia. *American Industries*, representing the National Association of Manufacturers, carried only one signed article commenting on the official policy between 1918 and 1925, and the author of even that article did not give specific support. The twenty-ninth annual NAM convention scheduled a session entitled "The Truth about Russia Industrially," and before the three speakers were introduced, it was announced that the NAM was not responsible for any statement made and that the convention "would not be called upon to express an opinion with respect to Russian affairs from any standpoint." See *American Industries* 24 (June 1924): 9. While *Iron Age* commented on the official policy and appeared to support it, the editors began to publish fewer articles criticizing the Soviets and supporting the official policy at the beginning of 1923 and published instead articles on the improving trade situation and economic opportunities present in Russia. This shift in outlook was a characteristic response on the part of the steel industries and other specialized producers of export products. See Alexander Gumberg (quoting Charles M. Schwab) to William E. Borah, December 11, 1925, Box 271, Borah Papers; editorial published in the company organ of the Modern Hiller Company, May 23, 1925, Russian File, HHCD.

35. L. J. Lewery to Hoover, September 22, 1924, Russian File, HHCD.

committed to the practical implementation of the anti-Soviet policy as were most political and financial leaders and those economic groups who feared competition from Russian products. Strong evidence also suggests that a number of the businesses or industries that began to trade with the USSR—particularly the cotton-textile manufacturers and a number of small machine-tool companies and engineering firms—were not fully participating in the general corporate prosperity of the period. Such businesses, as well as those involved in agriculture and soft coal mining, were victims of changing consumer habits, a glut on the domestic market of their particular product or service, or their own chaotic and inefficient business practices. Their inability either to organize their operations along traditionally centralized, oligarchic lines or to change to the decentralized, associational patterns suggested by Hoover as Secretary of Commerce may have moved them to abandon the ideologically and economically consistent position of opposing Soviet recognition in fact as well as theory.[36]

It is also possible that, given the basic contradictions within official Government circles on the question of recognition, these less well organized or more destructively competitive enterprises found the tightrope act that Washington officials were performing too difficult and too unprofitable to master, and so the division of opinion within the business community became increasingly pronounced after 1925. During this same period, trade relations with the Soviets steadily began to improve, reaching a climax in 1931 and then precipitously declining a full two years before the United States recognized the USSR in 1933.

During the first half of the 1920s, the Soviet leaders hoped that this tiny, woefully uninfluential, and disorganized mi-

36. Joan Hoff Wilson, *Herbert Clark Hoover: Forgotten Progressive*, chaps. 4, 5; Louis Galambos, *Competition and Cooperation: The Emergence of a National Trade Association*, pp. 89–92; Ellis W. Hawley, "Secretary Hoover and the Bituminous Coal Problem, 1921–1928," *Business History Review* 42 (Autumn 1968): 253–70; Gary Harlan Koerselman, "Herbert Hoover and the Farm Crisis of the Twenties: A Study of the Commerce Department's Efforts To Solve the Agricultural Depression, 1921–1928" (Ph.D. dissertation, Northern Illinois University), 1971.

nority within the U.S. business community would be able to force the U.S. Government to grant the USSR recognition. The Soviets seem to have been convinced that despite the presence of Hughes and Hoover in the Harding and Coolidge cabinets, the business-oriented Republican party would ultimately grant recognition to the USSR in return for Russian trade concessions to the few U.S. firms that would take the risk. The Soviets either underestimated or did not know the degree to which the ideological position assumed by the State and Commerce departments was fast becoming institutionalized and thus how insulated from outside pressure those who agreed with that position were.

Therefore Soviet leaders and their representatives in this country continued to urge U.S. companies conducting business with the USSR to advocate recognition. Although the leaders were unsuccessful, their repeated attempts clearly indicate that they shared with many contemporary Americans (and later generations of historians) the idea that recognition was a diplomatic gesture that could be purchased with the right business contacts.[37] Perhaps the Soviets had become victims of their own theories about capitalist motivation. In fact, they had to overcome the entire bureaucratized opposition within top business and Government circles before recognition could become a reality, which was finally accomplished only after Franklin D. Roosevelt personally by-passed or ignored these rigid bureaucratic thought patterns and procedures.

37. Maddox, *Borah and Foreign Policy*, 47, 185–86, 209n. 75.

IV

CONFUSION: VIEWS OF
BUSINESS AND GOVERNMENT
LEADERS, 1925–1931

During the slow but steady development of economic
relations between the United States and the USSR, many
businessmen gradually changed their attitudes about trade
with Russia, but they did not automatically become the fer-
vent advocates of recognition that Soviet leaders desired.
Business relations dated back to a few scattered contracts
and concessions made from 1918 to 1923 with Royal Keeley,
Charles H. Smith, and other engineers and with such firms as
the Ford Motor Company, the International Barnsdall Corporation, Armand Hammer's Allied American Corporation,
the Sinclair Exploration Company, and Sidney Hillman's
Russian-American Industrial Corporation.[1] In spite of these

1. Young (Baltic Provinces) to State Department, September
13, 1921, DeWitt C. Poole (Division of Russian Affairs, State
Department) to Charles Evans Hughes, October 18, 1921, Poole
to Hughes, November 9, 1921, Young to State Department, September 28, 1922, Poole, memorandum, January 11, 1923, Coleman (Latvia) to State Department, March 2, April 1, 1923,
State Department to Peter T. Swanist, June 2, 1923, Coleman to
State Department, June 21, 1923, Hanson (Harbin, Manchuria)
to State Department, November 20, 1923, U.S. Department of
State, Records Relating to Internal Affairs of Russia and the
Soviet Union, Record Group 59, Files 861.50/234, 861.50/280,
861.50/353, 861.6464/123, 861.602/76, 861.602/78, 861.602
/81, 861.602/87, 861.9111/286; Allan Nevins and Frank Ernest
Hill, *Ford*, Vol. 2, *Expansion and Challenge, 1915–1933*, p. 673;
Floyd James Fithian, "Soviet-American Economic Relations,
1918–1933: American Business in Russia during the Period of
Nonrecognition" (Ph.D. dissertation, University of Nebraska,
1964), pp. 307–9.

early contracts and the tempting rumors about gigantic concessions being offered Washington B. Vanderlip, W. Averell Harriman, and Leslie B. Urquhardt, trade and investments were negligible, and U.S. businessmen remained naturally cautious about dealing with the new Russian regime before 1923. Then, several changes in the USSR's economic policy stimulated greater U.S. business interest, an interest that increased as the decade progressed.

Beginning in 1923, Soviet officials modified their concession policy in order to make the system less subject to political machinations. As noted earlier, Lenin had hoped to obtain the United States' recognition through the Vanderlip and Sinclair concessions. When his hopes were not realized and after the Genoa, Hague, and Lausanne conferences did not produce the political or economic results the Bolsheviks desired, they began to subordinate their political goals to the practical problem of rebuilding their country's economic productivity. They had assumed since the November Revolution that the problem could be solved only with the aid of foreign capital investment and foreign credit. To encourage both, the Soviet Government issued a series of decrees that modified and clarified the original concession policy.[2]

Like the domestic changes introduced in 1921 as the New Economic Policy, the new concession policy appeared to hostile foreign observers to be a "retreat from communism."[3] In fact, none of the modified concession rules weakened the Soviet Government's control of foreign trade or foreign eco-

2. Coleman, report on Joseph A. Meyerowitch, business representative of Allis-Chalmers in Russia to State Department, July 17, 1923, U.S. Department of State, Records Relating to Internal Affairs of Russia and the Soviet Union, Record Group 59, File 861.602/88; E. Dana Durand to Christian Herter, April 1, 1922, Box 267, L. J. Lewery to Julius Klein, September 22, 1924, Box 266, HHCD; Paul Scheffer, *Seven Years in Soviet Russia*, p. 261; Anthony C. Sutton, *Western Technology and Soviet Development*, Vol. 1, *1917 to 1930*, pp. 6–7.

3. Calvin B. Hoover, *The Economic Life of Soviet Russia*, p. 153; Simon Liberman, *Building Lenin's Russia*, p. 149; Louis Fischer, *The Soviets in World Affairs*, 2: 583–85; Stuart Chase, Robert Dunn, and Rexford Guy Tugwell, eds., *Soviet Russia in the Second Decade*, p. 342; Fithian, "Soviet-American Economic Relations," p. 109; Herbert Hoover, address to International Chamber of Commerce, May 15, 1922, 227-HHPS.

nomic policy, and absolute ownership was still forbidden under the legal doctrine of *usufruct,* which meant the concessions carried no property rights with them. Limits were placed on the number of years the property could be leased, on the amount of profit that foreign concessionaires could earn, and on the percentage of profits they could export from the country. In addition, the Soviet State Bank insisted that, despite the actual value of the postwar ruble's having fallen by about 50 per cent, the ruble be exchanged on a parity with foreign currencies. Nonetheless, the modified policy did make concessions easier to obtain, and even with the economic restrictions, net profits of from 20 per cent to 30 per cent were not uncommon. And at least one foreign concession, a Swedish ball-bearing factory, reportedly made a 200 per cent profit. According to one contemporary observer, rumors of such profits were tempting only to those businessmen who had "steady nerves and strong stomachs" because foreign concessionaires tended either to prosper enormously or to fail miserably.[4] There was little middle ground for them under the new concession policy.

In addition to obtaining concessions, U.S. businesses could trade with Russia in the early years of the New Economic Policy by signing commercial contracts with authorized purchasing firms. The NEP authorized three types of trading organizations. Some were Soviet-controlled agencies, such as Arcos, the Products Exchange Corporation, and ARTS (All Russian Textile Syndicate); others were semiofficial organizations that had once been private cooperatives, such as Centrosoyus (Central Union of Consumers Cooperatives) and Selskosoyus (Union of Agricultural Producers Cooperatives). There were also a few private trading companies estab-

4. Coleman to State Department, April 26, June 8, June 21, 1923, December 19, 1929, U.S. Department of State, Records Relating to Internal Affairs of Russia and the Soviet Union, Record Group 59, Files 861.602/79, 861.602/85, 861.602/87, 861. 602/207; Saul G. Bron, *Soviet Economic Development and American Business,* pp. 138–39; Chase, Dunn, and Tugwell, eds., *Second Decade,* pp. 344–56; Scheffer, *Seven Years,* pp. 260–71; Alexander Baykov, *Soviet Foreign Trade,* pp. 10–11; William Henry Chamberlin, *Soviet Russia: A Living Record and History,* pp. 362–69; Sutton, *Western Technology,* Vol. 1, *1917 to 1930,* pp. 8–9.

lished by special permission of the Soviet Government.[5] The only prominent example of this kind of purchasing firm operated by a U.S. citizen was Armand Hammer's Allied American Corporation (ALAMERICO).

Hammer had originally traveled to Soviet Russia in August 1921, when he was twenty-three years old, as a physician interested in famine relief. Several months later, in November, he became one of the first U.S. concessionaires by signing a contract to operate an abandoned asbestos mine in the Urals. Not completely content with this line of endeavor and knowing next to nothing about producing asbestos, Hammer briefly returned to the United States for advice. By January 1922 he obtained an agency to sell Ford products in Russia, and after making similar arrangements with other U.S. manufacturers, he, his brother, and his father arranged for their Allied American Corporation to represent these companies in Russia. A little over a year later, in July 1923, the Soviets gave the firm a trading concession that permitted it to obtain import and export licenses without direct approval of the Commissariat of Foreign Trade.[6]

By 1924 ALAMERICO had offices in Moscow and New York and was the most successful of the private export-import firms doing business with the Soviets. In that year the company was the selling agent for approximately thirty-eight major U.S. manufacturers, representing a combined capitalization of over $1,000,000,000. Ford Motor, U.S. Rubber, Union Twist Drill, and the American Tool Works were among those represented by Allied American. Between 1921 and 1923 Hammer personally contributed to breaking down many

5. E. Dana Durand, confidential circular, "Trade with Russia," April 9, 1923, Russian File, HHCD; L. J. Lewery to Chicago district manager, BFDC, August 23, 1924, U.S. Department of Commerce, Records of the Bureau of Foreign and Domestic Commerce, Record Group 151, File 448–U.S.; Baykov, *Soviet Foreign Trade*, pp. 12–14.

6. Armand Hammer, *The Quest for the Romanoff Treasure*, pp. 67, 84, 101–2, 107–9, 121, 174–75; E. Dana Durand to Allied American Corporation, July 17, 1922, Hammer to Durand, August 11, 1923, U.S. Department of Commerce, Records of the Bureau of Foreign and Domestic Commerce, Record Group 151, File 448–U.S.; Fithian, "Soviet-American Economic Relations," pp. 113–14; Sutton, *Western Technology*, Vol. 1, *1917 to 1930*, pp. 108–9, 268–70.

of Henry Ford's inhibitions about dealing directly with the Soviets. Then, in 1924 the Soviet Government instituted a program aimed at abolishing all private trading organizations, and by 1926 the Hammer firm was no longer an important force in U.S.-Russian trade relations. In the interim Hammer had obtained a concession to manufacture pencils in the Soviet Union.[7]

From 1922 to 1924, the Department of Commerce recommended the services of the Allied American Corporation to U.S. businessmen. Officials in Washington were impressed by the company's $2,500,000 turnover for the year ending in June 1924 and by the fact that most of the purchases had been made on a cash basis. Leonard J. Lewery, the assistant chief of the European Division of the Bureau of Foreign and Domestic Commerce, issued a "friendly warning" to the U.S. trade commissioner at Riga for reporting to the bureau that the Allied American Corporation was "a pretty rotten bunch" that operated as a "propaganda organ of the Soviet government." Lewery told the commissioner, Carl J. Mayer, that he would have to modify his views of the Hammer firm, not only because of its impressive record, but also because there had been complaints from the Hammer family and from businessmen to whom Mayer had spoken unfavorably about the company.[8]

While it was true that Armand Hammer and other company officials commented enthusiastically about conditions in the Soviet Union and opportunities for trade there, none of them advocated recognition in the 1920s, and consequently Washington members of the Commerce Department did not think the enterprise represented a threat to the Government's ideological opposition to recognition. In addition, Commerce officials insisted that it was not "the object of the Bureau [of Foreign and Domestic Commerce] to interfere

7. L. J. Lewery to Carl J. Mayer (trade commissioner, Riga), July 7, 1924, U.S. Department of Commerce, Records of the Bureau of Foreign and Domestic Commerce, Record Group 151, File 488–U.S.; Fithian, "Soviet-American Economic Relations," pp. 114, 116, 309–12. See Appendix A for further details about Hammer's activities in the USSR.

8. L. J. Lewery to Carl J. Mayer, July 7, July 23, 1924, U.S. Department of Commerce, Records of the Bureau of Foreign and Domestic Commerce, Record Group 151, File 448–U.S.

with business relations of any American concern in Russia."[9] From the standpoint of the department, it was better to have trade between the countries conducted by a private U.S. firm than by a Soviet-controlled agency.

Another trading organization associated with a U.S. citizen was ARTS, the All Russian Textile Syndicate, which was formed in December 1923. It was not a private trading organization like ALAMERICO, but a subsidiary of the All Union Textile Syndicate of Moscow, and its purpose was to purchase cotton to be used in the Russian textile industry. Its promoter in the United States, Alexander Gumberg, was a friend and adviser of some well-known advocates of Russian recognition, including Raymond Robins and Senator William E. Borah. Unlike Armand Hammer, Gumberg worked after 1923 to coordinate the activities of businessmen who were interested in trading with Russia and the intellectuals and politicians who wanted to recognize the Soviet Union in the interest of world peace. He, Robins, Borah, and their associates worked with such organizations as the National Council for Prevention of War, the National Women's Trade Union League, the League of Women Voters of the United States, the Women's International League for Peace and Freedom, and the National Committee for the Recognition of Russia in a sporadic and futile campaign for recognition during the decade.[10]

Alexander Gumberg was a native-born Russian who had lived for fourteen years in New York, where he engaged in Socialist activity, and for a short period he managed the Russian-Socialist newspaper *Novy Mir*. After the March 1917 Revolution he went to Russia and served intermittently as an aide and interpreter for the members of the Elihu Root

9. Fithian, "Soviet-American Economic Relations," pp. 115–16; Herbert W. Gruber (acting chief, Commercial Intelligence Division, BFDC) to Machinery Division, BFDC, August 13, 1924, U.S. Department of Commerce, Records of the Bureau of Foreign and Domestic Commerce, Record Group 151, File 448–U.S.

10. Fithian, "Soviet-American Economic Relations," pp. 127, 129–30, 132; Peter G. Filene, *Americans and the Soviet Experiment, 1917–1933*, pp. 88–92; Anne Vincent Meiburger, *Efforts of Raymond Robins toward the Recognition of Soviet Russia and the Outlawry of War, 1917–1933*, pp. 55–101, 143–62.

Mission, the American Advisory Commission of Railway Experts, the Red Cross Commission, the Bullard Committee on Public Information, and the Associated Press. He returned to the United States with Raymond Robins in the summer of 1918 as the official representative of the Petrograd Telegraph Agency. This position made him the leading public-relations agent for Lenin's Government, and as such he immediately became an object of suspicion for the State Department and several congressional investigating committees.

Fortunately, Gumberg acquired influential political and business friends in the United States. As a result of the contacts he had made during his work with the various commissions from the United States that visited Russia in 1917, Gumberg met prominent financiers after his return, notably, Dwight Morrow of the House of Morgan, Reeve Schley, of the Chase National Bank, and Schley's associate Louis Adamic. He could also count on the friendship of financier and mining magnate William Boyce Thompson, Samuel Zemurray of the United Fruit Company, former Governor of Indiana James P. Goodrich, Senator Burton K. Wheeler, Progressives Robert and Philip La Follette, and of course Robins. In addition, two Wall Street lawyers—Allen Wardwell of Davis, Polk, Wardwell, Gardiner and Reed, and Thomas D. Thacher of Thacher and Bartlett—were among his supporters and legal advisers. Both Wardwell and Thacher had met Gumberg while touring Russia in the summer of 1917.[11]

The importance of Gumberg's role in promoting U.S.-Russian trade was viewed in one way by the U.S. businessmen with whom he came into contact and in another by the officials of the Government. As vice-president and treasurer of the All Russian Textile Syndicate and as Russian consultant for the Chase National Bank, Gumberg made a number of business trips to the USSR. His business associates extolled the astuteness of his economic activities, but Government

11. Biographical information about Gumberg can be found in William Appleman Williams, *American-Russian Relations, 1781–1947*, pp. 110–11, 211; George F. Kennan, *Russia Leaves the War*, pp. 65–67; George F. Kennan, *The Decision to Intervene*, pp. 226–32, 236; Meiburger, *Efforts of Raymond Robins*, pp. 21, 151; Fithian, "Soviet-American Economic Relations," pp. 130–31; Robert James Maddox, *William E. Borah and American Foreign Policy*, p. 198.

officials discounted his effectiveness. For example, Judge Thacher told Dwight Morrow that Gumberg alone was responsible for the successful cotton purchases of ARTS and that these transactions "had done more than any other thing to establish that degree of confidence and credit necessary to the future development of Russian-American trade." Cotton merchants with whom Gumberg dealt voiced similar praise for his competence. Reeve Schley was apparently sufficiently convinced of his ability to arrange a $2,000,000 loan for Gumberg's newly formed company in 1923.[12] Although State Department officials were aware of his "convincing and impressive acquaintances in Washington and New York," they had no confidence in the advice and information he gave them because he obviously disagreed with official policy and because they were convinced that he "had been a Bolshevik agent." While the Commerce Department was willing to accept any economic information Gumberg possessed, it dismissed his importance within ARTS by saying that his position was "merely a clerical one" and that he did not have "any executive authority whatsoever" because all purchases by the company were directed from Moscow.[13]

Thus, Gumberg occupied a unique position in the 1920s. He was a businessman who advocated recognition of Russia without alienating his influential Wall Street friends and who had political views that found sympathy among a small group of intellectuals and Republican politicians. His potentially significant position as a liaison between businessmen interested in trading with the Soviets and noneconomic groups predisposed toward recognition was substantially

12. Williams, *American-Russian Relations*, pp. 110, 211; *The Wall Street Journal*, December 14, 1925, p. 12; Fithian, "Soviet-American Economic Relations," pp. 131–32; Hans Heymann, *We Can Do Business with Russia*, p. 76; Meiburger, *Efforts of Raymond Robins*, pp. 100–101.

13. J. G. Rogers (Assistant Secretary of State), memorandum, May 5, 1931, U.S. Department of State, Political Relations between the U.S. and Russia and the Soviet Union, Record Group 59, File 711.61/223; Paul S. Clapp (Hoover's personal assistant) to Sidney Brooke, December 5, 1925, Box 268, HHCD; L. J. Lewery to Lehman Brothers, July 23, 1924, U.S. Department of Commerce, Records of the Bureau of Foreign and Domestic Commerce, Record Group 151, File 448-U.S.

weakened, however, by the failure of government officials to accord him the same respect and importance given by his business and political associates. Consequently, Gumberg personally exercised little influence over Government policy on the question of recognition between 1923 and 1933, although he did stimulate interest within business circles for trade with the Soviets.[14] Among other things, his company contributed to the pressure that brought about a more liberal visa policy for Russian businessmen in 1925. In 1927 he retired from ARTS but continued to work to improve economic and political relations between the United States and the Soviet Union, primarily through the auspices of the American-Russian Chamber of Commerce.

In the second half of the decade the various kinds of trading organizations, whether private or semiofficial, were either forced out of existence entirely or reduced in significance by the Soviet Government as it consolidated its control over foreign trade. The Soviet agency that grew to dominate U.S.-Russian trade by the end of the decade was the Amtorg Trading Corporation. It was formed on May 27, 1924, as the result of a merger of the state-controlled Arcos and the Products Exchange Corporation, and by 1929 Amtorg was placing orders in the United States for approximately $94,500,000. Between October 1929 and September 1930, 1,700 U.S. firms sold goods to Amtorg; their transactions represented more than half of the total sales to the Soviets for that year. It has been estimated that between 1924 and 1930 Amtorg handled 53 per cent of the sales between the two countries; the All Russian Textile Syndicate, 35 per cent; Centrosoyus and Selskosoyus, 5 per cent each; and the remaining 2 per cent was

14. Williams, *American-Russian Relations*, pp. 178–79. Williams notes that despite Gumberg's activities, there never was "an exact community of interests" established among the politicians, intellectuals, and businessmen who were sympathetic toward Russia. Christopher Lasch agrees in *The American Liberals and the Russian Revolution*, pp. 216–17. Fithian and Maddox attribute greater importance to Gumberg's role than I do; they do not consider his lack of influence with Washington administrators and the structural process that groups and individuals must follow to affect foreign policy. See Lester W. Milbrath, "Interest Groups and Foreign Policy," in James N. Rosenau, ed., *Domestic Sources of Foreign Policy*, pp. 231–51.

handled by other trading firms and U.S. companies with concessions or individual trade contracts.[15]

Some businessmen and Government officials strongly suspected that Amtorg was in reality a Russian propaganda agent carrying on subversive activities in the United States. In addition, several large U.S. companies initially reacted with hostility toward Amtorg because they could not deal directly with the various Soviet industrial monopolies or departments of government but had to route all their business through Amtorg officials.[16]

The Commerce Department was initially less concerned than the State Department about the propaganda functions of Amtorg. In 1925 it reported favorably to business inquiries about the Soviet firm. Nonetheless, department officials pointed out to businessmen that the credit rating of Amtorg was based exclusively on the credit rating of the Soviet Government, and until the latter obtained "a little better standing in this country" they did not recommend granting lenient credit terms to any Communist purchasing agent. The Commerce Department consistently disparaged the claims made by Amtorg officials about future market possibilities and industrial progress in the Soviet Union and noted with satisfaction that no banks in the United States would discount Amtorg trade acceptances.[17]

15. American-Russian Chamber of Commerce, *Handbook of the Soviet Union*, pp. 350, 352; U.S. Congress, House, Committee on Ways and Means, *Hearings on H.R. 15597, H.R. 15927, H.R. 16517*, 71st Cong., 3d sess., January 27–28, 1931, pp. 114, 125–45; National Association of Manufacturers, *Proceedings*, October 1926, p. 34; State Department, translation from *Moscow Soviet Trade*, March 14, 1929, U.S. Department of State, General Records, Record Group 59, File 661.1115 Amtorg Trading Corp./39.

16. White, report of interview with Eybye (General Motors representative) to State Department, June 16, 1926, U.S. Department of State, Records Relating to Internal Affairs of Russia and the Soviet Union, Record Group 59, File 861.797/7; Donald G. Bishop, *The Roosevelt-Litvinov Agreements: The American View*, pp. 35–36; National Association of Manufacturers, *Proceedings*, October 1926, p. 35.

17. J. C. White (chargé d'affaires, Riga) to State Department, September 30, November 29, 1924, U.S. Department of State, General Records, Record Group 59, File 661.1115 Amtorg Trad-

By 1927 only two reliable companies—Amrusco and the Industrial Credit Corporation—discounted Amtorg paper. The rates ran as high as 40 per cent, a rate that made the cost of providing credit to Amtorg too exorbitant for small manufacturers. One of them complained in vain to the Department of Commerce, saying that he would have been "perfectly willing to finance sales [to Russia] through a third party if it could be done on ordinary banking terms" but that his business could not stand the cost involved in dealing with one of the discount companies.[18] Discount rates for Amtorg acceptances declined during the First Five-Year Plan, but the entire process remained so unnecessarily complicated because of the negative attitude of the Government and U.S. bankers that even the Russian specialist of the BFDC had a difficult time tracing it. In one instance, E. C. Ropes, chief of the Slavic Section of the Eastern European Division, described the situation in 1931 in these terms:

Delgass, formerly, as you know, with Amtorg, some months ago set up the Amrusco, nominally for service to American firms selling to Russia. Recently he announced his intention of insuring acceptances, or discounting them without recourse. I find that the American company which insured some $30,000 worth for him, at 10 percent flat, has had a bad smash [because of the Depression] and has ceased to insure. He is therefore limiting himself to discounting, which he does with the assistance of Boris Said, who protects himself by holding the money due to the Amtorg from

---

ing Corp./2,4: Harold Dotterer to T. L. Gaukel, February 26, 1925, BFDC memorandum on Amtorg, February 25, 1925, Carl J. Mayer to Julius Klein, May 14, 1925, E. C. Ropes (chief, Slavic Section, European Division, BFDC) to T. L. Gaukel, April 28, 1927, Ropes to London office, March 2, 1931, U.S. Department of Commerce, Records of the Bureau of Foreign and Domestic Commerce, Record Group 151, File 448-U.S. Within the Department of Commerce only the Division of Commercial Laws was overly concerned with Amtorg as "an instrumentality of the Soviet." See memorandum, May 18, 1925, U.S. Department of Commerce, Records of the Bureau of Foreign and Domestic Commerce, Record Group 151, File 448-U.S.

18. E. C. Ropes to T. L. Gaukel, April 28, 1927, Ropes to F. L. Roberts (Chicago district office, BFDC), March 7, 1931, U.S. Department of Commerce, Records of the Bureau of Foreign and Domestic Commerce, Record Group 151, File 448-U.S.; Fithian, "Soviet-American Economic Relations," pp. 187–89.

the Standard New York for oil. The sums, which must be considerable, thus act as a reserve in case of Amtorg default. Said told us all about this scheme a year ago, and evidently could not find any way to make it operative except in this round-the-corner manner. Naturally Delgass is not telling how he does it.[19]

In addition to high discount rates there were other problems that hampered commercial exchanges between Russia and the United States. Soviet businessmen experienced difficulty obtaining visas, the Soviet Government had no recourse to U.S. courts, the absence of consular officials made notarizing legal documents and handling bills of lading more cumbersome, each country imposed exececcive port charges on the ships of the other country, and finally, there were no mutual regulations governing patent or copyright matters. The removal or clarification of most of these legal and commercial obstacles after recognition gave some justification to the argument of Amtorg and protrade businessmen in the United States that the establishment of diplomatic relations would facilitate trade.[20]

Despite these difficulties, trade with the USSR more than doubled prewar levels during the course of the 1920s, and the balance of trade remained, as it had been before 1914, disproportionately in favor of the United States. By the end of the fiscal year 1924–1925, U.S. businessmen were exporting more than $68,000,000 in goods to the Russians—more than the businessmen of any other nation. Then, between 1925 and 1926, exports declined because European countries began to extend long-term credit to Soviet trading agencies. By the end of 1927, however, the United States was second only to Germany in exports to the USSR, even though the U.S. Government was encouraging harsh credit terms.[21]

19. Ropes to London office, March 2, 1931, U.S. Department of Commerce, Records of the Bureau of Foreign and Domestic Commerce, Record Group 151, File 448-U.S.; *Business Week,* September 2, 1931, p. 34.

20. American-Russian Chamber of Commerce, *Handbook of Soviet Union,* pp. 355–61; Bron, *Soviet Economic Development,* p. 94; Sutton, *Western Technology,* Vol. 1, *1917 to 1930,* pp. 299–304.

21. Amtorg to E. C. Ropes, November 10, 1926, T. L. Gaukel to Ropes, February 15, 1927, Ropes to Gaukel, April 28, 1927,

In that same year the Commerce Department predicted that the U.S. portion of Soviet trade had peaked because Russian industrial progress was beginning to falter under communism. The concomitance of the First Five-Year Plan and the Depression, however, created greater commercial activity between the two nations. During 1930 the United States once again became the leading exporter to the USSR, with Soviet purchases totaling $114,399,000. This amount was an increase of 35 per cent over the preceding year, and it represented 3 per cent of the total export trade of this country and 25 per cent of all Russian imports. While Soviet-U.S. trade still constituted only a little over 1 per cent of the total commerce of the United States, the increase in 1930 impressed U.S. businessmen who engaged in foreign trade because it happened when exports to other major nations were declining. In view of the Depression, *Business Week* told its readers "to sell the misguided [Soviet] fanatics all they are willing to pay for."[22]

Government officials were not as sanguine about the situation. In fact, the Commerce Department, for reasons more ideological than economic, became increasingly negative toward trade with the USSR as the Depression continued. Although the department denied that it was discouraging business orders and questioning Amtorg's credit rating after 1929, letters from such Commerce officials as E. C. Ropes to individual businessmen and statements in business journals

Ropes to Des Moines district office, BFDC, December 13, 1927, U.S. Department of Commerce, Records of the Bureau of Foreign and Domestic Commerce, Record Group 151, File 448-U.S.; Fithian, "Soviet-American Economic Relations," pp. 180–81, 213; Robert Paul Browder, *The Origins of Soviet-American Diplomacy,* pp. 223–25; Baykov, *Soviet Foreign Trade,* tables 1 and 7, appendix; American-Russian Chamber of Commerce, *Handbook of Soviet Union,* pp. 292–93. Soviet figures tend to be higher than U.S. figures.

22. Ropes to Gaukel, April 28, 1927, U.S. Department of Commerce, Records of the Bureau of Foreign and Domestic Commerce, Record Group 151, File 448-U.S.; Browder, *Soviet-American Diplomacy,* p. 225; *Business Week,* May 14, 1930, p. 12. Robert L. Morris also notes that the breach in diplomatic relations between England and the USSR helped to stimulate American-Russian trade between 1927 and 1930. See Robert L. Morris, "A Reassessment of Russian Recognition," *The Historian* 24 (August 1962): 473.

and newspapers proved the contrary. A particularly bitter exchange took place between the Bureau of Foreign and Domestic Commerce and the Kennedy–Van Saun Manufacturing and Engineering Corporation in 1931. Upset over the Depression, Joseph E. Kennedy accused the Commerce Department in general of arrogance in the handling of economic foreign policy, and in particular of lying when it claimed not to have taken sides about trading with the Soviets. The department, Kennedy contended, had "meddled in other people's business" by making false statements about Amtorg and the USSR in U.S. newspapers. Nonetheless, a year after Kennedy and other businessmen made these kinds of accusations, Julius Klein, then Assistant Secretary of Commerce, privately recommended that the publications of Amtorg be considered nothing more than propaganda.[23]

Ultimately, the new director of the BFDC, Frederick M. Feiker, did admit in 1932 that, as *Business Week* and other business sources had been pointing out for some time, Amtorg had a perfect credit record. He asserted, however, that other things—among them the total of the outstanding obligations of the Soviet Government—had to be considered in trading with the USSR. It was a "matter of general knowledge that credits extended by Germany, England and other countries have now reached an amount of about $500 million, or about the sum of all exports from Soviet Russia in one year." He also noted that in 1931 the country experienced an unfavorable balance of trade, which came to almost $150,000,000. Because he did not think the United States would lift its ban on the sale of Soviet bonds or that the Reconstruction Finance Corporation could legally advance loans for the acceptances

23. *Business Week*, May 14, 1930, p. 12; E. C. Ropes to Wickwire Spencer Steel Company, June 24, 1930, Ropes to Crocker First National Bank of San Francisco, September 15, 1930, Ropes to Manufacturers Association of Connecticut, October 1, 1930, Ropes to Storm Manufacturing Company, October 14, 1931, Kennedy to Frederick M. Feiker (director, BFDC), November 23, December 3, December 18, 1931, Feiker to Kennedy, November 27, December 15, 1931, Julius Klein to Robert P. Lamont (Secretary of Commerce), September 27, 1932, U.S. Department of Commerce, Records of the Bureau of Foreign and Domestic Commerce, Record Group 151, File 448-U.S.

of orders from Amtorg, he concluded that it was "impossible for this Bureau to encourage or support the granting of credits to facilitate the sale of goods to Amtorg at the present time." Other officials within the BFDC also implied in letters to businessmen that they should begin to sell to Russia on a strictly cash basis. As the Depression continued they repeatedly had to deny that there were any plans for establishing Government-guaranteed credit for U.S. manufacturers who wanted to sell their products to Amtorg.[24]

Thus, a year before recognition of the USSR, top officials within the Commerce Department were discounting Amtorg's statements and activities as pure propaganda and no longer recommending that agency's services to U.S. businessmen.[25] This stubborn refusal to remain open to whatever trade might be available in time of depression clearly indicated the degree to which long-time Government servants like Feiker had accepted the ideological aspects of the anti-Communist nonrecognition policy as it became institutionalized throughout the bureaucracy during the 1920s. Despite the Commerce Department's misuse of the Depression to justify an ideologically motivated attack against Amtorg, the

24. Feiker to Farm Tools, Inc., August 23, 1932, W. H. Rastall (chief, Industrial Machinery Division, BFDC) to Sullivan Machinery Company, August 16, 1932, E. C. Ropes to Sundstrand Machine Tool Company, February 6, 1932, Ropes to Door Company, November 11, 1931 (about November 5 statement by David Lawrence in the *New York Sun* that the Commerce Department was telling businessmen to require cash for all future sales to the USSR), U.S. Department of Commerce, Records of the Bureau of Foreign and Domestic Commerce, Record Group 151, File 448-U.S. For favorable business comments about Soviet credit, see *Business Week*, February 12, 1930, p. 39; *Nation's Business* 18 (April 1930): 265; National Association of Manufacturers, *Proceedings*, October 1926, p. 27.

25. Protrade groups repeatedly reminded the Commerce Department in 1932 and 1933 that Amtorg remained the only authorized purchasing agent to the Soviet Union in the United States and, as such, should be recommended to businessmen. For one such reminder, see American-Russian Chamber of Commerce to John Dickinson (Assistant Secretary of Commerce), September 11, 1933, U.S. Department of Commerce, Records of the Bureau of Foreign and Domestic Commerce, Record Group 151, File 448-U.S.

firm remained the largest purchasing agent for the USSR throughout the 1930s, and the company still plays an important, if less-publicized role in U.S.-Soviet trade relations.

Amtorg was not the only organization of its kind to experience the more openly expressed hostility of Government officials as the Depression deepened. The American-Russian Chamber of Commerce also fell into disfavor. This organization did not originally suffer from the stigma of communism that marked Amtorg in the 1920s because the chamber had indigenous roots that antedated the war. The organization had been incorporated on January 22, 1916, "to foster trade, encourage and generally promote the economic, commercial and industrial relations between the United States of America and Russia." During the war and in the immediate postwar years the chamber was dominated by such conservative New York financial and insurance firms as the House of Morgan, the National City Bank, the New York Life Insurance Company, the Chase National Bank, the Guaranty Trust Company, and the First National Bank of New York. The House of Morgan exercised the strongest influence within the organization because it was responsible for floating most of the wartime loans to tsarist Russia. Under such leadership, the organization opposed both trade with Russia and recognition of the Soviet Government after the Bolshevik Revolution.[26]

Although New York banking and insurance houses no longer completely controlled the chamber by 1920, it continued to oppose trade and recognition because its members feared that Germany, if not restrained by the former Allies and other countries, would come to dominate Russia's political and economic life. In other words, the chamber's policy from the Bolshevik Revolution to 1925 was to oppose trade and recognition and at the same time to exhort the U.S. Government to preserve equal commercial access to Russia so that U.S. businessmen could take advantage of the markets there sometime in the future.[27]

26. American-Russian Chamber of Commerce, *Handbook of Soviet Union*, p. 544; Williams, *American-Russian Relations*, pp. 85, 174, 180; Heymann, *We Can Do Business*, pp. 77–78.

27. William C. Redfield to State Department, January 13, 1922, U.S. Department of State, General Records, Record Group 59, File 661.115/362; S. R. Bertron to State Department, Feb-

Since the original purpose of the American-Russian Chamber of Commerce had been to promote trade with Russia, its immediate postwar hostility to commercial relations undermined its reason to exist. Recognizing this, the chamber tried to obtain State Department approval in 1922 and 1923 to send a delegation of representatives of U.S. industry to Soviet Russia in order to impress the Soviets "with the futility of government recognition as affecting business unless they are prepared to do business on well-recognized business principles." Neither the State Department nor the Commerce Department was willing to approve such a commission. When the chamber's desire to serve the administration by acting "as a means of unofficial contact with Russia" was also turned down, the organization unofficially disbanded in 1923.[28]

The American-Russian Chamber of Commerce was reorganized on June 11, 1926. There was a drastic change in leadership and in the members' attitudes toward trade with Russia. Apparently upon Alex Gumberg's urging, Reeve Schley, vice-president of the Chase National Bank, revived the chamber and became its president, and in 1928 Charles Haddell Smith, a former U.S. representative on the wartime Siberian Railway Commission and a perennial promoter of U.S.–Soviet trade relations and Communist propaganda, became vice-president.[29] At the same time, the influence of the tightly organized and highly disciplined financial and insurance interests diminished; the power shifted to the law firms of Thacher

---

ruary 27, 1922, U.S. Department of State, Records Relating to Internal Affairs of Russia and the Soviet Union, Record Group 59, File 861.50/274. Both men were executives of the American-Russian Chamber of Commerce.

28. S. R. Bertron to State Department, October 23, 1922, Evan E. Young (chief, Eastern European Division) to Hughes, October 22, 1923, Hughes to Berton, June 7, October 27, 1923, Bertron to State Department, September 18, 1923, U.S. Department of State, Records Relating to Internal Affairs of Russia and the Soviet Union, Record Group 59, Files F.W. 861.50Am3/37, F.W. 861.50Am38, F.W. 861.50Am3/39; memorandum of conversation between Hughes and Bertron, December 20, 1922, U.S. Department of State, Memoranda of Conversations of the Secretary of State, 1921–1923, Record Group 59.

29. Heymann, *We Can Do Business*, p. 78; Williams, *American-Russian Relations*, p. 213; Sutton, *Western Technology*, Vol. 1, *1917 to 1930*, pp. 284–85, 289–90.

and Wardwell and to a different conglomeration of export firms and industrial, commodity, engineering, and oil companies. All in all, the new leadership of the chamber was made up of considerably more unstructured, competitive, and volatile economic groups than the previous one.

For example, Schley and Gumberg were associated with the Chase National Bank, which had been granting short-term credit to the Soviets since the mid-1920s, but by 1932 it was the only bank represented on the board of directors. The composition of the rank-and-file membership, which had always been predominantly heavy-duty equipment companies, specialized commodity groups, electrical firms, and exporters, did not change radically, but the members' attitudes and actions did. Moreover, a greater number of these concerns joined, as did oil companies and engineering firms. By 1932 there were approximately 135 members in the chamber, some of whom represented the giants of U.S. industry—the Standard Oil Company of New York, the General Motors Corporation, the International Harvester Company, the International General Electric Company, and Westinghouse Electric International Company. Otto Kahn was the single individual financier of world prominence who was listed as a member in 1932.[30]

Writing to Secretary of State Frank B. Kellogg in December 1926, Schley did not display the former hostility to trade with the Soviets or the diffidence apparent in the pre-1925 correspondence between the chamber and the State Department. In a matter-of-fact manner Schley simply informed Kellogg that his group was setting up a Moscow office under the direction of Charles Smith, an American engineer who had been publicly in favor of recognition of Russia since 1918 and who had been privately categorized by the State Department in 1923 as an "agent of the Soviet Government."[31] Adding somewhat facetiously that he realized that this latest ac-

30. U.S. Congress, House, Committee on Ways and Means, *Hearings on H.R. 15597, H.R. 15927, H.R. 16517*, pp. 122–25.

31. Schley to State Department, December 15, 1926, Hanson to State, April 27, 1923, U.S. Department of State, Records Relating to Internal Affairs of Russia and the Soviet Union, Record Group 59, Files F.W. 861.50Am3/41, 861.602/82.

tivity of the American-Russian Chamber of Commerce was "nothing in which the State Department is interested," Schley promised nonetheless to keep the Government informed, upon request, of the progress Mr. Smith might have in "bringing the businessmen of both nations into closer contact through mutual understanding."[32]

At the same time, Schley's instructions to Smith specifically reminded him that the chamber "was in no way interested in politics or political discussions." The public statements of the organization from 1926 until the summer of 1933, when a resolution calling for recognition was passed, were in strict accordance with this advice. In fact, the bylaws of the chamber forbade it to "take any part in any political matter affecting the United States and the Soviet Union."[33] Individuals and companies belonging to the organization, such as Gumberg, Smith, and the Amtorg Trading Corporation, could continue to advocate the resumption of diplomatic contact with the USSR, but they were not allowed to use the chamber as a sounding board for their prorecognition sentiments. Therefore, despite the reorganization, the American-Russian Chamber of Commerce did not officially become an advocate of political recognition of the USSR between 1926 and the summer of 1933.

In 1930, however, the chamber began to criticize the Commerce Department's increasingly negative comments about Amtorg and the Soviet economy. Robert P. Lamont, Hoover's Secretary of Commerce from 1929 to 1932, immediately denied the charges that the department had changed its attitude toward trading with the Soviets and that such a change had placed the Government in opposition to the activities of the chamber. As long as Commerce and chamber officials confined their activities to the distribution of information about the Soviet Union, Lamont could not see any basic conflict between them or any need for the chamber to discontinue its work. He admitted that they did disagree about the health

32. Schley to State Department, December 15, 1926, Schley to Charles Smith, n.d., ibid., File F.W. 861.50Am3/41.

33. Schley to Smith, n.d., ibid.; U.S. Congress, House, Committee on Ways and Means, *Hearings on H.R. 15597, H.R. 15927, H.R. 16517*, p. 146.

of the Soviet economy "due to a difference in interpretation or in source of information."[34]

Nevertheless, under the leadership of Col. Hugh L. Cooper, an engineer who succeeded Schley as president, as well as Schley, Wardwell, Thacher, and Gumberg, the American-Russian Chamber of Commerce proceeded to lodge a series of complaints against the Commerce Department from 1930 until the United States recognized Russia in 1933. These complaints convinced department officials that there was little difference between the propaganda tactics of Amtorg and those of the chamber and that, given "the deterioration of conditions in Russia," there was absolutely no need for the department to heed the chamber's suggestion to change its attitude. By the time the chamber officially endorsed recognition of the Soviet Union in the summer of 1933, Commerce officials had already stopped listening to the group for ideological reasons, and Cooper was considered a *persona non grata* at both the Commerce and the State departments.[35]

In part, their rejection resulted from Cooper's vacillating position on recognition. In 1928, for example, in a speech to the American section of the All Union Western Chamber of Commerce, he contended that trade relations depended on recognition. In the same year, he stated in an article that he supported recognition if the Soviets met the conditions stipulated by the State Department. Yet he told the House Ways and Means Committee in 1931 that he was not in favor of recognition and never had been, and in a letter to *The New York Times* he denied having made any overtures to Hoover or Stimson about recognition. As president of the American-Russian Chamber of Commerce, he did not publicly advocate recognition until July 1933, but he maintained that he had privately told FDR and Secretary Hull in April that "the only

34. Lamont to Allen Wardwell, November 19, 1930, Klein to Lamont, September 27, 1932, Col. Hugh L. Cooper to John Dickinson (Assistant Secretary of Commerce), September 11, 1933, Louis Domeratsky (chief, Regional Information Division), memorandum, September 15, 1933, U.S. Department of Commerce, Records of the Bureau of Foreign and Domestic Commerce, Record Group 151, File 448-U.S.

35. Robert P. Lamont to Cooper, January 20, 1931, Klein to Lamont, September 27, 1932, ibid.; Fithian, "Soviet-American Economic Relations," pp. 190, 274.

practical course to pursue is outright recognition, to be followed by a well-considered trade agreement." To complicate matters further, Roosevelt denied, in an off-the-record remark at a press conference, having talked to Cooper about recognition. Thus, Cooper both confused and annoyed Government officials, particularly those of the Hoover administration, but they did not consider him a possible subversive. According to a 1931 State Department description, he was "hard boiled, clear headed, a veteran engineer, strongly anticommunist but eager to make money and achieve professionally," who probably had been allowed to see only the best aspects of life in Russia.[36]

Despite this moderate assessment of Cooper, members of the State and Commerce departments and other opponents of recognition unjustly relegated the American-Russian Chamber of Commerce under his leadership and the Amtorg Trading Corporation to the same category, that is, they viewed both as excessively pro-Soviet propagandists whose motive for favoring recognition was economic self-interest. They did not consider the chamber's effort to dissociate itself from the alleged political activity of Amtorg and all prorecognition agitation before July 1933. At the 1931 embargo hearings, for example, Cooper publicly denied that his organization was receiving most of its financial support from Amtorg or any foreign government and that it was engaging in any kind of propaganda activity of a political nature[37] What had happened was that between 1918 and 1933, the

---

36. Sussdorff (Riga) to State Department, September 26, 1928, January 10, 1929, U.S. Department of State, Records Relating to Internal Affairs of Russia and the Soviet Union, Record Group 59, Files 861.6463/31, 861.6463/34; *Annals of the American Academy of Political and Social Sciences* 138 (July 1928): 119; U.S. Congress, House, Committee on Ways and Means, *Hearings on H.R. 15597, H.R. 15927, H.R. 16517,* p. 95; *The New York Times,* July 11, 1933, p. 16; *Complete Presidential Press Conferences of Franklin D. Roosevelt,* Vols. 1–2, *1933,* no. 12 (April 14, 1933), 1: 143–44; J. G. Rogers (Assistant Secretary of State), memorandum, May 5, 1931, U.S. Department of State, Political Relations between the U.S. and Russia and the Soviet Union, Record Group 59, File 711.61/223.

37. U.S. Congress, House, Committee on Ways and Means, *Hearings on H.R. 15597, H.R. 15927, H.R. 16517,* pp. 96, 146.

chamber had drastically changed its attitude toward trade with the USSR. In the process, the Government's ideological opposition to recognition became increasingly irrelevant to chamber members. During the same period, but primarily after the Depression began, the attitude of President Hoover and the departments of State and Commerce had become more negative about trade and consequently more defensive about the Government's nonrecognition policy.

Commercial relations with Russia gradually improved until 1931 despite all obstacles, but the concession policy proved a dismal failure for the Soviets, as well as the American concessionaires. Between 1921 and 1930 more than 2,600 applications for Soviet concessions had been received, but slightly fewer than 500 were actually granted. The major reason given by Soviet officials for rejecting so many applicants was that they were "too irresponsible or otherwise undesirable for the government to enter into contracts with them." According to a 1929 report by the president of the Soviet People's Commissars, the growth of Russian industry over the decade had not depended on foreign concession enterprises, the total output of which was less than 1 per cent of the total industrial production of the USSR in 1929. In 1928 Soviet industry produced approximately 14,000,000,000 rubles in goods and services; for the same year, the contribution of these foreign concessions was valued at only 86,000,000 rubles. As of March 1929, there were only 68 foreign concessions still operating in the Soviet Union, 8 of which were American.[38]

Armand Hammer's concessions, which originally included an asbestos mine, a trading contract, and finally a pencil factory, proved to be the most successful of the 8 U.S. concessions. According to State Department estimates, he made

38. Coleman to State Department, April 8, December 19, 1929, U.S. Department of State, Records Relating to Internal Affairs of Russia and the Soviet Union, Record Group 59, Files 861.602/181, 861.602/207; Elisha M. Friedman, *Russia in Transition: A Business Man's Appraisal*, p. 256; Chase, Dunn, and Tugwell, eds., *Second Decade*, pp. 344–48; Paul Haensel, *The Economic Policy of Soviet Russia*, pp. 170–71; Liberman, *Building Lenin's Russia*, p. 143; Amtorg, *Soviet-American Trade Outlook*, p. 9; Chamberlin, *Soviet Russia*, pp. 362, 366; Sutton, *Western Technology*, Vol. 1, *1917 to 1933*, p. 9. In 1930 the ruble was valued at 51.46 cents.

about 50 per cent profit on his original capital outlay for manufacturing pencils, and in one year alone, his profits purport-
edly amounted to more than $1,000,000.[39] On the other hand,
W. Averell Harriman was the least successful of the U.S. concessionaires, as he was in all of his Russian ventures in the
decade. The Harriman concession, one of the two largest
granted by the Soviets, was for the development of extensive
manganese fields in the Chiaturi district of Georgia. After
receiving the concession in 1925, Harriman struggled for
three years against labor problems, competition from a
Soviet-operated manganese monopoly, and a fall in the world
price of manganese. He finally dissolved the Georgian Manganese Company in September 1928. Unable to obtain cash
from the Soviets for this concession, he had to accept USSR
bonds instead.[40]

This failure and similar ones prompted the Soviets to abandon their concession policy in 1928 in favor of more direct
trade and contracts with foreign companies and individuals
for manufactured goods and technical aid. By the end of the
decade the number of technical agreements with the United
States had increased sharply—from 15 through mid-1929 to
more than 40 by the beginning of 1930.[41] The increase in

39. Hammer, *Quest*, pp. 179–80, 185–89; Coleman to State
Department, March 9, 1925, U.S. Department of State, Records
Relating to Internal Affairs of Russia and the Soviet Union, Record
Group 59, File 861.602/130; Chase, Dunn, and Tugwell, eds.,
Second Decade, p. 353; *The Saturday Evening Post*, (March 17,
1966): 88. See Appendix A for further details about Hammer's
pencil concession.

40. Belgian Embassy to State Department, November 8, 1923,
Coleman to State Department, June 26, 1925, Tobin (Netherlands) to State Department, June 18, 1926, Schurman (Berlin)
to State Department, December 7, December 9, 1926, Robert F.
Kelley, memorandum, December 26, 1926, Bevan (Hamburg)
to State Department, June 11, 1927, Schurman to State Department, June 28, 1927, U.S. Department of State, Records Relating to Internal Affairs of Russia and the Soviet Union, Record
Group 59, Files 861.637/2, 861.637/17, 861.637/24, 861.637/25,
861.637/27, 861.637/28, 861.637/39, 861.637/40; Hammer,
Quest, p. 121; Sutton, *Western Technology*, Vol. 1, *1917 to 1930*,
pp. 86–91, 298–99. See Appendix B and Chapter II, pp. 37–
39, for further details about Harriman's activities in the USSR.

41. Schurman, translation of Paul Scheffer's article in *Berliner
Tageblatt* (April 14, 1929), to State Department, April 17, 1929,

trade agreements was significant but not as dramatic until the concomitant effects of the First Five-Year Plan and the Depression had their impact on commercial activity between the two nations during 1930 and 1931. The major trade and technical-assistance contracts signed between 1928 and 1930 were with International General Electric, Standard Oil of New Jersey, Ford Motor, and the Radio Corporation of America (RCA).

In particular the IGE Purchase and Sales Agreement of October 9, 1928, represented a major breakthrough in Soviet-U.S. commercial relations and caused a flurry of rumors about recognition because it had been negotiated with the knowledge of the State Department. It involved a contract that granted credits to Amtorg of approximately $25,000,000 over a six-year period. This contract set the stage for other long-term corporation credit, not only because of the sum involved, but also because General Electric had been in contact with the Soviets since 1922 and had been trading with them in ever-increasing amounts through its European affiliates—despite the company's claim that it lost almost $2,000,000 when the Russian General Electric Company was nationalized by the Bolsheviks. Explaining his company's precedent-setting action fifteen years after it occurred, IGE President Clark Minor said:

> Real business with Russia started in 1928. We disregarded the two-million dollar tsarist debts and never regretted having forgotten them. Indirectly we recovered the claim amply. We went on the theory that if a person wants credit he must take certain risks, especially if a great area like Russia had to be industrialized. Walther Rathenau, former head of the German Allgemeine Electrisitaets-Gesellschaft [an IGE affiliate] . . . followed the same principle.

U.S. Department of State, Records Relating to Internal Affairs of Russia and the Soviet Union, Record Group 59, File 861.602 Hammer/4; Edward Hallett Carr, *Socialism in One Country*, 1: 454–55; Friedman, *Russia in Transition*, p. 256; Sutton, *Western Technology*, Vol. 2, *1930 to 1945*, pp. 16–31, *passim*. For details of the technical assistance that the Soviet Union had been receiving the entire decade from the United States, see Sutton, *Western Technology*, Vol. 1, *1917 to 1930*, 346–47.

Obviously the fulfillment of this contract was looked upon as settlement of all IGE claims against the Bolshevik policy of nationalization.[42]

This breakthrough in Soviet-U.S. trade and credit relations coincided almost exactly with the appearance of Stalin's First Five-Year Plan and a little before the 1929 Depression. It was under the contract method, therefore, not the concession method, that large quantities of U.S. goods, credit, and technical aid began to flow into the Soviet Union for the first time since the Bolshevik Revolution.

Prior to the IGE contract, for example, the USSR had not been able to obtain long-term commercial credit from any U.S. source. The few banks that had been dealing with Amtorg or the Soviet State Bank avoided long-term credit transactions because of the Government's policy against them. Even the Chase National Bank under Schley's influence had provided only short-term financing for the All Russian Textile Syndicate's purchases of U.S. cotton in 1925. In general, U.S. bankers continued to refuse direct long-term credit to the USSR, even after the large manufacturing firms, such as General Electric and Ford, began granting it. In 1929, however, a number of smaller manufacturers chose to follow the lead of IGE, rather than the advice of the State and Commerce departments; several manufacturers began granting credit for three years or more, and approximately 200 firms began, for the first time, to grant one-year credit. By the end of 1931, credit from U.S. manufacturers constituted the second-largest source of short-term financing for the USSR; 80 per cent of all foreign short-term creditors of the Soviets were industrial firms, and 20 per cent were banking establishments. (Before World War I, 36 per cent of Russia's

42. M. A. Oudin (vice-president, IGE) to State Department, June 28, 1922, DeWitt Poole, memorandum, October 18, 1922, Washburn (Austria) to State Department, November 4, 1927, Sussdorff to State Department, October 22, 1928, U.S. Department of State, Records Relating to Internal Affairs of Russia and the Soviet Union, Record Group 59, Files 861.6463/11, 861.6463/18, 861.6463/30, 861.602/159; Fischer, *Soviets*, 2: 766–67; Bishop, *Roosevelt-Litvinov Agreements*, p. 144; Heymann, *We Can Do Business*, p. 41; Fithian, "Soviet-American Economic Relations," pp. 279–83.

short-term creditors were foreign manufacturers, and 64 per cent were foreign bankers.)[43]

To a certain degree the statistics for 1931 misrepresent the economic relationship between foreign banking houses and the USSR. As one contemporary observer noted, "Though these figures show that foreign banks are disinclined to invest money directly in the USSR, they are, to all intents and purposes, carrying the whole burden of Soviet Russia's foreign debts, for inasmuch as they discount Soviet bills drawn by industrial firms, they are, as a matter of fact, supplying the capital necessary for her purchases abroad and for the production and delivery of commodities which she exports." Long before the Depression of 1929, therefore, it must be assumed that the theoretical opposition of the American Bankers Association to dealing with the Soviets was undermined in practice by loans to foreign countries and financial services to domestic manufacturers.[44]

There are a number of reasons that, even if the Depression had not intervened, the First Five-Year Plan and the shift to a contract system would have brought such dramatic changes in relations. The success of the First Five-Year Plan was absolutely dependent upon credit facilities, heavy equipment, and technology of the Western nations, particularly the United States, and it was predicated upon the assumption that the capitalist world would remain prosperous for some time to come and thus that Russia could obtain the necessary credit to finance imports from the West.[45] Also, the number of U.S. businessmen who responded positively to the First Five-Year Plan and to Stalin permitted a significant increase in commercial and technical-aid contracts between the two nations after 1928, and the Depression initially gave additional momentum to this trend. Businessmen never gave

43. Fischer, *Soviets*, 2: 768; Thomas D. Campbell, *Russia: Market or Menace?* pp. 138, 141; Bron, *Soviet Economic Development*, p. 57.

44. Friedman, *Russia in Transition*, pp. 312–16. *Journal of the American Bankers Association* 23 (March 1931): 737–39; 23 (June 1931): 969; 24 (July 1931): 13, 19.

45. Gerhard Dobbert, *Red Economics*, pp. 300, 309–10, 321; H. R. Knickerbocker, *Soviet Trade and World Depression*, p. vi; C. B. Hoover, *Economic Life*, p. 166.

Stalin the unqualified approval they did Mussolini,[46] but "socialism in one country" sounded considerably less radical and safer than had the rhetoric of the early Bolsheviks and of Trotsky about world revolution.[47] Further, a small group of U.S. companies unconsciously contributed to the consolidation of Stalin's power and to at least the partial success of the First Five-Year Plan after the business community in general had shunned a weak and internally divided Communist Russia for over a decade. (In this sense, the contribution was similar to the one that the American Relief Administration made to Soviet stabilization under the New Economic Policy; both contributions have been minimized by ideologues in each country, especially since the onset of the Cold War.)

Finally, very few spokesmen for the business firms signing contracts with the Soviets between 1928 and 1933 publicly or privately advocated recognition of the USSR. Although an Amtorg official claimed that, by the trade and technical agreements of Ford Motor, IGE, and RCA, these companies had "decided to recognize officially our Union," none of them participated in the recognition movement. The Ford Motor Company was not even a member of the American-Russian Chamber of Commerce.[48]

Henry Ford, who was known to be hostile toward the Bolsheviks in the early 1920s, apparently subordinated his initial

46. John P. Diggins, "Mussolini's Italy: The View from America, 1922–1941" (Ph.D. dissertation, University of Southern California, 1964), chap. 3; *Literary Digest* 77 (June 9, 1923): 72–74; *Nation's Business* 15 (December 1927): 62. The author of this last article said that Mussolini had all the qualities of a "successful American executive."

47. Coleman to State Department, March 26, 1928, Schurman to State Department, April 11, 1929, U.S. Department of State, Records Relating to Internal Affairs of Russia and the Soviet Union, Record Group 59, Files 861.50/586, 861.602 Hammer/3; Campbell, *Russia*, pp. 14–18; Lewis S. Feuer, "American Travelers to the Soviet Union, 1917–1932: The Formation of a Component of New Deal Ideology," *American Quarterly* 14 (Summer 1962): 139.

48. Coleman to State Department, June 23, 1929, U.S. Department of State, Records Relating to Internal Affairs of Russia and the Soviet Union, Record Group 59, File 861.797/9.

political aversion to his business sense by 1929, when his company signed a major contract with Amtorg. The following year *Nation's Business* described him as a practical man who had no interest in political theory. Between 1918 and 1933 he did not make the issue of recognition or nonrecognition one of his personal crusades. According to one biographer, Ford convinced himself that business with the Soviets was "a means of promoting world concord" and that the advanced nations had a responsibility to help the underdeveloped areas of the world become more self-sufficient. Like most mammoth concerns of the period, Ford Motor could deal with the USSR regardless of the position of the U.S. Government; thus, the firm regarded recognition of the USSR as unessential—and perhaps undesirable, because it would allow smaller firms to compete for the Russian market.[49]

Both New York and New Jersey Standard Oil had signed contracts to market Soviet oil by 1929, but the only major oil representative to work for recognition of the USSR was Ivy L. Lee, a publicity agent for the Rockefeller family and an "adviser on public relations" for New York Standard. Immediately before and after the conclusion of a contract in March 1926 between the Soviets, the Standard Oil Company of New York, and the Vacuum Oil Company, Lee wrote to prominent individuals and influential business groups, such as Senator Borah, Elihu Root, the New York Chamber of Commerce, and the Chamber of Commerce of the United States, urging recognition of the Soviet Union. Lee's campaign was distinguished by its general naïveté, short duration, and singular failure. Only men like Borah, who were already in favor of the idea, responded favorably, and most important, the departments of Commerce and State were completely unimpressed by his one-man propaganda effort.[50]

49. *Nation's Business* 18 (June 1930): 20–23; Nevins and Hill, *Ford*, 2: 673–74; Maddox, *Borah and Foreign Policy*, p. 209. For details of Ford's activities in the USSR, see Appendix C.

50. Louis Fischer, *Oil Imperialism: The International Struggle for Petroleum*, pp. 144–48; Fischer, *Soviets*, 2: 568–69; Lee to Borah, February 16, March 3, 1926, Borah to Lee, February 16, 1926, Box 271, William E. Borah Papers; *Nation's Business* 15 (September 1927): 13. In the early 1920s Ivy Lee had served as a publicity agent for New Jersey Standard as well, but after

By the end of 1927, having been rebuked by the business community in general and by the executives of Standard Oil of New Jersey and the Royal Dutch–Shell Company in particular (neither of whom had yet signed a Soviet contract),[51] Lee resigned himself to writing letters that called simply for more trade with the Soviet Union.

Even Lee's modified position found no sympathy in Government circles. In 1927 Julius Klein, the director of the BFDC, reported to Hoover from Geneva about a conversation he had had with this public relations agent. To Klein, Lee was "very much of a 'light weight' " whose ideas were not at all original. The following year Lee sent to the State Department a fourteen-page memorandum giving his "estimate of American public opinion toward Russia." He did not propose recognition, and he conceded that the USSR would have to assume at least a portion of the "Tsarist and Kerensky debts" and conduct its diplomacy in "good faith"; however, the chief of Eastern European affairs, Robert F. Kelley, summarily dismissed Lee's views. Tersely noting in the margin of Lee's memorandum that "there is no good faith from the Bolshevik standpoint," Kelley informed Assistant Secretary of State Robert E. Olds that Lee was suffering from

> a complete misapprehension of the essential character of the present regime in Russia and of the real difficulty lying in the way of establishment of friendly relations between the United States and Russia. He does not understand, or possibly he cannot bring himself to believe, (1) that the present regime in Russia is a regime dedicated to the promotion of "the world revolution," that is the extension throughout the world of the political, economical, and social system set up in Russia in 1917; (2) that the fundamental purpose of the Bolshevik leaders precludes the observance by them of obligations ordinarily accepted as governing relations between nations; and (3) that, consequently, relations on a basis usual between friendly nations cannot

---

Chairman of the Board A. C. Bedford died in 1925, Lee's connections with that company appear to have ended; see George Sweet Gibb and Evelyn H. Knowlton, *History of Standard Oil*, Vol. 2, *The Resurgent Years, 1911–1927*, p. 614; Sutton, *Western Technology*, Vol. 1, *1917 to 1930*, p. 292.

51. See Appendix D for details about New Jersey Standard's activities in the USSR.

be established with the present regime in Russia until its leaders have abandoned their world revolutionary aims and practices.

Kelley occupied an influential position within the State Department, and his statement and those issued by secretaries Frank B. Kellogg and Henry L. Stimson in 1928 and 1929 show that Lee's short-lived campaign had not swayed anyone in that branch of the federal bureaucracy.[52]

The businessman who became strongest advocate of recognition before 1933 was James D. Mooney, vice-president of General Motors. When he returned from Russia in the fall of 1930 he told the American Automotive Club of France that only U.S. recognition of the USSR could bring about "normal trade relations" with the Soviets. Later in the year he wrote to Senator Borah that it was "simply good old-fashioned common sense" to trade with the USSR, especially in time of depression. Curiously enough, having used the economic stability and good credit rating of the Soviets to justify his support of recognition between 1930 and 1933, Mooney published a book in 1934 in which he warned the U.S. public, then experiencing the New Deal, against "letting economic difficulties muck us down into socialism, fascism, communism, a cult of incompetence, or any of the other so-called new but in reality historically stale experiments in political economy that are now being tried throughout the world."[53] Like so many of the politicians and intellectuals who declared themselves in favor of recognition of the USSR, Mooney did not base his desire to establish commercial and diplomatic relations with the Soviets on any ideological understanding or approval of their economic and political system. Mooney might, then, seem to have favored recognition for purely mercenary reasons, but if this were the case, he and his com-

52. Klein to Hoover, May 19, 1927, Economic Conferences and Commission File, HHCD; Lee to State Department, February 2, 1928, Kelley to Robert E. Olds (Assistant Secretary of State), February 10, 1928, U.S. Department of State, Political Relations between the U.S. and Russia and the Soviet Union, Record Group 59, File F.W. 711.61/130½; Meiburger, *Efforts of Raymond Robins*, p. 153.

53. *The New York Times*, October 8, 1930, p. 11; Mooney to Borah, December 29, 1930, Box 328, Borah Papers; James D. Mooney, *The New Capitalism*, p. 223.

pany did not profit as they might have anticipated, because General Motors did not sign a major contract with the Soviets in the immediate years preceding or following recognition.

Had Mooney been joined, as he was not, by a well-organized group of other prominent businessmen in an effort to bring direct pressure on the Government for recognition, the Hoover administration probably would not have reacted to their demands. The increase in Russian trade that had developed during the 1920s still represented too small a percentage of the total foreign commerce of the United States to warrant a major change in foreign policy, even if the Government's ideology had permitted recognition. The attitude of those in the Department of Commerce was emphatic on this point. After Hoover's election in 1928 the Slavic expert of the BFDC reiterated the bureau's stand that "in spite of the constantly increasing participation of American business in Russian trade, the developments like the General Electric contract, or any other action by individual firms, *there is no reason as yet for the Bureau to depart from its previous custom on Russian matters* [Emphasis added.]." This statement does not reflect exactly the attitude Hoover brought with him to the Presidency, but it is the one he propounded as Secretary of Commerce. Although partisan press releases written with his approval during the 1932 campaign and again at the time recognition was accorded in November 1933 indicate that his attitude had mellowed slightly, he had not altered his views enough to take definite steps toward recognition.[54]

Hoover's attitude was a complex one that evolved from his strong public stand against Bolshevik Russia during World War I, to his defense of civil liberties during the Red Scare, to his relief efforts in Soviet Russia in the early 1920s, to a modification of his opposition to trading with the Soviets when he was Secretary of Commerce, to his refusal when he

54. E. C. Ropes to H. C. MacLean (commercial attaché, Paris), November 23, 1928, U.S. Department of Commerce, Records of the Bureau of Foreign and Domestic Commerce, Record Group 151, File 448–U.S.; Hoover, *Memoirs*, 2: 182; William R. Castle, Jr. (Under-Secretary of State) to Hoover, August 17, 1932, Hoover to Castle (including undated press release), November 15, 1933, Castle Papers; Maddox, *Borah and Foreign Policy*, pp. 211–12; Edward M. Bennett, *Recognition of Russia: An American Foreign Policy Dilemma*, pp. 74–80.

was President to engage the White House in "Red hunting" or to arrest peaceful Communist picketing, to a reported announcement in July 1929 before a business group en route to the USSR that he was reconsidering the question of recognition because he did not want U.S. businesses to lose potential Soviet trade to foreign competitors, to his tacit support of the Government's actually financing exports to the Soviet Union in 1932 and 1933 through short-term credit advances from the Reconstruction Finance Corporation. As President, Hoover did not act decisively on the changes in his attitude toward the Soviet Union largely because the Depression of 1929 made him rigidly defensive about any action that might seem to repudiate earlier ideological or economic positions he had taken.[55] Instead, he retreated to the bureaucratized anticommunism of both the Commerce and State departments and imposed his Depression-bred defensiveness about nonrecognition on Henry L. Stimson, his Secretary of State, who appeared inclined toward reconciliation with the Soviets during the Manchurian crisis.

55. Joan Hoff Wilson, *Herbert Clark Hoover: Forgotten Progressive*, chaps. 6 and 8.

V

MYTH: THE VIEW CONCERNING
BUSINESS AND RECOGNITION

Fortunately for the Hoover administration's defensive anti-Soviet policy, trade with the Soviet Union did not continue to increase at the impressive rate it had in 1930 and 1931. By 1932, instead of supplying 25 per cent of all Soviet imports, the United States was supplying only 4.5 per cent, or $12,641,000, in goods,—a 90 per cent decline from 1931.[1] Such a severe drop in exports naturally weakened the arguments of the politicians, industrialists, and exporters who had been taking advantage of the Depression to cement U.S.-Russian economic relations and who were urging the Government to remove the remaining financial and commercial restrictions against the Soviet Union. Thus, when former Secretary of State Frank B. Kellogg suggested to Henry L. Stimson in November 1932 that the United States should recognize the USSR so a commercial treaty could be negotiated between

1. Peter G. Filene, *Americans and the Soviet Experiment, 1917–1933*, pp. 230, 235; American-Russian Chamber of Commerce, *Handbook of the Soviet Union*, pp. 355–56; Floyd James Fithian, "Soviet-American Economic Relations, 1918–1933: American Business in Russia during the Period of Nonrecognition" (Ph.D. dissertation, University of Nebraska, 1964), pp. 186–87, 213–15. Fithian notes that the decline stemmed from a continued lack of long-term credit and discounting services by U.S. banks for Amtorg acceptances, as well as a decline in value of Soviet products on the world market during the Depression. Consequently, the Soviets purchased fewer goods from U.S. firms, except heavy equipment essential for the First Five-Year Plan, and increased their exports to offset the low prices being received for them. An attempted embargo of certain Soviet products, which began in 1930, worsened relations between the two countries, but it was not a major cause of the precipitous decline in trade, as charged by the American-Russian Chamber of Commerce.

the two nations, he did so at a very poor time.[2] Trade had declined so drastically that such a treaty seemed unnecessary. Furthermore, the Government's determination not to change its economic and political policy toward Russia had been temporarily strengthened by the actions of a strong anti-Soviet, antitrade group within the business community and Congress.

This group of nationalists partially neutralized the impact of the internationalist, protrade businessmen and politicians and gave the Government a rationalization not only for maintaining its original nonrecognition policy, but also for increasing commercial restrictions against the USSR. These antitraders, like many Government officials, had feared increased trade with the Soviets in the early 1930s because it seemed to indicate that the Depression, which was devastating the U.S. economy, was not having the same effect on the Communist system. Ironically, these businessmen and politicians, who throughout the 1920s had called the Communist system unworkable and unrealistic, now looked for reasons to block trade because the Soviets were apparently beating Western capitalists at their own game.[3] In part they appear to have been duped by Soviet propaganda that described the Depression as a purely capitalist phenomenon, and therefore they did not view the increase in Soviet exports for what it was: largely a reflection of the negative impact that worldwide deflation was having on Russia's socialized economy. Instead, the antitraders tried to gain acceptance for their intensified ideological campaign against the Communists by accusing the USSR of exporting to the United States goods that had been produced by forced or convict labor and therefore of violating the 1930 tariff act. They also maintained that the USSR was dumping such commodities as wheat, oil, anthracite, and cotton on the world market.[4]

2. Frank B. Kellogg to Stimson, November 18, 1932, U.S. Department of State, Records Relating to Internal Affairs of Russia and the Soviet Union, Record Group 59, File 861.01/1841.

3. Jerome Davis, "Russia: 'The Acid Test,'" in Samuel D. Schmalhausen, ed., *Behold America!* pp. 166, 175–76; Filene, *Americans and the Soviet Experiment*, pp. 230–31.

4. U.S. Congress, House, Committee on Ways and Means, *Hearings on H.R. 15597, H.R. 15927, H.R. 16517,* 71st Cong., 3d sess., January 27–28, 1931, pp. 1–6, 21–22. The forced-labor

The Commerce Department took no direct part in the activities of the antitraders, but the Treasury Department did. In 1930, Treasury officials temporarily prohibited the entry of Soviet pulpwood and manganese and ordered an investigation of the use of forced labor in the production of Russian coal and lumber. At the same time a congressional hearing on the threat of communism in the United States attempted in vain to discredit the Amtorg Trading Corporation. A Treasury decision in 1931 upheld charges that the Soviets were dumping matches and asbestos on the world market, and by 1932 more than 100 organizations, in addition to individual businessmen and politicians who were nationalists, petitioned Congress for a general embargo on all Soviet imports. Although their effort failed, they did impede the exchange of certain products between the United States and Russia and encouraged frequent, protracted investigations that were deliberately designed, according to Senator William E. Borah, not to protect U.S. producers, but "to embarrass the situation with reference to Russia."[5]

Probably the most significant result of the antitraders' increased activity was the disharmony it produced within the

---

provision of the 1930 Tariff was of dubious intent. If the products involved were needed in the United States they could be admitted regardless of the conditions under which they were produced. Therefore, the provision was used to ban only those Soviet products that competed with U.S. goods. The convict-labor provision of the act was also applied in this selective manner. It is now acknowledged that the Soviets were not engaging in dumping practices in the early 1930s because their increased exports were not aimed at monopolizing a market, nor did they result from overproduction. Instead, they involved a national sacrifice, for most of the products, such as grain, could have been consumed domestically. Far from being an attempt to undermine capitalism, as the antitraders claimed, they were undertaken to pay for needed imports. See Filene, *Americans and the Soviet Experiment*, pp. 230–31; Fithian, "Soviet-American Economic Relations," p. 204, 208–9.

5. E. C. Ropes to Dudley Harmon (executive vice-president, New England Council), February 9, 1931, U.S. Department of Commerce, Records of the Bureau of Foreign and Domestic Commerce, Record Group 151, File 448-U.S.; Filene, *Americans and the Soviet Experiment*, pp. 231–32; Fithian, "Soviet-American Economic Relations," pp. 203–4, 210–11; Borah to Ann Louise Strong, December 10, 1930, Box 328, William E. Borah Papers.

business community. Businessmen seemed to divide according to their particular economic function. The paper manufacturers opposed the ban on Soviet pulpwood while the U.S. lumber and pulpwood producers favored it. In this case the antitraders won. The ban on manganese, however, was lifted because the American Manganese Producers' Association could not overcome the opposition of the American Iron and Steel Institute and United States Steel. After much adverse publicity, protraders, led by the Chicago Board of Trade, also prevented the ban on wheat that was being considered because Secretary of Agriculture Arthur M. Hyde and the American Farm Bureau Federation had charged that the Soviets were dumping grain. In addition, the protrade coal dealers successfully denied that Soviet anthracite was being dumped when mine owners and the United Mine Workers said it was.[6] Thus, the disagreement within the business community about Russian trade, which had existed on a minor scale since the mid-1920s, became a major divisive force in the early 1930s.[7]

6. U.S. Congress, House, Committee on Ways and Means, *Hearings on H.R. 15597, H.R. 15927, H.R. 16517*, pp. 6, 22; *Commercial and Financial Chronicle* 131 (October 11, 1930): 2316–17; Filene, *Americans and the Soviet Experiment*, pp. 232–33; Fithian, "Soviet-American Economic Relations," p. 206; William Appleman Williams, *American-Russian Relations, 1781–1947*, pp. 223–24; Davis, "Russia: The Acid Test,'" p. 170.

7. The following information on these divisions can be found in U.S. Congress, House, Committee on Ways and Means, *Hearings on H.R. 15597, H.R. 15927, H.R. 16517*, pp. 21–22, 99, 168–76; Smith W. Brookhart to Borah, September 2, 1933, Box 353, Borah Papers; Jerome Davis, "Capitalism and Communism," *Annals of the American Academy of Political and Social Science* 156 (July 1931): 67; Robert Paul Browder, *The Origins of Soviet-American Diplomacy*, pp. 31, 38–39, 77; Filene, *Americans and the Soviet Experiment*, pp. 232–34; Fithian, "Soviet-American Economic Relations," pp. 205, 211; American Coalition of Patriotic Societies to Hoover, February 28, 1931, U.S. Department of State, General Records, Record Group 59, File 611.616/192; *Business Week*, May 14, 1930, p. 12. *American Industries* 30 (February 1930): 21–26; 30 (April 1930): 24. *Nation's Business* 17 (June 1929): 27, 168; 18 (March 1930): 27–29, 166, 168; 18 (April 1930): 56, 58, 62, 265, 267; 21 (January 1933): 19. *Iron Age* 130 (July 7, 1932): 45; 132 (October 26, 1933): 48–49.

By 1932 most of the antitrade nationalists were the domestic producers of lumber, pulpwood, manganese, matches,
glue, fur, sausage casings, coal, and wheat, and their national
associations. This hard-core group of specialized interests
received varying degrees of support from more than fifty
patriotic and fraternal societies, the American Federation of
Labor, and such economic organizations as the American
Bankers Association, the Joint Conference on Unfair Russian
Competition, the New York Chamber of Commerce, the
Philadelphia Board of Trade, and many state and city chambers of commerce. The approximately thirty-five antitraders
in Congress were led by Senator Tasher L. Oddie from
Nevada and by Representative Hamilton Fish from New
York. The editors of the *Chicago Tribune, The Wall Street
Journal,* and the *Journal of the American Bankers Associa-
tion* also supported the antitrade group.

The internationalists who wanted continued trade with
Russia were exporters, importers, steamship companies, several banking firms in New York and San Francisco, and manufacturers of many kinds of export products—among them,
small producers of heavy machinery, as well as the larger
plants of Westinghouse, General Motors, the American Locomotive Company, the International Paper Company, the
American Tool Works, and International General Electric.
The only national business organization officially supporting
the protrade position by 1932 was the American-Russian
Chamber of Commerce, although some members of the National Association of Manufacturers and the Chamber of
Commerce of the United States also endorsed trade with the
Soviets. In addition, such local groups as the Commonwealth
Club of San Francisco and St. Louis business organizations,
were motivated by sectional self-interest to support the
protrade cause. In Congress, Senators Borah, Burton K.
Wheeler, Smith W. Brookhart, Bronson Cutting, Key Pitt-
man, Joseph T. Robinson, Hiram Johnson, Robert M. La
Follette, Jr., George W. Norris, and Representatives Fiorello
La Guardia and Adolph Sabath advocated continuing trade,
and such journals as *Business Week, Iron Age, Nation's
Business, American Industries,* and the *Chicago Journal of
Commerce* were also encouraging trade by the end of 1932.

Neither the protraders nor the antitraders in the early

1930s achieved their immediate economic goal. The internationalists failed to remove all remaining commercial and financial restrictions on trade with the USSR, and the nationalists failed to obtain a complete ban on Soviet exports to the United States. Both sides so overstated their cases that their public debate did not contribute to a better understanding of the economic and political relations between the two nations, and the private statements by Treasury and Commerce Department officials were less than candid about the significance of the proposed restrictions. Under-Secretary of the Treasury Ogden L. Mills told Colonel Cooper and a delegation of businessmen that he did not think U.S. importers "had anything to worry about," and the director of the BFDC told a machine-tool company in 1932 that none of the new "Treasury regulations have . . . kept out a single shipment from Soviet Russia." In fact, costly delays, loss of commercial opportunities, and in some instances canceled orders and contracts accompanied the uncertainty and irritation created by temporary embargoes and investigations of the forced labor and dumping charges.[8] Also, since many officials of the State, Commerce, and Treasury departments were in basic ideological agreement with the antitraders, the increasingly untenable Government policy toward the USSR was momentarily reinforced.

The protraders exercised no discernible impact on official policy. State Department officials, in particular, were dismayed but unmoved by the growing number of editors, commercial leaders, and even bankers who were expressing an interest in dealing with the Soviets and opposing continued Government interference with trade.[9] The protraders did

8. Robert Kelley, memorandum, January 23, 1931, U.S. Department of State, General Records, Record Group 59, File 611.616/185; Frederick M. Feiker (director of BFDC) to Sundstrand Machine and Tool Company, February 6, 1932, U.S. Department of Commerce, Records of the Bureau of Foreign and Domestic Commerce, Record Group 151, File 448-U.S.; Fithian, "Soviet-American Economic Relations," pp. 206–11, 215–16.

9. John F. Carter, Jr. (Division of Western European Affairs, State Department) to William R. Castle, Jr. (Under-Secretary of State), February 13, 1931, U.S. Department of State, Political Relations between the U.S. and Russia and the Soviet Union, Record Group 59, File 711.61/201.

achieve a measure of success by removing a few of the new bans on Russian products and by persuading some businessmen to modify or eliminate their ideological opposition to trade with the USSR, but at the same time, they unfortunately gave credence to the misleading idea that unrestricted U.S.-Russian commerce was a panacea for the Depression.

This less-than-decisive confrontation between two groups of businessmen and politicians is significant, nonetheless. In retrospect, the Depression was a primary factor in the controversy. The economic crisis not only exacerbated the negative attitude of Washington toward Moscow, making it all the more defensive, but it also forced down the prices of Russian exports; the lowered prices, in turn, triggered U.S. accusations about dumping and subsequent restrictions. These restrictions led to an undetermined amount of Soviet economic retaliation in the form of reduced imports from the United States. The continued refusal of U.S. bankers to extend long-term credit to Soviet agencies, coupled with the Depression, prevented any general increase in trade between the two nations between 1931 and 1933, despite all the actions of the protraders. Even in the face of the nationalists' opposition, trade in manufactured goods would probably have continued to increase to meet the demands of the First Five-Year Plan and subsequent ones if the Depression had not affected Russia's capacity to pay for needed imports and to obtain long-term credit in Europe. Agricultural imports by the USSR, on the other hand, were doomed to decline, regardless of the Depression, because after the initial dislocation and famine caused by forced collectivization in the early 1930s, domestic production in the Soviet Union gradually increased.[10]

Although the terms "nationalist" and "internationalist" have been used to describe the antitraders and protraders respectively, some businessmen who were normally nationalists did support trade with Russia when Amtorg dangled trade contracts in front of them, and some important financiers who traditionally were internationalists did not believe that

10. Browder, *Soviet-American Diplomacy*, pp. 35, 46–47; Fithian, "Soviet-American Economic Relations," p. 216; Robert L. Morris, "A Reassessment of Russian Recognition," *The Historian* 24 (August 1962): 472–73.

the United States should trade with Communists. Among Government officials, Hoover typified the dilemma of all those internationalists who sacrificed their expansionist views to nationalist ideological considerations without being able to find any effective unilateral action that would force the Soviets to conform to U.S. standards of economics and politics so that trade with them would become ideologically acceptable. On this point the protraders and antitraders in government and business circles agreed—it would be better if the Soviet system did not exist, but neither side knew how to do away with it.

Finally, most of the businessmen who wanted the Government to remove trade restrictions did not advocate the recognition of Russia. Many of them were in communication with the Commerce Department and were aware of the Government's firm commitment to nonrecognition; they, unlike some of the better-known protraders who were politicians or liberal intellectuals, did not insist that the Government recognize the USSR, as well as remove restrictions on trade, because they did not want to jeopardize the possibility that the Government might be persuaded to extend trade relations. The businessmen writing to Senator Borah during the Depression usually confined their support of him to his promotion of trade with the Soviets. Joseph E. Kennedy, one of the most outspoken business critics of the Government's policy toward Russia, did not stress recognition but rather "assistance from the United States government agencies in obtaining a share" of Soviet commerce. Kennedy told Commerce Department officials that he did not approve of the Communist regime in Russia but that the kind of governments foreign countries established was not "any of our business." A machine-tool manufacturer told the BFDC that from his "narrow, selfish viewpoint," there was no reason not to do business with the Soviets as long as satisfactory terms could be arranged.[11] Business correspondence with Senator Borah and the State Department clearly shows that most of the businessmen deal-

11. Kennedy to Borah, July 21, 1932, Box 328, Borah Papers; Kennedy to Feiker, December 18, 1931, Barnes Drill Company to W. H. Rastall (chief, Industrial Machinery Division, BFDC), January 12, January 20, January 22, 1932, U.S. Department of Commerce, Records of the Bureau of Foreign and Domestic Commerce, Record Group 151, Files 448-U.S., 221-Russian.

ing with the Soviets, including those who represented such giant companies as IGE, Ford, New Jersey Standard, and RCA, consciously avoided the issue of recognition between 1930 and 1933. Their economic attitudes toward trading evolved while those ideological ones about recognition did not.

This evolution is particularly evident in the statements of such national business organizations as the National Association of Manufacturers, the Chamber of Commerce of the United States, and the American Iron and Steel Institute. In October 1929 the NAM passed a resolution in favor of an official investigation of the "alleged activities of Russian agencies to illegitimately enter and influence our markets," but by 1930 the journal of the NAM was promoting the expanding Russian market for U.S. products. In June 1929 *Nation's Business*, the official publication of the national Chamber of Commerce, commented on the "noticeable change in the American businessman's interest in Russia." In the spring of 1930 this journal carried a series of protrade, proinvestment articles, and by 1933 the chamber had authorized a delegation to visit the USSR to explore further trade possibilities and general economic conditions there. As W. M. Kiplinger confidently predicted to the readers of *Nation's Business* in January 1933, recognition was a long way off but the chances were good that Roosevelt would appoint an "unofficial" trade commission to promote United States interests in Russia. According to *Iron Age*, an early advocate of trade relations between the two countries, U.S. business views on Russia were "rapidly changing" because of the partial success of the First Five-Year Plan. This publication recommended in 1931 that an RFC loan be granted to the Soviets or that "some method of acceptance or discounting Soviet purchases" be worked out by the RFC or leading manufacturers in order to stimulate the economy of the United States. Despite these statements, neither the NAM, the United States Chamber of Commerce, nor the American Iron and Steel Institute passed a resolution in favor of recognition before diplomatic relations had, in fact, been established.[12]

12. National Association of Manufacturers, *Proceedings*, October 1929, p. 53. *American Industries* 30 (February 1930): 21–

Although business spokesmen did sometimes criticize the policy of nonrecognition as irrelevant or shortsighted, there is no evidence that organized business pressure prompted recognition. One contemporary proponent of recognition impatiently complained in 1931 that "the persons who stand most to gain have remained silent. The large companies and banks trading with the Bolsheviks seem to believe that they must assume an attitude of neutrality, and keep out of 'politics.' They do not work for recognition, although as American citizens, they have as much right to fight for recognition as Matthew Woll and Hamilton Fish have to fight against it." Senator Borah, for example, as late as February 1933 sadly acknowledged that there was as yet no movement among businessmen supporting recognition. The Manhattan Board of Commerce informed Borah in June that it was "about to endorse and sponsor a campaign to bring about the recognition of Soviet Russia by the United States government," but in October 1933 Secretary of State Cordell Hull was still wondering whether business groups interested in Russian trade were going to make "a strong effort" to promote recognition and a large loan. Only two national business organizations—the United States Board of Trade and the American-Russian Chamber of Commerce—officially endorsed the policy of establishing diplomatic relations before Roosevelt negotiated the terms of recognition with the Soviet Government in November 1933.[13]

26; 30 (April 1930): 24. *Nation's Business* 17 (June 1929): 27, 168; 18 (March 1930): 27–29, 166, 168; 18 (April 1930): 56, 58, 62, 265–67; 21 (January 1933): 19. *Iron Age* 130 (July 7, 1932): 45; 132 (October 26, 1933): 48–49. Browder, *Soviet-American Diplomacy*, p. 77.

13. Charles M. Muchnic, "A Business Man's View of Russia: Letters from an American Executive," *Harper's* 149 (September 1929): 437–53; Louis Fischer, *Why Recognize Russia?* pp. 139–40; Borah to George Kent, February 24, 1933, Box 352, Manhattan Board of Commerce to Borah, June 28, 1933, Box 521, Borah Papers; Hull to Frank C. Walker (Treasury Department), October 28, 1933, Box 18, R. Walton Moore Papers. The San Francisco Commonwealth Club had endorsed recognition in 1932 because it anticipated economic benefits to California. See U.S. Board of Trade to Borah, July 8, 1933, American-Russian Chamber of Commerce, press release, July 13, 1933, Box 352, Borah Papers; Browder, *Soviet-American Diplomacy*, p. 38.

Nevertheless, during the 1920s and early 1930s there were predictions that "from pure self-interest," the United States would eventually come to terms with the Communists in order to permit U.S. businessmen to take full advantage of the extensive commercial opportunities of the Russian market.[14] Writing in 1927, Chester H. Rowell, a Progressive from California, asserted that recognition was a "business question" that would be settled only after "our businessmen conclude that it will be profitable to them for us to recognize Russia." On the eve of recognition *Bankers Magazine* assumed that "considerations of trade rather than that of politics have no doubt promoted this change in the American attitude toward the Soviet Regime." As late as 1965 the national magazine of the American Legion reminded its readers that business pressure had brought recognition, "over all objections to the Soviet Union as an international outlaw." Yet there is almost no structural or organizational evidence that individual businessmen or specialized business groups took any of the steps that social scientists now know are necessary to effect as great a change of policy as the one toward the USSR that occurred under FDR.[15] So why did such a popular myth arise and why does it still persist?

Historians and laymen who have given credence to this myth have overlooked the time at which most prominent business figures and business organizations began publicly to support recognition—not only after Roosevelt had made up his mind to recognize the USSR in the spring of 1933,[16]

14. Hanson (Harbin, Manchuria) to State Department, April 27, 1923, Coleman to State Department, July 7, 1923, U.S. Department of State, Records Relating to Internal Affairs of Russia and the Soviet Union, Record Group 59, Files 861.602/82, 861.602/88; Gerhard Dobbert, *Red Economics*, p. 326; Elisha M. Friedman, *Russia in Transition: A Businessman's Appraisal*, pp. 555–57; Louis Fischer, *The Soviets in World Affairs*, 2: 570; Fischer, *Why Recognize Russia?* pp. 147–53.

15. Rowell to Janet Speakman, March 12, 1927, Box 3, Chester H. Rowell Papers, Bancroft Library, University of California, Berkeley; *Bankers Magazine* 127 (November 1933): 492; *American Legion*, October 1965, p. 56; Lester W. Milbrath, "Interest Groups and Foreign Policy," in James N. Rosenau, ed., *Domestic Sources of Foreign Policy*, pp. 231–51.

16. Beatrice Farnsworth, *William C. Bullitt and the Soviet*

but also after he had issued an invitation to the Soviet Government on October 10 to negotiate the question. This tardiness is often obscured by the Democrats' use of economic necessity as their public justification of recognition. Another feature of the myth requiring reconsideration is the misleading emphasis that has been placed on certain private polls conducted between 1930 and 1933. The one usually cited was made in 1931 by Jerome Davis, a Yale professor and long-time Russian sympathizer. Davis had published several books about the USSR and had visited that country at least six times from 1917 to 1931. He was a friend of such early pro-recognition Democrats as Col. Edward M. House and businessman Edward A. Filene, as well as Senator Borah and Raymond Robins. Early in 1929 he confided to Borah that he hoped to be appointed to any future commission to investigate the possibilities of recognition, and by 1933 Davis's ambition was to become the first U.S. Ambassador to the Soviet Union.[17]

Davis conducted his 1931 poll to counter the attempt of the antitraders to ban certain Russian commodities. After writing to "some fifty of the largest and best known firms" dealing with the Soviets, he reported he had received 47 replies, "most of them requesting that their attitudes be kept confidential." All but 2 of the 47 claimed the USSR had been a reliable customer. Also, 22 said they were in favor of immediate recognition, while only 4 expressed complete disapproval of the idea; 11 preferred that Hoover appoint a trade commission, and 10 were noncommittal, saying "it was a political issue on which they did not wish to express an opinion."[18] Thus, 25—more than half—of the respondents did not specifically endorse recognizing the Soviet Union, although most accounts of this poll simply cite the fact that 22 did approve.

Union, p. 89; Herbert Feis, 1933: Characters in Crisis, p. 307; Browder, Soviet-American Diplomacy, pp. 99–100.

17. Davis, "Russia: 'The Acid Test,' " p. 164; Davis to Borah, March 20, 1929, Box 308, Davis to Borah, February 13, February 15, March 20, March 21, 1933, Borah to Raymond Robins, November 8, 1933, Box 352, Borah Papers. Borah's first choice for an ambassador to Russia was Robins; his second choice was Davis.

18. Davis, "Capitalism and Communism," pp. 65–67, 72.

This poll hardly represented a scientific sampling of a cross section of companies doing business with the Soviets, since more than 1700 U.S. firms utilized the services of Amtorg to sell their products to Russia in 1931. It is far from conclusive about the attitude of big business, let alone the average company engaging in Russian trade. Finally, the information Davis received was given in the strictest confidence and does not demonstrate the existence of any organized movement within the business community for recognition. In a March 1933 memorandum on recognition requested by Secretary of State Cordell Hull, Davis claimed to have received letters from most of the 150 members of the American-Russian Chamber of Commerce supporting recognition.[19] This response anticipated a resolution the organization passed in support of recognition the following July, but there is no evidence that the new administration was influenced by this information.

The career personnel in the departments of State and Commerce definitely were not. Such officials in the State Department as Assistant Secretary of State R. Walton Moore, Special Assistant to the Secretary of State William C. Bullitt, and Robert F. Kelley continued to draft memoranda categorically opposing "immediate and unconditional recognition." Moore, for example, in October and November 1933 insisted that there would be "very widespread adverse criticism" of such action from the U.S. public unless recognition was accompanied by agreement "pertaining to propaganda, religion, espionage, et cetera." Moore, apparently ignoring the results of polls by the American Foundation, as well as those by the State Department, said his estimate of public opinion came from his own reading of newspapers across the country.[20]

Two general public opinion polls were conducted in 1931 and 1933. The State Department's was a survey of editorials that Secretary of State Henry L. Stimson had ordered in March 1931. It indicated that only 13 per cent of 183 newspapers favored recognition and 63 per cent opposed any change in official policy. After Roosevelt issued his invitation

19. Davis to Louis McHenry Howe, March 23, 1933, Official File 220–A, Box 4, Franklin D. Roosevelt Papers.
20. Moore, memoranda, October 4, November 9, 1933, Box 18, Moore Papers.

to the Russian Government in October 1933, a very limited poll by the State Department involving only 63 newspaper editorials revealed approximately two-thirds in favor of recognition and one-third opposed. According to the department's analysis the argument most often cited for recognition was the possibility of increased trade. This reversal in opinion from 1931 was confirmed at the end of October in the results of a more extensive poll made by the Committee on Russian-American Relations of the American Foundation. In this survey 1,139 newspaper editors were asked specifically whether they approved of immediate recognition followed by negotiations to resolve existing points of controversy between the two nations; 718 (63 per cent) responded positively while 306 (26.9 per cent) responded negatively. The South and the industrial states in the East were more strongly for what amounted to unconditional recognition than were the Midwest and New England areas. The two reasons for recognition most often cited were the possibility of increased trade opportunities and the awareness of Japanese aggression in the Far East. This poll also suffered from methodological defects, but it did show that general opinion was markedly changed from the spring of 1931, largely because of the Depression and the Manchurian crisis.[21]

The American Foundation's announcement of the results of its survey came well after Roosevelt had started to progress toward recognition. In fact, earlier in the summer of 1933 Roosevelt had refused to meet publicly or privately with the Russian-American Relations Committee of the foundation, even though it included such important business figures as Thomas Lamont and James D. Mooney, because "it would be taken as an out and out announcement of recognition." Roosevelt's refusal came after he and his wife had been assured several times by a close friend, who was also a member of the committee, that the group "fully realized . . . recognition is al-

21. Farnsworth, *Bullitt and the Soviet Union*, pp. 89, 206–7 n. 5; Filene, *Americans and the Soviet Experiment*, pp. 265, 290–91; Browder, *Soviet-American Diplomacy*, pp. 85–86; American Foundation, press release, October 30, 1933, Official File 20, Box 1, Roosevelt Papers; Meno Lovenstein, *American Opinion of Soviet Russia*, p. 139–46.

ready in train and . . . the object in proposing this [meeting] is not to 'urge' the President to interest himself in recognition," but to advise him about how to proceed.[22] As it turned out, Roosevelt proceeded on his own.

By the time FDR came to office the American Foundation's committee was only one of a variety of groups and individuals he could have turned to for advice on either side of the recognition controversy. Many labor unions, with the exception of the AFL, were in favor of recognizing the USSR; such influential Democrats as Owen D. Young, Al Smith, Colonel House, Josephus Daniels, Samuel Untermeyer, and Edward Filene advocated establishing diplomatic relations, as did many of the protrade senators and congressmen mentioned earlier and the usual sprinkling of educators, clergymen, and women's peace groups.[23]

Most of the U.S. engineers employed by the Soviet Union in the early 1930s were for recognition of the USSR.[24] A few

22. Esther E. Lape to Eleanor Roosevelt, July 10, July 12, July 18, 1933, Lape to FDR, July 21, 1933, FDR to Lape, July 28, 1933, official file 220-A, Box 4, Roosevelt Papers. Other members of the committee were George H. Houston, president of Baldwin Locomotive Works; Thomas A. Morgan, president of Curtis Wright Corporation; J. H. Rand, president of Remington Rand; Col. Hugh Y. Cooper; and Allen Wardwell.

23. Among the labor groups endorsing recognition were Amalgamated Clothing Workers of America; International Ladies Garment Workers Union; United Textile Workers of America; Cloth Hat, Cap and Millinery Workers International Union; American Federation of Teachers; Marine Workers Industrial Union; and the Conference for Progressive Labor Action. Many more labor organizations than business organizations were publicly in favor of recognition by the fall of 1933. For these and other prorecognition groups and individuals, see Browder, *Soviet-American Diplomacy*, pp. 77, 82–83; Feis, *1933*, pp. 307–8; Marian C. McKenna, *Borah*, p. 303; Farnsworth, *Bullitt and the Soviet Union*, pp. 75–76, 89; Frank Freidel, *Franklin D. Roosevelt*, Vol. 3, *The Triumphs*, p. 272; Official File 220-A, Box 4, Roosevelt Papers; Box 352, Borah Papers.

24. For the following information about engineers, see Friedman, *Russia in Transition*, pp. 251, 257–58; Hans Heymann, *We Can Do Business with Russia*, pp. 26–28, 81, 84; Lewis S. Feuer, "American Travelers to the Soviet Union, 1917–1932; The Formation of a Component of New Deal Ideology," *American Quar-*

engineers had worked in the USSR before 1928, but their numbers increased when the First Five-Year Plan created an extraordinary demand for foreign technical aid. About one-third of the technical assistance contracts granted under the plan went to U.S. firms, and by 1931 approximately 1000 U.S. engineers were working in the USSR. Of all the technical aid that the United States supplied to the Soviets, the work of Charles E. Stuart in coal mining, H. J. Freyn in the steel industry, the Ford engineer John Calder in manufacturing, Walter A. Rukeyser in the asbestos-mining industry, and Hugh L. Cooper in power-plant construction along the lower Dnieper, stand out as major U.S. contributions to the technological industrialization of the USSR. Stuart, Freyn, and Cooper became actively involved in the recognition movement. Most engineers—even those who were not involved in the movement to recognize Russia—returned from Russia overly enthusiastic about the experimentation and large-scale planning that characterized the Five-Year Plan, and their views were often exploited by those already in favor of recognition.

Although U.S. engineers were quick to criticize "the in-

---

terly 14 (Summer 1962): 138–43; Davis, "Capitalism and Communism," p. 74; Edmund Wilson, *The American Earthquake: A Documentary of the Twenties and Thirties*, pp. 269–73; Filene, *Americans and the Soviet Experiment*, pp. 207, 217–20; H. J. Freyn, "An American Engineer Looks at the Five-Year Plan," *New Republic* 66 (May 6, 1931): 317–19; Walter A. Rukeyser, "Do Our Engineers in Russia Damage America?" *Scribner's Magazine* 90 (November 1931): 521–24; W. J. Austin, "Why Fear Russia?" *Scribner's Magazine* 90 (September 1931): 291–95. George A. Burrell, "Experiences of an American Engineer in Russia," *National Petroleum News* 23 (September 16, 1931): 43, 45–46, 48; 23 (September 30, 1931): 43–45; 23 (October 14, 1931): 43–44, 46–47; 23 (October 21, 1931): 34–37. J. G. Rogers, memorandum, May 5, 1931, U.S. Department of State, Political Relations between the U.S. and Russia and the Soviet Union, Record Group 59, File 711.61/223; William Phillips (Under-Secretary of State) to FDR, June 5, 1933, Arthur Upham Pope to FDR, April 15, 1933, Official File 220-A, Box 4, Roosevelt Papers; U.S. Congress, House, Committee on Ways and Means, *Hearings on H.R. 15597, H.R. 15927, H.R. 16517*, pp. 95, 110; Charles Stuart to R. Walton Moore, October 20, November 4, 1933, Box 18, Moore Papers.

herent procrastination of the Russian temperament," the inefficiency of the Soviet bureaucracy, the backwardness of Soviet industry, and the arbitrary and unnecessarily severe punishment meted out for honest errors in judgment, they were "instinctively at home with a government which aimed to rule by blueprints," and they openly admired the self-sacrificing, hard-working Soviet leaders with whom they had personal contact. Thus, they usually became much more sympathetic with what they thought the Russian leaders were trying to do than did the ordinary U.S. businessman who simply sold goods to the Soviets and never accepted the Communist concept of national planning. Despite their disapproval of such views, Government officials and businessmen thought of Cooper, Calder, and other prominent engineers as Russian experts who enjoyed the confidence of Soviet authorities and could "cultivate better trade relations between the two countries."

On the other side of the recognition issue were the powerful American Bankers Association, the law firm representing some of the financial institutions that had suffered from Russian nationalization of industries, the New York Chamber of Commerce, the Union League Club of Chicago, the AFL, the National Civic Federation, the American Legion and other patriotic organizations, plus the *Chicago Tribune, The New York Times,* and 673,568 voters from Massachusetts who signed a petition against recognition in March 1933. Most of those legislators and businessmen who had wanted continuing restrictions on trade also opposed recognition; they were joined by Bernard Baruch, John Spargo, Bainbridge Colby, and Father Edmund Walsh, the outspoken, conservative vice-president of Georgetown University. Significantly, the National Civic Federation's list of those "unequivocally against recognition of the Russian Soviet Regime" contained the names of more than 5,000 businessmen, clergymen, congressmen, and educators. None of the prorecognition groups were ever able to assemble as many prominent business figures as are found on that list, including Harvey S. Firestone; Howard Heinz; Samuel Insull; David M. Goodrich; Darwin P. Kingsley, president of New York Life; Walter S. Gifford, president of AT&T; E. M. Herr, president of Westinghouse; R. E. Wood, president of Sears Roebuck; John D. Ryan, chairman of the board of Anaconda Copper Company; and Alvan Macauley, president of Packard Motors.[25]

Possibly because sides were so clearly drawn by 1932, FDR straddled the issue of recognition during his campaign for the Presidency. He apparently convinced the executive board of the United Russian National Organizations that he had "no intention of granting diplomatic recognition" to the Soviets, while chemical engineer Alcan Hirsch came away from an interview with the candidate thinking that Roosevelt was contemplating recognition.[26] After taking office Roosevelt also did not consult extensively the leading representatives of either side; instead, he worked behind the scenes with a few personal advisers to establish diplomatic relations for essentially political reasons. Publicly, however, his administration justified its actions mainly in economic terms.

Ultimately Roosevelt based his decision to recognize the Soviet Union primarily on political, rather than economic, considerations; like Stalin, he feared the increasingly aggressive postures of Germany and, to a greater degree, Japan. As the tension between Japan and Russia increased during the spring of 1933, despite the President's endorsement of the Stimson Doctrine, recognition seemed to Roosevelt a subtle form of diplomatic pressure that might well give the Japanese reason to pause in their conquest of South Manchuria

25. Browder, *Soviet-American Diplomacy*, pp. 79, 84–85; McKenna, *Borah*, p. 393; Frank L. Polk to FDR, October 20, 1933, in Edgar B. Nixon, *Franklin D. Roosevelt and Foreign Affairs*, Vol. 1, *January 1933–February 1934*, pp. 433–34. Rep. Hon. C. Wallgren to FDR, October 24, 1933, Official File 20, Box 1; Union League Club to FDR, March 20, 1933, Official File 1; Marvin H. McIntyre (FDR's assistant secretary), memorandum, March 31, 1933, John Spargo to FDR, July 5, 1933, Father Walsh to McIntyre, October 21, 1933, Official File 220-A, Box 4, Roosevelt Papers. *Journal of the American Bankers Association* 26 (August 1933): 26; National Civic Federation to Hull, March 20, 1933, National Civic Federation to William Phillips, July 24, 1933, U.S. Department of State, Records Relating to Internal Affairs of Russia and the Soviet Union, Record Group 59, Files 861.01/1875, 861.01/1965; National Civic Federation list, February 1931, U.S. Department of State, General Records, Record Group 59, File 811.45 Council on Foreign Relations/63.

26. United Russian National Organizations to FDR, November 3, 1932, Presidential File, Box 18, Roosevelt Papers; Alcan Hirsch, *Industrialized Russia*, p. 251.

but would not unnecessarily antagonize them. Recognition, which the United States extended to the USSR just after Japan created the puppet state of Manchukuo, was the logical nonmilitary answer of the Democrats to a problem the Republican Stimson Doctrine had failed to solve. Stimson had considered this same course in the spring and summer of 1932 but had rejected it because Hoover's attitude remained unchanged, because the Far Eastern Division of the State Department advised against it, and because he himself believed that the United States would lose its "moral standing" in the Far East if it acted solely out of political expediency.[27] Even though Wilson had initiated the nonrecognition policy, the Republicans were the ones who had assumed the role of guardians of the original anti-Soviet doctrine in the 1920s and early 1930s. Thus, the Democrats could more freely repudiate the policy in 1933 than could the Republicans.

There were, however, personnel in the departments of State and Commerce who were not ready to abandon a policy that had become institutionalized. If anything, career men were more opposed to recognition in 1933 than they had been in the previous decade. Frederick Feiker, who was at this time director of the BFDC, and E. C. Ropes, the BFDC Slavic specialist, remained disdainfully impervious to the activities of groups advocating recognition and simply reiterated the standard position of the Commerce Department that recognition would not increase the amount of trade between the two countries because the credit difficulties of Amtorg would not be solved by such action.[28]

27. Morris, "Reassessment of Russian Recognition," pp. 471, 478–79; Browder, *Soviet-American Diplomacy*, pp. 68–69, 95, 97, 99; Farnsworth, *Bullitt and the Soviet Union*, pp. 90–91; Feis, *1933*, pp. 310–11; John Morton Blum, *From the Morgenthau Diaries: Years of Crisis, 1928–1938*, p. 54; Stanley K. Hornbeck (chief, Division of Far Eastern Affairs, State Department), memorandum, July 11, 1932, Stimson to Borah, September 8, 1932, U.S. Department of State, Records Relating to Internal Affairs of Russia and the Soviet Union, Record Group 59, Files 861.01/1785, 861.01/1786; George F. Kennan, *Memoirs, 1925–1950*, p. 57; Freidel, *Franklin D. Roosevelt*, Vol. 4, *Launching the New Deal*, pp. 104, 119–23.

28. Ropes to Whiting Corporation, March 18, 1933, Ropes to Buffalo district office, BFDC, June 1, 1933, Ropes to A. Dacks, August 1, 1933, Ropes to Julius Klein, October 17, 1932, Fred-

The State Department contained a broader spectrum of institutionalized negative opinion about recognition. Those under the influence of the East European chief, Robert Kelley—one of whom was the new Secretary of State, Cordell Hull—feared that the President would rush into diplomatic relations with the Soviet Union without receiving the proper ideological guarantees, namely, the cessation of Communist propaganda in the United States, settlement of the Russian debt, and confirmation of the economic, legal, and religious rights of U.S. citizens in the USSR. Uppermost in the minds of Kelley and Hull in the summer and fall of 1933 were not relations with Japan and Germany, but disturbing reports about Communist subversion in Cuba.[29] In addition, Kelley, Hull, Chief of the Far Eastern Division Stanley K. Hornbeck, Under-Secretary of State William R. Castle, Jr., Assistant Secretary of State R. Walton Moore, and members of the U.S. legation at Riga—Minister Robert P. Skinner, George F. Kennan, and Felix Cole—were convinced that recognition would not bring about a substantial increase in trade, except perhaps by artificially stimulating commerce through long-term government credit at a time when, according to them, Russia was a poor risk.[30]

---

erick M. Feiker to Henry S. Beale, October 5, 1932, U.S. Department of Commerce, Records of the Bureau of Foreign and Domestic Commerce, Record Group 151, Files 448-U.S., 221-Russia.

29. For the details of Kelley's and Hull's preoccupation with Communist activity in Cuba and of the unsuccessful attempt of the Secretary of State and other State Department officials to embarrass and possibly thwart the negotiations with the Soviets by publicizing Communist subversion in Cuba, see Robert E. Bowers, "Hull, Russian Subversion in Cuba, and Recognition of the USSR," *Journal of American History* 52 (December 1966): 542–54. Hull's memoirs and the *Foreign Relations Papers* confirm that his support of recognition was very qualified and very belated.

30. Stanley Hornbeck, memorandum, July 11, 1932, U.S. Department of State, Records Relating to Internal Affairs of Russia and the Soviet Union, Record Group 59, File 861.01/1785; Castle, memorandum to Fred L. Eberhardt, March 3, 1933, Kelley, memorandum, July 27, 1933, *FRP: The Soviet Union, 1933–1939*, pp. 3–11; Moore, memorandum, October 4, 1933, Hull to Frank C. Walker (Treasury Department), October 28, 1933, Moore Papers; Samuel N. Harper, *The Russia I Believe In: The Memoirs*

Some members of the State Department and other Government officials were more enthusiastic about recognition, because they thought it would help the domestic economy by improving U.S. commodity prices and thus the entire matter of farm relief. Russia's return to the international wheat market during the Depression had not only led to the unjustified charges from the United States about dumping, but also to three world wheat conferences between January 1930 and May 1931. At the last one, representatives from both the United States and the Soviet Union were present, and although they reached no agreement, their meeting and other contacts about the world price of wheat led some members of the Government to speculate that the wheat negotiations were laying the foundation for recognition. While Hoover was still in office, Under-Secretary of State Joseph Cotton and Assistant Secretary of State William Castle were made aware of the political implications of the wheat conferences by the economic historian Louis Fischer. Later, Fischer's book *Why Recognize Russia?* which suggested that diplomatic contacts between the two nations could easily be made during future wheat conferences, came to the attention of Secretary Cordell Hull. At the same time Herbert Feis, economic adviser to the State Department, Senator Smith W. Brookhart, Secretary of Agriculture Henry Wallace, and Henry Morgenthau, Jr., director of the Farm Credit Administration, were very much concerned with farm relief, commodity prices, and domestic-allotment proposals, especially for wheat and cotton. Consequently, these men considered obtaining a wheat-quota agreement with the Soviets and increasing cotton sales to Russia in return for recognition distinct possibilities, and they made their views known to the new President. Also, the Commerce Department had been concerned since 1925 about Russian grain exports and was generally aware of the interest in selling agricultural products to the USSR that had developed by August 1933 under the leadership of Senator Brookhart, the Agriculture Department, and the Agricultural Adjustment Administration.[31]

of *Samuel N. Harper, 1902–1941*, p. 200; Bernadotte E. Schmitt, "With How Little Wisdom . . . ," *American Historical Review* 66 (January 1961): 311; Kennan, *Memoirs*, pp. 47–52.

31. H. S. Smith (special representative, Commerce Depart-

After receiving this economic advice, Roosevelt also began to associate commodity prices and recognition, although he personally did not fear Russian wheat sales abroad as much as these men did.[32] In his first private attempt to make contact with the Soviets at the beginning of his administration, he ignored the departments of State and Commerce by instructing Morgenthau to arrange meetings through intermediaries with Amtorg representatives about financing the sale of farm products and industrial goods. By May, Roosevelt displayed his impatience with the inconclusive Amtorg meetings, as well as his ignorance of the increase in Russian-U.S. commercial relations before 1932, when he told Morgenthau that he wished he could meet personally with a single individual representing the Soviets to "break the ice between the two countries and in that way gradually get people of the United States used to doing business with the Russians." Later in the month he "broke the ice" in his own fashion by sending a personal plea for peace, economic cooperation, and disarmament to the heads of fifty-four foreign nations, including the titular head of the Soviet Union Mikhail Kalinin. Roosevelt's spontaneous action did not constitute recognition, but he did set a significant precedent by obviously by-passing Hull and the anti-Communist bureaucracy of the State Department and communicating directly with foreign leaders.[33]

---

ment), report, September 15, 1925, Box 266, HHCD; BFDC to Edward S. Cannon, August 10, 1933, U.S. Department of Commerce, Records of the Bureau of Foreign and Domestic Commerce, Record Group 151, File 448-U.S. For further details of the wheat issue and recognition, see Robert E. Bowers, "American Diplomacy, the 1933 Wheat Conference, and Recognition of the Soviet Union," *Agricultural History* 11 (January 1966): 39–52; AAA, memorandum, September 22, 1933, Official File 1–K, Roosevelt Papers; AAA, memorandum, November 4, 1933, Box 18, Moore Papers; Henry Wallace to FDR, November 7, 1933, Official File 220-A, Box 4, Roosevelt Papers.

32. In an off-the-record remark at one of his first press conferences FDR told newsmen that "Russia is today probably . . . not in a position to do very much wheat exporting. They need their own wheat." See *Complete Presidential Press Conferences of Franklin D. Roosevelt*, Vols. 1–2, 1933, no. 3 (March 13, 1933), 1: 43.

33. Freidel, *Franklin D. Roosevelt*, Vol. 4, *Launching the New Deal*, p. 498; John Callan O'Laughlin to Hoover, May 18, 1933,

FDR's personal advisers who worked most closely with him on recognition were Raymond Moley, William C. Bullitt, and Morgenthau. Moley and Bullitt had recommended establishing relations with the USSR for exclusively political reasons in 1932. Moley was the first to be put in charge of all material on recognition in the fall and winter of 1932–1933. After Bullitt returned from Europe in the spring of 1933, he was appointed to the State Department and handled the political aspects of recognition. Then toward the end of September, the White House let it be known that Morgenthau had been in charge of coordinating all proposals for financing exports to the USSR for the last three months. Although a long-time advocate of recognition, Bullitt was not as eager to push ahead with unconditional recognition as were Moley and Morgenthau—one for political, the other for economic reasons. In fact, Bullitt shared all of Kelley's and Moore's reservations about rushing into recognition without the proper guarantees. Thus, Bullitt can be found complaining about the general antirecognition, anti-Russian bias within the State Department, yet agreeing with the conditions for recognition set by career men like Kelley, who were considerably less enthusiastic about recognition than he was.[34]

No discernible progress toward recognition was made until June and July, when the wheat problem brought Morgen-

Box 43, O'Laughlin Papers; Morgenthau, Diary, May 8, 1933, p. 17; FDR to Heads of Nationals Represented at the London and Geneva Conferences, May 16, 1933, and press conference, May 16, 1933, in Nixon, *Roosevelt and Foreign Affairs*, Vol. 1, *January 1933–February 1934*, p. 126–29; Bowers, "Hull, Russian Subversion," p. 554. The timing of this message was determined by Hitler's intention to address the Reichstag on May 17. Norman Davis wanted a statement from the United States to precede Hitler's in order to save the Geneva Disarmament Conference. Although the State Department cooperated in the preparation of the message, Hull disapproved of the fact that it was not sent through the respective foreign offices. See Cordell Hull, *Memoirs*, 1: 226–27, 297–98.

34. Feis, *1933*, pp. 312–14; Bowers, "Hull, Russian Subversion," p. 545; Farnsworth, *Bullitt and the Soviet Union*, pp. 95–96; Henry Morgenthau, Jr., Diary, September 27, 1933, pp. 63, 65; FDR, press conference, September 22, 1933, President's Personal File 1–P, Box 225, Roosevelt Papers; Morris, "Reassessment of Russian Recognition," pp. 474–75.

thau, Senator James Couzens, Bullitt, Moley, and Hull into direct conversations with Soviet Foreign Minister Maxim Litvinov at the London Economic Conference. Sometime during the course of these discussions, Litvinov candidly asked Bullitt about Roosevelt's intention to recognize the USSR but received only a noncommittal answer. On July 3, however, the day after Moley talked with the Soviet minister, the Reconstruction Finance Corporation announced its approval of a short-term credit advance of $4,000,000 to Amtorg for the purchase of U.S. cotton. FDR had delayed approving this arrangement earlier in the year, and later in August—after a conference between representatives of agricultural and industrial interests recommended the establishment of a Russian-Export Discount Corporation to facilitate trade—he cautioned Morgenthau to set an over-all limit of $100,000,000 for the next several months on raw material and machinery sales to Russia.[35]

FDR exercised this economic restraint despite his agricultural advisers' eagerness for more trade, many businessmen's inquiries about it, and his own desire to improve relations between the two countries. There were several reasons for his hesitation. He was receiving repeated warnings from both the pro-Soviet and anti-Soviet men in the State Department not to enter into any major economic transactions, especially long-term loans, until the Communists agreed to recognition terms that were satisfactory to the United States. Also, the Soviets did not respond as eagerly to the idea of long-term loans as the President had been led to believe they would by Bullitt and others, who were overestimating the immediate Soviet need for U.S. credit. Moreover, Roosevelt was perfectly willing to employ economic pressure to gain recognition on U.S. terms if that pressure would bring the desired results quickly, but it did not. He had never placed international trade relations above the domestic economic problems the Depression had generated, and since the domestic situation occupied most of his time in the spring and summer of 1933, he simply did not pursue his initial economic approach to reconciliation with the USSR as intensely as he might have otherwise. Finally, his primary interest in recog-

35. Bowers, "American Diplomacy," pp. 48–50; Morganthau Diary, August 16, 1933, p. 59.

nition remained political, and he was not going to let the lack of a financial settlement be an impediment; indeed, there was no formal economic agreement in the official exchange of notes establishing recognition.[36]

Consequently, when nothing significant materialized from his economic tactics by the end of September, Roosevelt confided to Morgenthau that he was tired of the "back door" approach and had a more direct, personal plan in mind to bring about recognition. The result was the October 10 invitation to the USSR to send a representative to the United States. Once again Bullitt and Morgenthau, rather than Secretary of State Hull, were the men involved in contacting the Soviets. In fact, some evidence indicates that the State Department was not apprised of the action until a few hours before it was taken.[37] Clearly the impetus toward recognition from March through September of 1933 came from the President and several of his closest personal advisers in the executive branch and not from the departments of State or Commerce. Roosevelt also carefully concealed his move toward recognition in his off-the-record statements to the press. In typically eclectic fashion he met sporadically with both proponents and opponents of recognition until just before diplomatic relations were established, all the while denying in press conferences that any progress toward establishing relations was being made. Hence, there is no indication that any of the well-known advocates of recognition, such as Borah, Gumberg, Robins, or Cooper, exercised any significant influence on his actions or knew about them in advance.[38]

36. W. K. Shuman (Treasury Department), memorandum, August 12, 1933, Official File 220-A, Box 4, Bullitt to FDR, July 8, 1933, Presidential File, Box 54, Roosevelt Papers; Hull to FDR, September 21, 1933, Kelley to William Phillips, September 25, 1933, Bullitt to Hull, October 4, 1933, Bullitt to FDR, November 15, 1933, *FRP: Soviet Union, 1933–1939*, pp. 12–17, 25–26; Feis, *1933*, pp. 310–13; Browder, *Soviet-American Diplomacy*, pp. 81, 92–93.

37. Morgenthau, Diary, September 26, 1933, p. 61; Harper, *Russia I Believe In*, pp. 200–201; Bowers, "Hull, Russian Subversion," p. 554.

38. FDR, press conferences, March 22, April 14, 1933, Box 224, July 5, September 22, September 29, October 11, 1933, Box 225, President's Personal File 1–P, Roosevelt Papers.

Cooper's influence on the new administration was probably

In retrospect, federal officials interested in the farm problem, not U.S. manufacturers who had pioneered in trading with the Soviets, appear to have introduced the economic considerations that temporarily colored Roosevelt's thinking about recognition. Roosevelt did nothing, of course, to discourage the impression among business groups and the general public that recognition was largely an economic move designed to improve conditions in the United States. To allow such an impression was cruelly misleading because only an inadequate "gentlemen's agreement" about the war-debt question had been reached; no arrangements had been made for long-term credit or trade contracts during the recognition negotiations. In January 1934 the Treasury Department refused to consider arguments for banning Soviet goods because of forced-labor conditions and proceeded to remove all the remaining Government restrictions on trade with the Soviet Union. In February 1934 FDR approved the establishment of an Export-Import Bank under powers granted to the RFC and NRA to finance trade with the Soviet Union.[39] At

---

greater than it had been under the previous Republican governments—both Roosevelt and Hull had requested him to present his views in April—but the influence of both Borah and Robins diminished in 1933. By his own admission Borah was not kept informed of the private actions of Roosevelt and his advisers, and illness kept him from actively participating in any kind of politics during the spring and summer of 1933. Robins also suffered from ill health. In September and November of 1932 he became a victim of amnesia; he was still recovering at the beginning of 1933. In April he left for a trip to Moscow, and upon his return in July he went to Washington to promote recognition. His political enemies, however, made the most of his mysterious disappearance during part of the time that he had amnesia, and his position in governmental circles was generally weakened. See Anne Vincent Meiburger, *Efforts of Raymond Robins toward the Recognition of Soviet Russia and the Outlawry of War, 1917–1933*, pp. 168–78; McKenna, *Borah*, pp. 306–7; Borah to A. Wunstorff, May 27, 1933, William P. Simms to Borah, October 20, 1933, Box 352, Borah Papers; Robins to FDR, October 14, October 28, 1933, FDR to Robins, October 17, December 8, 1933, in Nixon, *Roosevelt and Foreign Affairs*, Vol. 1, *January 1933–February 1934*, pp. 428–29, 431, 514; Robert James Maddox, *William E. Borah and American Foreign Policy*, p. 213.

39. Donald G. Bishop, *The Roosevelt-Litvinov Agreements:*

this point Roosevelt and the State Department belatedly and unsuccessfully tried to get Congress to exempt Russia from the Johnson Debt-Default Act of June 1934, which prohibited further credit to countries in default, by arguing that the Soviets were in the process of negotiating a settlement as part of the terms of recognition. Consequently, no significant loans to, or trade with, the USSR materialized until World War II —when Lend-Lease programs circumvented the Johnson act —because no satisfactory settlement of the debt problem could be reached.[40]

U.S. importers and exporters had long been in favor of an Export-Import Bank, and they were quick to complain about the continued lack of long-term credit and discount services. However, the State Department and bankers on the board of trustees of the Export-Import Bank, with Roosevelt's approval, held firm on the point that the bank would not facilitate "any credit transaction . . . until the Soviet government . . . submitted a debt adjustment proposal acceptable to the President." By April 1934 Assistant Secretary Moore was distressed that Roosevelt seemed more "inclined to . . . modify the original debt proposals," but Ambassador Bullitt's increasingly negative reports from Moscow about the Soviets' reluctance to honor the recognition agreement apparently hardened FDR's attitude on the one point of controversy between the two nations that he had considered least important,

The American View, pp. 27–31, 149–52; Treasury Department, press release, January 24, 1934, in Morgenthau Diary, pp. 120–21; FDR, press conference, February 2, 1934, in Nixon, *Roosevelt and Foreign Affairs*, Vol. 1, *January 1933–February 1934*, pp. 623–26; Orville H. Bullitt, ed., *For the President: Personal and Secret Correspondence Between Franklin D. Roosevelt and William C. Bullitt*, p. 52.

40. Moore to Senator Joseph T. Robinson (with enclosed memorandum by FDR on Johnson bill), January 27, 1934, in Nixon, *Roosevelt and Foreign Affairs*, Vol. 1, *January 1933–February 1934*, pp. 615–16; J. Chal Vinson, "War Debts and Peace Legislation: The Johnson Act of 1934," *Mid-America* 50 (July 1968): 215–16; Hull, *Memoirs*, 1: 303; Warren F. Kimball, *The Most Unsordid Act: Lend-Lease, 1939–1941*, pp. 2, 41–42, 93–94, 107, 121, 124–25, 189, 200, 216; Robert Huhn Jones, *The Roads to Russia: United States Lend-Lease to the Soviet Union*, pp. 215–39.

namely, the debt claims.[41] Thus, the Government continued to inhibit the development of U.S.-Russian economic relations even after recognition, in defiance of much of the business community and in contradiction to its major public justification of recognition—improved trade in a time of depression.

Therefore, recognition did not increase U.S.-Russian understanding but instead created greater ideological suspicion and distrust because the Roosevelt administration so heavily used economics to justify its action. That recognition should cause increased animosity is somewhat ironic because FDR had ignored or by-passed the bureaucratized opposition to recognition that existed in the State and Commerce departments. After diplomatic relations were established through strong executive initiative, however, the traditional, institutionalized, anti-Communist ideology prevailed once more. Nothing but enlightened leadership could have changed the popular misconceptions about the USSR that had developed in the decade following World War I, and FDR did not provide such leadership in his personal and private progression toward recognition, nor did the other members of his administration who publicly defended the policy after diplomatic relations were established on November 16. Trade was deliberately used as a ruse to ensure the acceptance of recognition that the President desired for essentially noneconomic reasons. As several contemporary observers pointed out, there was a glaring inconsistency by 1933 between U.S. economic and political relations with the Soviets.[42] The former had progressed until at least 1932, whereas the latter had languished. It was this inconsistency or lack of coordi-

41. Kelley, memorandum of telephone conversation with president of Wright Aeronautical Corporation, February 23, 1934, Kelley to Bullitt, March 17, 1934, Moore to Bullitt, March 3, April 24, May 8, June 4, August 13, 1934, Bullitt to Moore, March 29, May 4, September 8, October 6, 1934, Moore Papers; Bullitt to State Department, March 15, March 28, April 8, 1934, *FRP: Soviet Union, 1933–1939*, pp. 66–67, 71–75, 79–81; Kennan, *Memoirs*, pp. 56–57; Bullitt, ed., *For the President*, pp. 154–57; Freidel, *Roosevelt*, Vol. 4, *Launching the New Deal*, pp. 134–35.

42. Fischer, *Why Recognize Russia?* pp. 195–96; Friedman, *Russia in Transition*, pp. 571–72.

nation upon which Roosevelt was able to capitalize in his executive drive for recognition of the USSR *without changing the ideological orientation of the original nonrecognition policy.*

In the United States, the problem of establishing normal economic and political relations with the USSR between 1917 and 1933 was complicated by institutionalized ideological considerations. Government officials maintained consistent ideological opposition to the new Communist regime, but a growing number of businessmen, who still were a minority within the business community, were enticed by the possibility of trading with Soviets. These businessmen either became increasingly indifferent to the original ideological basis of nonrecognition or consciously chose to separate economic from political foreign policy, at least in the case of the Soviet Union. Nevertheless, they were aware of the Government's firm ideological commitment and so did not generally advocate recognition, for they, too, were affected by the abstract ideological threat posed by communism.

During the same period, Soviet experts within the State and Commerce departments stubbornly continued the ideological position formulated in 1920, refusing to admit that a contradiction had developed in the economic and political treatment of the Soviet Union. Consequently, policy makers in the departments did not represent those businessmen who were most strongly in favor of firmly establishing U.S.-Soviet economic relations, and they did not reflect the dramatic change in favor of recognition that occurred in public opinion between March 1931 and October 1933. Instead, they tried to curb action they considered precipitous on the part of President Roosevelt and to promote the establishment of diplomatic relations on only sound ideological standards. Although they succeeded in having a number of such conditions included in the recognition agreement, their victory was, in the long run, meaningless because it did not alleviate ideological hostility between the two nations.

Therefore recognition, when it occurred in 1933, was not the product of business influence because the business community, which privately had divided into protrade and antitrade groups, had not made a united effort on this issue. In a very real sense, those antitrade businessmen who supported without reservations the Government's stand on recognition were in a less-ambiguous position in terms of reconciling their economic self-interest with their ideological predisposition than were those who had reservations about the policy for economic reasons but who continued to speak against recognition out of minimal ideological convictions and strong Government encouragement. Furthermore, the publicly organized business support for recognition that did exist came belatedly—after Roosevelt had decided to achieve U.S. recognition of Russia because he feared the growing Japanese power in the Far East. As a result, neither the opinion of businessmen nor general public opinion influenced the process leading to recognition, despite the new administration's defending this diplomatic act as a measure to alleviate the Depression.

The way in which the United States came to recognize the USSR offers an excellent opportunity to misinterpret the business community's effect on the formulation of U.S. foreign policy. At the very most, those businessmen who advocated trade with the Soviets helped to create a popular rationale for recognition that did not require acceptance or understanding of the Communist system. The policy of nonrecognition also provides one of the best examples of twentieth-century U.S. diplomacy at its worst because it fostered a lack of reconciliation and coordination between economic and political foreign policy. This inconsistency was the direct product of an ideologically based diplomacy that became bureaucratized and obsolete but nonetheless self-perpetuating. As such, it represents an endemic weakness in the subsequent conduct of U.S. foreign policy that has not allowed the United States to achieve the international humanitarian goals it proclaims and that, carried to its logical extreme during the Cold War, became an almost fatal liability in the United States' relations with foreign nations.

VI

INTERPRETATIONS: CONFLICTING
VIEWS AMONG U.S. HISTORIANS

There are several reasons why most studies of Soviet recognition have not placed the role of business into a proper perspective. One of the most important is the absence of any detailed consideration of the contradictions which developed among ideological, economic, and organizational forces during the sixteen years when no official diplomatic contact existed between the United States and the USSR. This oversight is directly related to the development of two distinct historiographical schools within the U.S. historical profession in the early twentieth century, to the ultimate fragmentation of both schools, and finally to the lack of any new comprehensive historical synthesis to replace them. At the moment, the relatively new field of organizational history, which is based on economic, intellectual, social, and bureaucratic analysis, appears to offer the greatest possibility of synthesizing historical scholarship for the remainder of the century.

Since 1900, historians have tended to divide into two opposing camps, which John Higham has called the "conservative evolutionists," and the "New Historians," or progressive historians.[1] Generally speaking, conservative evolutionists emphasize consensus and the unity or continuity of U.S. history and its evolving institutions, whereas progressive or liberal historians stress the diversity and conflict of specific historical events or time periods. The first school was outward-looking in the sense that it sought European origins for U.S. institutions; the second was more introspective, seek-

1. John Higham, *History: Professional Scholarship in America*, p. 148; Charles E. Neu, "The Changing Interpretive Structure of American Foreign Policy," in John Braeman et al., eds., *Twentieth-Century American Foreign Policy*, pp. 1–2.

ing the uniqueness of the U.S. domestic experience, but at the same time critical of tradition and institutional continuity.

Only a few of the many areas of disagreement between these two groups of scholars have affected the writing of diplomatic history and hence have directly inhibited understanding of the ways in which ideology, economics, and organizational theories are related to the United States' recognition of the USSR and to other important actions in U.S. foreign policy in this century. Of these few areas, the primary one concerns the merit of capitalism. Conservative historians have been procapitalist, or at least probusiness, and the progressive historians have been very suspicious of big business and often anticapitalist—although not necessarily Marxist— in orientation. The influence of these two groups has ebbed and flowed among successive generations of U.S. historians since the turn of the century and for the last seventy years has prevented the development of a balanced view of economic motivation in the formulation of American foreign policy.

For most of this time conservative evolutionists have been considered probusiness because they have usually followed the Rankian tradition of describing the origins and development of economic institutions without commenting on individual intention or possible negative results. The probusiness faction among historians which has been the most influential in recent years came out of World War II. In 1941, for example, the Social Science Research Council appointed a committee on Research in Economic History to investigate the role of the U.S. Government in economic development. Creating this committee represented not only a significant shift away from the study of the "political organization of economic progress" that was so characteristic of earlier conservative historians, but also a shift away from the value-laden progressive approach that had dwelled on the conflicts between good and bad economic groupings and promulgated a "robber baron" image of most successful businessmen. The contemporary brand of entrepreneurial history, that is, probusiness revisionism, almost exclusively concentrates on the positive "historical causes of economic development," rather than on the negative "economic causes of historical development." Between 1948 and 1958 it was greatly encouraged and influenced by the Harvard University Research Center in Entrepreneurial History and by the Committee on Historiography of the Social Science Research Council. Among the first postwar entrepreneurial historians were Allan Nevins, Fritz Redlich, Thomas C. Cochran, and Edward Chase Kirkland.[2]

In contrast, the origins of the anticapitalist school ultimately go back to Marx, rather than Ranke, and can be first seen in the political, moral, and economic predispositions held by intellectuals of the Populist and Progressive eras. This school reflects the impact of Marxist thought on essentially non-Marxist historians and was first made respectable in the writings of Frederick Jackson Turner, Charles A. Beard, Vernon Louis Parrington, Matthew Josephson, and Chester M. Destler. Their outlook was dominant between the two world wars but succumbed to fragmentation and disillusionment in the 1950s as their theories about the glories of the frontier, rural values, and the gradual ascendency of liberal reform in U.S. history were increasingly challenged. The eclipse of the progressive synthesis and of a critical approach to the U.S. economy corresponded to the rise of entrepreneurial history, with its positive emphasis on urban, capitalist development.[3]

2. Higham, *History*, pp. 163, 177–82, 217–20. The first publication of the center, *Change and the Entrepreneur: Postulates and Patterns for Entrepreneurial History*, contains essays by leading spokesmen for this school, such as Joseph Schumpeter, who generally praise the virtues of corporate liberalism. The number of publications in the area of entrepreneurial history has increased very rapidly, and the best guide to this literature can be found in the articles and reviews in *Business History Review*. Two early articles containing both summaries of the entrepreneurial interpretation and representative bibliographies are Hal Bridges, "The Robber Baron Concept in American History," *Business History Review* 32 (Spring 1958): 1–13, and Gabriel Kolko, "The Premises of Business Revisionism," *Business History Review* 33 (Autumn, 1959): 330–44.

3. See Higham, *History*, pp. 172–82, 199–211; Richard Hofstadter and Walter P. Metzger, *The Development of Academic Freedom in the United States*, pp. 413–67; Richard Hofstadter, *The Progressive Historians*; Lee Benson, *Turner and Beard, American Historical Writing Reconsidered*, p. 103; Cushing

A considerably more radicalized version of the original progressive, antibusiness school reappeared with new vigor in the early 1960s in the writings of "New Left," or neo-Marxist, historians. The foreign-policy studies of Walter LaFeber, Lloyd C. Gardner, N. Gordon Levin, Gabriel Kolko, Robert F. Smith, Carl P. Parrini, and Ronald Radosh were influenced indirectly by Beard and directly by William Appleman Williams, who in the 1950s almost single-handedly maintained a critical approach to the impact of corporate liberalism on U.S. diplomacy.[4]

The significant difference between this postprogressive generation of anticapitalist revisionists and their precursors is that they, like the procapitalist historians, are now searching for an explanation of continuity, rather than change, in the U.S. past. Both groups are, in other words, searching for an explanation of the lack of stability in contemporary society and a historical explanation of how to create new order, and it is from the probusiness, entrepreneurial approach that the first steps have been taken toward creating a post-World War II historical synthesis. Using interdisciplinary methods, which include collective biographical techniques and quantitative, as well as system, analyses, some business historians began after 1945 to study specific socioeconomic organizations and the bureaucratization of American life in general. This new organizational school emerged to challenge the assumptions and methods not only of conservative evolution-

---

Strout, *The Pragmatic Revolt in American History: Carl Becker and Charles Beard*, pp. 86–95; John Tipple, "The Anatomy of Prejudice: Origins of the Robber Baron Legend," *Business History Review* 33 (Winter 1959): 510–23; Bridges, "Robber Baron Concept," pp. 5–6; F. A. Hayek, ed., *Capitalism and the Historians*, pp. 76, 83, 113–23.

4. Neu, "Changing Structure of Foreign Policy," pp. 51–57; David F. Trask, "Writings on American Foreign Relations: 1957 to the Present," in Braeman et al., eds., *Foreign Policy*, pp. 58–65; Irwin Unger, "The 'New Left' and American History: Some Recent Trends in United States Historiography," *American Historical Review* 72 (July 1967): 1237–63; Barton J. Bernstein, ed., *Towards a New Past: Dissenting Essays in American History*; idem, "Our Empire's Roots," *The Progressive* (June 1970), pp. 45–48; H. Wayne Morgan, ed., *The Gilded Age: A Reappraisal*; Joseph M. Siracusa, *New Left Histories and Historians*, pp. 3–49.

ists and progressives, but also of the first entrepreneurial historians.[5]

Studies of U.S. foreign policy reveal the basic division within U.S. historiographical circles: those historians who assume a strong anticapitalist position, and hence who are very critical of the current managerial corporate state, are also those who more often attribute more economic motivation and ideological characteristics to U.S. diplomacy than do those historians who assume a predominantly procapitalist point of view. However, critics of the impact of corporate liberalism on the formulation of foreign policy are not found exclusively among advocates of left-of-center politics. "New Right," as well as "New Left," writers have relentlessly attacked the basically probusiness "liberal ideology of mainstream corporate America and its academic and intellectual servants."[6] In the process, these historians have also contributed to a new historical synthesis, albeit one that is much more pessimistic about modern society than is the synthesis proposed by their entrepreneurial peers. They use many of the same interdisciplinary methods but insist on asking "*why* political power operates in a class society," rather than simply describing *how* it operates, and usually assume that "diplomacy is essentially a response to forces generated by America's economic and social structure," rather than to external factors.[7]

5. For representative bibliographical examples and a general discussion of the search for order through organizational history, see Higham, *History*, pp. 212–32; Samuel P. Hays, "The Social Analysis of American Political History, 1880–1920," *Political Science Quarterly* 80 (September 1965): 373–94; and Louis Galambos, "The Emerging Organizational Synthesis in Modern American History," *Business History Review* 44 (Autumn 1970): 279–90.

6. Ronald Radosh and Murray N. Rothbard, eds., *A New History of Leviathan: Essays on the Rise of the American Corporate State*, p. ix; and Murray N. Rothbard, *For a New Liberty*, pp. 1–22, 279–317. Rothbard serves as an excellent example of a right-wing libertarian who, in his criticism of corporate liberalism, advocates "anarcho-capitalism" based on an entirely free market economy. In contrast, Radosh and other Socialist critics of the corporate state favor the formation of a decentralized Socialist economy.

7. Alvin W. Gouldner, "Metaphysical Pathos and the Theory

Another development worth noting about this historiographical dualism as it relates to foreign-policy studies is that conservative, evolutionary views prevailed among the original generation of serious diplomatic historians who emerged in the 1920s. They initially ignored ideological, economic, and organizational concepts, preferring to write about diplomacy through a "mastery of public documents" in order to place the origins of U.S. foreign policy in an international setting. As a result, scholars in the field of diplomatic history adopted the standard progressive approach to scholarship, which is based on conflict rather than consensus, less quickly than other historians and hence lagged behind the prevailing historiographical climate until after World War II.[8]

Succeeding generations of foreign-policy specialists divided during the Cold War years into groups that have been called the liberal realists and the radical revisionists. The liberal realists, led by George Kennan and Hans J. Morgenthau, were concerned with the confusion, uncertainty, moral obscurantism, and U.S. leaders' general lack of appreciation of diplomatic theory and vital national interests insofar as they rejected a balance-of-power, or *realpolitik*, approach to foreign affairs. The radical revisionists, led by William Appleman Williams, revived an economic critique of U.S. diplomacy based not on the incompetence of foreign-policy makers implied by the liberal realists, but on the conviction that Washington officials knew only too well what they had to do abroad to serve the best interests of the liberal corporate state at home. Just as the liberal realists represented a modified version of the conservative evolutionary school, so the radical revisionists were carrying on the progressive historiographical tradition.[9]

---

of Bureaucracy," *American Political Science Journal* 49 (June 1955): 496–507; Gabriel Kolko, *The Roots of American Foreign Policy*, p. 5; Robert W. Tucker, *The Radical Left and American Foreign Policy*, p. 30.

8. Higham, *History*, pp. 187–88; Galambos, "Emerging Organizational Synthesis," p. 285; Neu, "Changing Structure of Foreign Policy," pp. 21, 28–30.

9. Tucker, *Radical Left and Foreign Policy*, pp. 21–39; Trask,

Despite their conflicting interpretations, there are points of agreement between these two camps of diplomatic historians. They both have become increasingly critical of the conduct of foreign affairs by the United States during the entire century and especially since the onset of the Cold War. Both are disturbed by the pervasive counterrevolutionary tendencies of U.S. policy and beset by frustration and concern as they see peoples in various parts of the world resisting the overextension of U.S. power.[10]

These points of convergence should not obscure the fact that in the last decade, foreign-policy studies continued to divide sharply into those that emphasize the impact of the U.S. political economy upon foreign policy, largely along the lines suggested by Williams, and those that are more in keeping with the liberal realists' critique, which makes perversion of an earlier, sound diplomacy, not systematic economic expansion, central to the formulation of foreign policy. This division is especially evident in studies dealing with the origins of the Cold War.[11] Employing ideological value judgments and economic statistics, the radical revisionists deny the "innocence" and altruism of U.S. foreign policy. Carried to its logical extreme, this approach leads to a theory of economic conspiracy or economic determinism, but applied judiciously, it can help the writing of diplomatic history avoid excessive chauvinism, superficial anecdotes, and the one-dimensional exchange of international communiqués so characteristic of the first diplomatic historians. After providing an invaluable initial critique of post-World War II foreign policy, some liberal realists, in turn, have retreated to an ubiquitous definition of national interest to produce their own excessive noneconomic defense of U.S. foreign policy,

"Writings on Foreign Relations," pp. 59–65; Neu, "Changing Structure of Foreign Policy," pp. 46–54.

10. Tucker, *Radical Left and Foreign Policy*, p. 40; Trask, "Writings on Foreign Relations," p. 64.

11. Tucker, *Radical Left and Foreign Policy*, pp. 26–28, 35–39, 88–108. For bibliographical information on both camps, see Robert James Maddox, *The New Left and the Origins of the Cold War*, Joseph M. Siracusa, *New Left Histories and Historians*, and Neu's article.

which brings up the question of how realistic certain realists are, particularly on the origins of the Cold War. Neither extreme has been able to overcome the tempting, yet highly questionable assumption that foreign-policy formulation is a completely rational, calculated process.[12]

Now that the general isolation of diplomatic history from the major trends in U.S. historiography is over, one can hope that the excessive and futile debate between the "orthodox scholars" and the "hard" or "soft" revisionists will also shortly disappear[13] and that diplomatic historians will begin to

---

12. Although the "rational actor" model is still the most widely employed of all the process models used by diplomatic historians, it is considered virtually obsolete by those organizational historians who study foreign-policy decision making because it assumes that diplomacy is the exclusive result of rationally calculated national self-interest based on value-maximizing choices. For a discussion of the various decision-making theories, see James E. Dougherty, *Contending Theories of International Relations*, pp. 312–44; Graham T. Allison, *Essence of Decision: Explaining the Cuban Missile Crisis, passim*.

13. These terms are used by Maddox, *New Left and Cold War*, pp. 3–4. Although he does not precisely define them, they generally refer to the split between the liberal realists and the radical revisionists. For reactions to this controversial book, see Francis Loewenheim, review, *The New York Times Book Review*, June 17, 1973, pp. 6–10; Joseph Alsop, "A Far-Reaching National Scandal," *San Francisco Chronicle*, June 22, 1973; Gabriel Kolko, "Memorandum on Robert James Maddox' *The New Left and the Origins of the Cold War*," May 1, 1973, mimeographed; Lloyd Gardner, "On Robert Maddox's *The New Left and the Origins of the Cold War*: A Reply Intended for the Persistent and the Patient," May 1973, mimeographed. Maddox's book carries this debate between the liberal realists and the radical revisionists to its absurd conclusion. In 169 very short pages he purports to refute methodology contained in well over 2,500 pages of writings by seven New Left historians without ever proving any ideological affinity among these authors or ever indicating the rationale behind his own methodology. In other words, Maddox makes no attempt to explain or justify his highly selective attack on relatively few portions of each work of this nebulous group of historians. In this highly personal and vituperative process, Maddox maintains he has uncovered "pervasive misuse of source materials" and comes up with his own conspiracy theory about the reasons that publishers and reviewers have neglected to expose this alleged New Left fraud, a theory that is in the same league with the most extreme economic conspiracy theories

examine the complex impact of ideological and economic motivation as it is affected by structural relationships and role playing within Government agencies and business organizations. To date, they have applied this comprehensive, socioeconomic, psycho-organizational kind of historical method almost exclusively to decision making in time of major Cold War crises.[14] Such an approach may provide not only a conclusive answer about the origins of the Cold War, but also the key to a new synthesis for understanding the general thrust of U.S. foreign policy since 1900, in terms that are not deludingly objective, ideologically chauvinistic, or economically reductionist. Particularly the studies of historians who have concentrated on collective biographical explanations of, or organizational investigations into, decision making now appear to offer one of the best vehicles for synthesizing twentieth-century historical scholarship before the year 2000. The greatest pitfall of such research to appear so far in entrepreneurial and structural studies is a tendency to encourage a deceptively amoral kind of historical writing. As always, conscious ideological analysis and a "value-laden historiography" that permits analysis of the present, as well as the past, remain essential prerequisites of any seminal synthesis for the future.[15]

One of the most inadequate features of recent U.S. diplomatic history has been the confusing and often contradictory portrayals of the relationship between self-interest and ideology by both orthodox realists and revisionists to the right or left of them. Under the conservative influence of Max Weber's descriptive social analysis, which stresses universal behavioral models rather than specific individual

---

he so detests. Surely, the point of diminishing returns has been reached and exceeded in this debate, with Maddox's book representing a new low in historical criticism.

14. The best single study of a specific example of decision making is Allison, *Essence of Decision*. For others, see the footnotes in Allison, and in Dougherty, *Theories of International Relations*, the essays in J. David Singer, ed., *Quantitative International Politics: Insights and Evidence*, and in James N. Rosenau, ed., *Domestic Sources of Foreign Policy*.

15. Howard Zinn, *The Politics of History*, pp. 12, 22–29, 31, 36; Kolko, "Business Revisionism," pp. 338–39; Arne Naess, *Democracy, Ideology and Objectivity*, pp. 141–233.

actions, most socio-psychological studies and the entrepreneurial histories utilizing them have substantially refuted the idea that economic self-interest alone can explain the behavior of people.[16] In particular, these studies do not consider the "interest theory" primary to interpreting or understanding the actions of businessmen or corporations and their respective ideologies.[17] They agree that it is a fallacy to equate economic self-interest with behavior because such an assumption reflects an inadequate understanding of the psychology of motivation and a simplistic notion of what constitutes self-interest.

Unfortunately, in an attempt to counter the widespread attack by succeeding generations of progressive historians on U.S. economic development—an attack that prevailed until World War II—early entrepreneurial historians initially went to the other extreme in trying to rehabilitate completely the "robber baron" image of businessmen. Using a structural-functional methodology, which presumably alleviated them from the responsibility of making value judgments about past actions of businessmen, they insisted that economic functions simply reflected societal standards that since the last quarter of the nineteenth century happened to encourage more and more business consolidation and bureaucratic organization. According to this interpretation,

16. Kolko, "Business Revisionism," pp. 336–37; idem, *Roots of Foreign Policy*, p. 5; idem, "Type," in Edward N. Saveth, ed., *American History and the Social Sciences*, pp. 340–56; Fritz Redlich, "The Business Leader in Theory and Reality," *American Journal of Economics and Sociology* 8 (April 1949): 223–37; Max Weber, *The Theory of Social and Economic Organization*, trans. by A. M. Henderson and Talcott Parsons, pp. 52–53, 148–73.

17. Francis X. Sutton, Seymour E. Harris, Carl Kaysen, and James Tobin, *The American Business Creed*, pp. vii, 3–6, 12–13, 303–4; Raymond Bauer, Ithiel de Sola Pool, and Lewis Anthony Dexter, *American Business and Public Policy: The Politics of Foreign Trade*, pp. 224–25, 229; Chester I. Barnard, "The Entrepreneur and Formal Organization," in *Change and the Entrepreneur*, p. 7; Stuart Bruchey, "The Inadequacy of the Profit Maximization as a Model of Business Behavior," *Business History Review* 34 (Winter 1960): 495–96; Karl Mannheim, *Ideology and Utopia: An Introduction to the Sociology of Knowledge*, pp. xxiii, 49–50, 61, 69, *passim*; Clifford Geertz, "Ideology as a Cultural System," in David E. Apter, ed., *Ideology and Discontent*, pp. 52–53, 56.

the activities of business leaders could not be reprehensible because they represented progress and because businessmen "could be influenced quite as often by their view of their social role in a given situation as by predatory motives."[18] Another entrepreneurial study has explained:

> The theory of self-interest as a complete and all-embracing explanation of behavior breaks down when we realize that self-interest is itself a set of mental images and convictions. Whose self-interest does a man see it as his role to serve— his own as a physical individual, that of the corporation for which he works, or that of some other unit? . . . What values does he pursue—solely money, or also respect and other values? The role businessmen played, the communications that impinged upon them, their ideology—all influenced their identifications and perceptions of their self-interest.[19]

The factor that self-interest plays in historical motivation cannot be entirely ignored even though it is difficult to determine. One way to begin to evaluate it is to view the "interest theory" as essentially an "empty box" model, one that has to be filled in with other determinants. This guideline allows the historian to view businessmen as responding not in terms of direct "perceived self-interest," but "when a self-interest was reinforced or at least not countered by a series of ideological and political considerations." In other words, "although self-interest stimulated action, just how much it did so depended on a number of attitudinal and political considerations," as indicated in this study by the fact that those businessmen who wanted most to trade with the USSR in the 1920s usually did not advocate recognition because of the Government's hostility to it.[20]

Probably the least useful assumption of the interest theory

18. Kolko, "Business Revisionism," pp. 331, 336–37; Redlich, "Business Leader," pp. 224–26; Robert F. Berkhofer, Jr., *A Behavioral Approach to Historical Analysis*, pp. 169–210; Bridges, "Robber Baron Concept," p. 12. Berkhofer notes that structural-functional methodology need not be the rigid, conservative approach it has become if historians would use it judiciously as a tool—as but one of many approaches to systems analysis.

19. Bauer et al., *American Business*, p. 226.

20. Bauer et al., *American Business*, pp. 207, 221, 229; E. E. Schattschneider, *Politics, Pressures and the Tariff*, pp. 162–63. Also see chaps. 3–5.

is that individuals act out of either rational calculation or a totally consuming power orientation. Such an assumption does not admit research demonstrating that members of modern societies obtain identity and motivation from "primary or reference groups" that are often not political, economic, or rational by nature, rather than from some logical, inner, political, or economic source of reference.[21] Confirmation of such role-determined behavior can be found in collective biographies of business and political leaders by such historians of vastly differing ideological points of view as Thomas C. Cochran and G. William Domhoff. However, role behavior of members of a power elite should not be accepted simply because their actual motivation cannot always be traced to a conscious or rational source of self-interest.

All of these complicating factors about the concept of perceived self-interest have increased the chances that it will be misinterpreted not only by those who originally try to determine what the self-interest is for themselves, but also by those academicians who study it and by Government officials who are the objects of pressure-group activity. The complexity of self-interest and motivation based upon it is such that the current socio-psychological literature tends to concur that people caught up in the chaos of modern life are seldom capable of determining what constitutes their own best self-interest. Yet social scientists in general, and historians in particular, as well as Government officials, blithely continue to generalize about self-interest when they describe countries, the general public, interest groups, and individual leaders.[22]

To admit that the issue of self-interest is complicated and not exclusively determined by rational economic or power

21. Geertz, "Ideology as a Cultural System," pp. 53, 60–61; Ernest R. May, "An American Tradition in Foreign Policy: The Role of Public Opinion," in William H. Nelson, ed., *Theory and Practice in American Politics*, pp. 108–12; Haggai Hurvitz, "Notes on the Orientation Guidance Approach to the Analysis of Ideologies" (M.A. thesis, Columbia University, 1968), pp. 6, 8–9.

22. Bauer et al., *American Business*, p. 128; May, "American Tradition in Foreign Policy," pp. 107–8, 112–22; Doris A. Graber, *Public Opinion, The President, and Foreign Policy: Four Case Studies from the Formative Years*, pp. 3–6, 329–34.

drives still does not clarify its relationship to ideology or to organizational structures. Ideology has been defined by Sutton as "any system of beliefs publicly expressed with the manifest purpose of influencing the sentiments and actions of others . . . a patterned reaction to the patterned strains of a social role."[23] This definition is not based on the interest theory described above, but upon the "strain theory" of ideological motivation. The strain theory is less simplistic because it takes into consideration both private and collective tension. Ideology, according to this interpretation, becomes an outlet for personal and social dislocation.[24] Yet this theory suffers from essentially the same negative concept of the function of ideology in modern times that flaws the interest theory.

These two basically negative approaches to ideology have led U.S. statesmen and social scientists to apply the term most often to such examples of foreign political movements as Russian bolshevism, Italian fascism, German national socialism, the Action Française, the North Vietnamese National Liberation Front, the Irish Republican Army, or the Front de liberation québecois. It has also led to a basically negative and conservative use of the technique of ideological analysis in historical writing because of the assumption that scholarship is not, or should not be, "socially relevant, value motivated, [and] action-inducing." Moreover, if ideology is viewed as a form of "radical intellectual depravity" or a "mode of thinking which is thrown off its proper course . . . something shady . . . that ought to be overcome and banished from our mind," then one could scarcely speak of the business ideology of any group without conjuring up a whole host of ulterior motives, propaganda tactics, and "cognitive insufficiencies."[25] For this reason the idea that ideological statements are basically hypocritical because they seldom conform to reality or produce actions or legislation consistent with stated goals, is still quite prevalent in writings about the

23. Sutton et al., *American Business Creed*, pp. 2, 307–8.
24. Geertz, "Ideology as a Cultural System," pp. 54–56.
25. Ibid., pp. 47, 49–51, 57, 64; Naess, *Democracy, Ideology and Objectivity*, pp. 141–233; Zinn, *Politics of History*, p. 2; Kolko, "Business History Revisionism," pp. 338–39.

business community, other interest groups, and reform movements.[26]

This suspicion about ideological statements is rooted in the assumptions that behavior and belief should correspond that such statements should accurately or empirically describe social conditions. The incorrectness of both assumptions is perhaps regrettable in terms of producing consistency between thought and action, but it does negate both as valid criteria for evaluating or defining contemporary ideologies.[27] Nonetheless, the criticism about the "glaring inconsistency between business behavior and business theory"[28] is periodically raised to discredit not only the ideology of the business community, but of practically any organized group that attempts political action.

Obviously the absence of an adequate definition of ideology prohibits understanding of the relationship between thought and action, the function of self-interest in the process of constructing an ideology, or the self-serving aspects of class-based organizations and bureaucracies. What is needed is a definition that will encompass the need felt by groups and individuals for guidance in times of flux and uncertainty—times like the post-World War I period. Such an approach would view ideology positively as an "ordered system of cultural symbols" that provides private, as well

26. This is especially true of writings about the Progressive Era, such as Gabriel Kolko, *The Triumph of Conservatism* (New York, 1963) Samuel P. Hays, *Conservation and the Gospel of Efficiency: The Progressive Conservation Movement, 1890–1920* (Cambridge, 1959); idem, "The Politics of Municipal Government in the Progressive Era," *Pacific Northwest Quarterly* 55 (October 1964): 157–69, and James Warren Prothro, *The Dollar Decade: Business Ideas in the 1920's.* Sutton et al., however, go to the other extreme when they state, "What businessmen actually do in the conduct of their own affairs may be a more treacherous guide to what they really believe about their society than is their ideology. We therefore do not regard the actual practice of American business as the ultimate criterion for the beliefs of businessmen." (p. 321)

27. Geertz, "Ideology as a Cultural System," pp. 71–72; Hurvitz, "Orientation Guidance Approach," pp. 26–27.

28. John Tipple, "The Robber Baron in the Gilded Age: Entrepreneur or Iconoclast?" in H. Wayne Morgan, ed., *The Gilded Age*, p. 27.

as public, identities and motivation. The cultural patterns thus formed could be cognitive, evaluative, or expressive and would act as orientation guides for patterning individual and collective life.[29] One such comprehensive and positive definition that has been suggested states, "Ideology is a system of ideas by which people who identify themselves as members of a certain social unit attempt to define and cope with problems of orientation of this unit, within the unit's conceived field of purposive action."[30] Another proposes that ideology is "any kind of consciousness that can relate itself to the ongoing activity of a class or group effective enough to make some sort of [limited] practical difference," and a third simply equates it with Karl Mannheim's "sociology of knowledge."[31] None of these definitions reduces the function of ideology to the level of mere propaganda, as implied in Sutton's quotation, because each allows for privately held, self-directed idea-systems. And even though they present ideology as a "coping mechanism" for individuals and social groupings, they do not necessarily limit its function only to releasing strains or power drives, nor do they remove from the scholar all responsibility for evaluating the outcome of ideological actions.[32]

29. Hurvitz, "Orientation Guidance Approach," pp. 13–14, 45, 49; Geertz, "Ideology as a Cultural System," 56, 60–62. According to Geertz, cultural symbols arise out of the normal thought process, which consists of the "construction and manipulation of symbol systems . . . a matching of the states and processes of symbolic models against the states and processes of the wider world."

30. Hurvitz, "Orientation Guidance Approach," p. 15. This author has also described ideologies as the "intellectual tools of a continuous learning process, by which concrete social units determine the directions in which they prefer to steer their activities, and what types of relations they choose to establish with whatever phenomena come their way." (p. 18)

31. George Lichtheim, *The Concept of Ideology and Other Essays*, p. 46; Kolko, Business Revisionism," pp. 337–38n.21; Naess, *Democracy, Ideology and Objectivity*, pp. 141–233. All these definitions reflect how, through the process of intellectual evolution, the contemporary definition of ideology differs from the limited one employed by eighteenth-century ideologues in France and how much it is peculiar to the twentieth century.

32. Hurvitz, "Orientation Guidance Approach," pp. 11, 20–21, 61; Geertz, "Ideology as a Cultural System," p. 64. Accord-

This kind of definition is absolutely necessary if one is to understand that postwar business ideology reflected not only immediate fears but ultimate confidence in the ability of technology, combined with traditional American values, to overcome domestic problems and hostile foreign ideologies. With one foot in the past and the other in the future, business leaders devised an ideology that gave the rank and file a certain amount of security and familiarity, that is, identity, to cope with rapidly changing social and economic conditions. Thus, the unwavering hostility of the ideology of the U.S. business community to the USSR in the 1920s, despite increased trade between U.S. businessmen and the Soviets, can be viewed not as ideological hypocrisy, but as the product of a rather jumbled combination of ideological fears, ignorance, national chauvinism, and belief in economic expansion. The same combination may well have impelled business circles to use the specter of bolshevism to attack certain aspects of postwar society. For example, everything from modern art and theater, to jazz and the NAACP, to the Wilsonian concept of internationalism was portrayed at one time or another between 1917 and 1933 by different segments of the business community as inspirations of the Bolsheviks. There is no way to cite legislation or other specific actions to prove or disprove the existence of this kind of orientation-guidance ideology. Its validity comes from its ability to fortify and justify for businessmen the American way of life in the face of the ideological challenge posed by communism.

The orientation-guidance approach to ideology appears, therefore, to offer the most flexible and least prejudicial methodological grounds upon which to discuss the actions and ideas of the business community on the related topics of trade with, and recognition of, the Soviet Union. The approach is not posited on a negative view of ideology, and it does not unrealistically demand that ideas and conduct,

---

ing to Geertz, "Whatever else ideologies may be—projections of unacknowledged fears, disguises for ulterior motives, phatic expressions of group solidarity—they are, most distinctively, maps of problematic social reality and matrices for the creation of collective conscience."

especially in a time of transition,[33] closely correspond. Likewise, it does not deny that actions can help to determine motives and self-interest, but as "systems of interacting [cultural] symbols" and "extrinsic sources of information" in the absence of traditional institutional guides for behavior, it does not require ideologies to describe empirical reality or to produce concrete results consistent with stated goals. What has been called the "dual-myth system of progress" —the idea that ideologies can both defend or criticize present conditions while projecting future utopias—is reflected in the difference between ideologies that praise or castigate the American Way while predicting how things could be according to some idealized version of the American Dream. And it is in the interplay between the "real" and "ideal," between what "is" and what "ought to be" that the business ideology of the 1920s served the all-important function of bridging the "emotional gap between things as they are and as one would have them be."[34] Thus, businessmen often predicted the disappearance of bolshevism because they *wanted* it to disappear, not because there was convincing evidence of its demise.

Given this function of ideology, it is not surprising to find that ideological statements can be most effective when they are most empirically inaccurate. This condition has led social scientists to describe ideological slogans as gross distortions or as "elaborate cries of pain" that oversimplify issues, when in fact they require careful stylistic analysis if

33. A discussion of the impact transitional periods have on ideology can be found in Harvey Wheeler, *Democracy in a Revolutionary Era*, pp. 146–60, and Geertz, "Ideology as a Cultural System," pp. 63–64, 75n.42.

34. Geertz, "Ideology as a Cultural System," pp. 55–56, 63, 70; Wheeler, *Democracy in a Revolutionary Era*, pp. 150–51; Lichtheim, *Concept of Ideology*, pp. 3, 45; Robert H. Wiebe, *Businessmen and Reform: A Study of the Progressive Movement* (Cambridge, Mass., 1962), p. 180. It is Wiebe's contention that "business maxims" should not be considered dogma as much as they should be considered a "predisposition about what American society ought to be." Along the same lines Lee Benson has suggested in *Turner and Beard* that statements about government, among other things, often reflect ideas about the ideal Good Society. (pp. 215–28)

their complex symbolic function is to be understood. An ideological expression employing tropes, metaphors, and personifications must be examined to determine, not the objective accuracy of the statement, but its success or failure as a form of communication between members of a particular social, economic, or governmental unit.[35]

One example of this kind of communication occurred when certain licensing, commercial, and financial restrictions remained to hamper trade with the USSR in the 1920s, despite the protests of the small business firms that were most negatively affected by these economic obstacles and that were not as adequately represented in Government circles as were such mammoth U.S. companies as General Electric, General Motors, Standard Oil, International Harvester, and the Ford Motor Company—all of which could and did do business with the Soviets long before recognition was accorded in 1933. To justify the contradiction of maintaining that there were no restrictions on such trade, when in fact there were, and to counter attempts to remove them, the State Department and members of the War Trade Board ascribed the motive for the protests and the attempts to remove the restrictions to "greed pure and simple." (One can only speculate what higher motives were displayed by General Electric, Ford, and the others.) The response of the Government official appears to be a good example of successful ideological communication that blocked their having to view the situation as one of an "in" group versus an "out" group, in this case, large manufacturing exporters versus small ones.

Another example occurred when Herbert Hoover stated in 1919 that Russia was like a "cesspool." His metaphor at one level instantly conveyed what his many statistical statements had, in this case, also documented— the internal breakdown of domestic production in postwar Russia. At the same time, however, and most importantly in terms of ideological impact, his words symbolically portrayed Bolshevik Russia as a filthy place whose problems went far beyond the temporary disruption of industrial and agricultural productivity.[36] Hoover was an ideologue, but he was not by tem-

35. Geertz, "Ideology as a Cultural System," pp. 57–58, 74 n.30.

36. Herbert Hoover, "What Thinking Men Are Saying," *The*

perament or training adept at speaking metaphorically. He preferred to use scientific, literal language. In many respects, therefore, his "cesspool" image of Russia and most of his other figurative statements about the young Communist regime in the early 1920s represent his most successful attempt to play the role of ideologue in his entire public career. Never again would he be so successful in using symbolic language to convey multifaceted meanings; never again would his words strike such responsive chords not only among businessmen, but among the American public; never again would his penchant for statistical analysis be so in tune with his ideological preconceptions. Increasingly after 1925, and especially twenty or thirty years later, his language and ideology no longer capsulized the mood of businessmen—let alone that of the country—by "making it a public possession, a social fact, rather than a set of disconnected, unrealized private emotions."[37]

Hoover's initial success and later failure in using such value-laden terms against the Soviet Union demonstrates the need for ideological analysis of language, as well as action, in discussions of foreign-policy formulation. Such an analysis has been used here to help determine when and why economic and political foreign policies toward the Soviet Union were not coordinated between 1918 and 1933, to help illumine specific documents, like the Colby Note, and to suggest the reasons for the United States Government's insisting that the ARA was nothing more than a private,

---

Magazine of Wall Street 25 (December 27, 1919): 191. One of the most popular metaphoric ways employed by Hoover and others to refer to bolshevism was as an infection or contagious disease.

37. Geertz, "Ideology as a Cultural System," p. 72. An example of an unsuccessful metaphor employed by Hoover against the USSR came in 1941 when he tried to convince the American people that collaboration with Stalin would be a "gargantuan jest." For details about the impact of Hoover's engineering background on his philosophy of life and government see Edwin T. Layton, Jr., *The Revolt of the Engineers: Social Responsibility and The American Engineering Profession*, pp. 189–95, *passim.* For Hoover's role as an ideologue, see Joan Hoff Wilson, *Herbert Clark Hoover: Forgotten Progressive*, chap. 2; for his views after 1933, see ibid., chaps. 7 and 8.

charitable organization when it functioned as a *de facto* arm of the State Department and for the Government's continuing to impose restrictions on trade with the USSR despite press releases to the contrary. Hence, the variance between public statements and private action became more understandable. Language analysis has also been employed here to demonstrate that although Government officials were consistent in their opposition to the new Communist regime, a growing number of businessmen, enticed by trading possibilities with the Soviets, either became increasingly indifferent to the original ideological basis of nonrecognition or chose to separate economic from political considerations. Finally, this method demonstrated that language used by businessmen to advocate trade with the USSR was not usually translated into actual or theoretical advocacy of recognition.

However, on the specific issue of recognition, examination of several kinds of organizational phenomena was probably more important than language analysis in explaining the discrepancy between action and theory. The surprisingly effective and dedicated Friends of Soviet Russia exerted significant psychological influence on decision making during the last months of the ARA's existence, but the inadequately organized and financed American Commercial Association utterly failed to impress bureaucrats within the State and Commerce departments. The scarcely less well organized, but considerably more influential and intensely competitive natural-resources industries, along with some highly specialized smaller industries, were among the first to ignore or try to modify the unofficial obstacles to trade condoned by the United States Government. It is significant that a number of these firms and industries were not as prosperous as they might have been in the 1920s.

The broadly based manufacturing and general business organizations, like the NAM and United States Chamber of Commerce, were unable to pass resolutions in favor of recognition until after the Government established relations with the USSR, although their official house organs had encouraged trade with the Soviets since the late 1920s. Finally, by the early 1930s those business organizations already involved in international operations, with the exception of a group of major New York banking and insurance firms, officially joined the ranks of the protraders, even though they had opposed trading with the Soviets during the first half of the 1920s. At the same time, those businesses whose activities were limited primarily to domestic sales remained antitraders in those first years of the Depression during the fight in Congress and the executive branch over commercial relations with the Soviet Union.

Key business and government officials also influenced the complex organizational, economic, and ideological forces at work during the sixteen-year period under discussion. Not only did the reorganization of both the departments of State and Commerce take place largely under the personal direction of Hughes and Hoover respectively, but it helped to institutionalize anti-Soviet ideology in the course of the 1920s. In addition, the personal competition between these two men—especially Hoover's unilateral administration of the ARA and his private success in convincing Congress and members of the Harding administration that food assistance would not help the Bolsheviks stabilize Russia and that trade had no relation to recognition—contributed significantly to the contradictions that developed between the economic and political treatment of the USSR during the 1920s. Secondary policy makers in these two departments, men like Julius Klein, Frederick M. Feiker, E. C. Ropes, Robert F. Kelley, Stanley K. Hornbeck, R. Walton Moore, and William R. Castle, Jr., also contributed as their ideological opposition to communism became bureaucratized.

In contrast, individual business spokesmen, such as Emerson P. Jennings, Alexander Gumberg, Reeve Schley, Hugh L. Cooper, James D. Mooney, and Ivy Lee, gave the impression that the entire business community backed recognition when the most cursory investigation of organization support for recognition does not confirm it. Despite the prominence of some of these men, they were outside the attitudinal and structural framework of the Government bureaucracy, so their effectiveness was much less than is usually thought and much less than it would have been, had their ideas and actions been favorably received by Washington officials.

Finally, the continuing search for a new sense of order and more efficient organizational techniques—a search in which Government and business leaders had participated since

the late nineteenth century—determined the nature of bureaucratic and economical structural change between 1918
and 1933. This quest and its effect during the early twentieth
century have heretofore been ignored in discussions of the
reasons behind the sixteen-year delay in recognizing the
Soviet Union.

APPENDIX A

ARMAND HAMMER

When the Soviet Government decided to abolish all private trading organizations after the formation of Amtorg in 1924, Hammer received another concession for a business he also knew very little about—pencil manufacturing. The factory was originally called American Industrial Concession; it proved to be his most profitable Russian investment. It is estimated that he made about 50 per cent profit on his original capital outlay, and in one year alone his profits are said to have amounted to more than $1,000,000.

These profit estimates, including those cited in Hammer's own account of his nine years in Soviet Russia, are very difficult to evaluate because the figures upon which they are based are never cited. There does exist, however, Hammer's confidential report to a member of the American Embassy at Berlin in which he stated that for the year 1926–1927 his total sales amounted to $2,500,000, of which $600,000 represented his net profit; for 1927–1928, the figures cited were $3,500,000, with a profit of $500,000. On the basis of these figures his average profit from sales for these two years would be around 20 per cent. Other State Department information indicates, however, that Hammer was able to export his net profits for only the first year that his pencil factory operated. Hammer had never publicly commented on this report, but his profits from sales probably were considerably less than most contemporary estimates, especially those that indicated profits of more than $1,000,000 a year. All concessionaires had difficulty exporting the excessive profits that could be made in the Soviet Union in the 1920s, and there is no reason to believe that Hammer completely avoided the legal and financial obstacles deliberately created by the Soviet government to thwart the exportation of profits.

The accuracy of contemporary estimates of Hammer's total profit on his original capital investment is even more difficult to determine. Here again State Department reports offer some help, but the data are far from complete. For example, the reports show that Hammer's total capital investment as of October 1, 1928, was 1,711,000 rubles or approximately $855,500. Assuming that he did not invest any significant additional amount between the end of 1928 and his decision in 1929 to sell out to the Soviet Government, and further assuming that he made on the average a net profit of $500,000 for the three years he operated his pencil concession, the percentage of his profit on his original capital investment could range all the way from a low of 50 per cent the first year to a high of 89 per cent the third year, depending on whether or not depreciation is figured into the calculations. Even the lowest estimate, however, represented an unusually large percentage of profit by Western standards. Some concessionaires in Russia during the 1920s are said to have made a profit of as much as 200 per cent on their original investment, but none of these were owned by U.S. citizens. Hammer was by far the most successful of the U.S. concessionaires, and although he admitted to labor and production difficulties, the profits he accumulated at least inside Russia clearly indicated that these problems did not constitute "insurmountable obstacles."

In 1926 the Soviet Government bought his asbestos concession, but in 1927 he failed to float a $500,000 loan in New York to expand his pencil and office-equipment concession because of the U.S. Government's policy against long-term loans. Finally in 1929 he decided that his expansion plans were requiring more investment capital than he could possibly obtain because the Depression further compounded his already serious credit problems, even though his operation was a complete success. Thus, according to his account of the situation, at that point the only "solution seemed to be to sell out to the Russian government ... [for] a fair price." The sales contract contained a provision allowing Hammer to take out of Russia all the art treasures he had collected. No doubt this was one way in which he was able to export his profits.

Hammer's acute business sense was apparently as highly

developed in this period as it ever became later because his decision to sell coincided with the First Five-Year Plan and the attempt on the part of the Soviet Government to buy back all concessions before their expiration dates. Despite his profitable and enjoyable nine years of holding court at the palatial "Brown House" in Moscow, Hammer did not return to the United States to become an advocate of recognition. He continued, however, to favor business contacts with the Soviets. As recently as 1964 Hammer tried but failed to negotiate a contract to build fertilizer factories in the USSR; he blamed the Vietnamese War for disrupting these talks. Finally in 1972, as chairman of the board of the Occidental Petroleum Corporation, Hammer announced "the biggest Russian deal ever completed by an American company" when he signed a five-year technical cooperation agreement for exploiting Soviet oil and natural gas. The contract is estimated to be worth $3,000,000,000 and covers four other fields besides gas and oil, including agricultural fertilizers.[1]

1. Armand Hammer, *The Quest for the Romanoff Treasure*, pp. 179–80, 185–89, 199–210; Coleman (Latvia) to State Department, March 9, 1925, April 8, 1929, Schurman (Berlin) to State Department, April 11, April 17, 1929, U.S. Department of State, Records Relating to Internal Affairs of Russia and the Soviet Union, Record Group 59, Files 861.602/130, 861.602/181, 861.602 Hammer/3–4; Stuart Chase, Robert Dunn, and Rexford Guy Tugwell, eds., *Soviet Russia in the Second Decade*, p. 353; Eugene Lyons, *Assignment in Utopia*, pp. 67, 251, 296–98, 417. *The New York Times*, November 22, 1927, p. 40; December 22, 1929, p. 31. *Nation's Business* 18 (March 1930): 166; *The Saturday Evening Post* (March 12, 1966): 88; *San Francisco Chronicle*, July 19, 1972, p. 1.

W. AVERELL HARRIMAN

W. Averell Harriman's economic experience with Russia was personally frustrating to say the least; he is a good example of both the unsuccessful financier and concessionaire as far as Russia was concerned. (It was noted in Chapter II that in 1926 he failed to float a loan intended to extend credit to German manufacturers who wanted to sell their products in the USSR, because the U.S. Government opposed such indirect, long-term financing of Soviet purchases abroad.) The Harriman concession, one of the two largest granted by the Soviets, was for the development of extensive manganese fields in the Chiaturi district of Georgia. Negotiations for the concession began in 1923, but a contract was not signed until June, 1925. Within a year, however, the State Department learned that the Harriman interests were "in perpetual conflict with Moscow to the extent that they are seriously considering withdrawal from Russia and renunciation of concession rights."

There were four major difficulties facing Harriman's Georgian Manganese Company. The first difficulty was competition from a Russian state monopoly known as the South Russian Ore Trust. Since the world demand for manganese remained fairly constant, the creation of a state monopoly posed a serious threat to the success of the Harriman concession. Also, there were excessive demands made upon the U.S. company by native workers who were represented by the Union of Georgian Miners. Further, Harriman had agreed to several unfortunate contract clauses. One called for the building of a railroad from Chiaturi to Sharopan, which proved to be a needless expense. The other was a clause requiring the company to pay a minimum royalty to the Soviet Government no matter what amount of ore production was attained. Finally, the world price of manganese fell after Harriman took over the concession, largely because of the development of newly discovered deposits in West Africa. All of these problems prompted Harriman to return to Moscow to negotiate a more favorable contract. It went into effect on January 1, 1928, but in March 1928, Harriman served notice upon the Soviet Government for cancellation of his manganese concession. The Georgian Manganese Company was formally dissolved in September of that year.

Harriman's abrupt action was apparently precipitated by his failure to gain influence in the South Russian Ore Trust. In particular, he felt that the Soviets should not have contracted with a German firm, Rawack and Grünweld Metal Company, to finance and sell abroad the ore produced by the state monopoly. The Soviet Government made this agreement with the German company *after* Harriman had been granted his concession. Harriman had tried for a number of years to alter the situation. After failing to get the Soviets to nullify their contract with the Germans he attempted to gain an interest in the state monopoly. By the spring of 1928 he decided that he was never going to succeed in removing what he considered to be the "greatest obstacle" to his concession—a combination of German-Soviet competition.

That a German firm had partially contributed to the failure of the second largest concessionaire in Soviet Russia seemed to confirm the fear of some State Department officials and U.S. businessmen who were interested in doing business with Russia that they had held since the beginning of the decade— the fear of German competition in Russia. U.S.-German competition for Russian markets increased markedly as a result of the Depression, which bore out a prediction made as early as 1926 by a member of the German foreign office. Also, beginning in 1931 U.S. traders lost to Germany large quantities of badly needed Russian trade because German bankers remained as willing in time of depression as they had been earlier in the 1920s to grant long-term credits to the Soviet Government. U.S. bankers had never granted such credits because of their excessive ideological hostility to the Soviet regime and the official State Department ban on long-term loans to the Soviets.

Harriman did not receive a cash settlement for his concession. Instead, for his total capital investment of $3,450,000 he received $4,450,000 in USSR bonds that were redeemable in fifteen years and that bore 7 per cent per annum. This settlement led a U.S. consul to conclude that "one of the ultimate results of Mr. Harriman's venture in the Soviet Union was a financial transaction amounting virtually to the granting to the Soviet government of a loan of $1,000,000."

Harriman's lack of success with both the Soviet and United States governments did not prevent him from becoming known as a U.S.-Russian business specialist in the latter half of the 1930s. That his reputation in this field endured was demonstrated in 1941 when he appeared the logical choice to negotiate the first lend-lease protocol with the USSR. Nevertheless, like Hammer, this U.S.-Russian business specialist was not among the ranks of those in favor of recognition before 1933.[1]

1. Belgian Embassy to State Department, November 8, 1923, Coleman (Latvia) to State Department, June 26, 1925, September 11, 1928, Tobin (Netherlands) to State Department, June 18, 1926, Schurman (Berlin) to State Department, December 7, December 8, 1926, June 28, 1927, Robert F. Kelley, memorandum, December 26, 1926, Bevan (Hamburg) to State Department, June 11, 1927, DeWitt C. Poole (Division of Russian Affairs) to Secretary of State, September 11, 1928, American-Russian Chamber of Commerce to Hughes, February 27, 1922, Young (Baltic Provinces) to State Department, September 13, 1921, Charles M. Muchnic (American Locomotive Sales Corporation) to State Department, April 1, 1926, Kelley, memorandum, November 3, 1928, Schurman to State Department, March 13, 1929, U.S. Department of State, Records Relating to Internal Affairs of Russia and the Soviet Union, Record Group 59, Files 861.637/2, 861.637/17, 861.637/44, 861.637/25, 861.637/28, 861.637/40, 861.637/27, 861.637/39, 861.637/43, 861.50/274, 861.50/234, 861.51Am3, 861.637 Harriman/20, 861.602/176; American-Russian Chamber of Commerce to Charles Evans Hughes, January 13, 1922, U.S. Department of State, General Records, Record Group 59, File 661.1115/362; Louis Fischer, *The Soviets in World Affairs*, 2: 764–69; Armand Hammer, *The Quest for the Romanoff Treasure*, p. 121; Elisha M. Friedman, *Russia in Transition: A Business Man's Appraisal*, p. 306; Thomas D. Campbell, *Russia: Market or Menace?* pp. 138, 143; Hans Heymann, *We Can Do Business with Russia*, p. 90; *Iron Age* 131 (January 5, 1933): 40.

HENRY FORD

Automotive products from the United States were not popular in Russia before World War I. Although U.S. cars had first appeared there in 1906, German and French automobiles and trucks dominated its small market until the end of the war. By 1912 there were still only 6,000 motor vehicles scattered among a population of 175,000,000 in Russia, and by 1925, there were approximately 20,000. Whatever the future potential of the Soviet market might have been, a delegation of Ford officials who visited Russia in 1926 reported negatively on the Soviet request that Ford build a factory inside the country. This judgment was confirmed later in the year by Mr. T. E. Eybye, a representative of the General Motors Company who also investigated the "prospects of automotive business in Soviet Russia." Eybye was even more pessimistic than the Ford group because he did not think the Soviets would be able to import more than 1500 automobiles, trucks, or autobuses a year, and his company was not willing to consider granting more than six months credit on such purchases. The Soviets, meanwhile, were demanding at least two years credit on any purchases. As far as building a General Motors plant in Russia was concerned, Eybye believed that "for years to come Russia would not become a large enough market for automobiles to warrant a plant for mass production."

Both Ford and General Motors, therefore, confined themselves to selling automotive products to Russia through Amtorg. Had the market seemed to warrant construction inside Russia, both companies would still have hesitated because of the rigid restrictions placed on concessionaires. More disconcerting to Ford and General Motors than the limitations placed on both the duration and profits of concessions was the Soviet practice of refusing to honor foreign patents. Nonetheless, by 1927 Ford claimed to be supplying 85 per cent of all trucks, cars, and tractors in the USSR. Despite this increasing trade the first major contract between Amtorg and Ford was not signed until May 31, 1929. It came about as a result of Soviet perseverance.

Undaunted by the wary attitude of U.S. motor companies, Soviet officials took the initiative in 1928 by asking the Ford Company to allow the State Automobile Trust to assemble Ford units in Russia from imported parts until Russian produced components could be made. Other U.S. automobile manufacturers, including General Motors, Durant, and Studebaker, were also contacted at this time, but the only large contract to materialize from these overtures was with Ford on May 31, 1929. The contract called for the Soviet Government to purchase $30,000,000 worth of automotive products over four years, in addition to building a plant at Nizhni-Novgorod capable of turning out 100,000 domestically produced units a year. After several New York bankers vouched for the "financial trustworthiness of the Soviet government," Ford agreed "to permit his engineers to assist in the construction" of this large automobile factory.

As a result company records show that between 1929 and 1935 total sales from the Amtorg contract amounted to $18,116,000, instead of the $30,000,000 stipulated in the original contract or the $40,000,000 that Charles E. Sorenson, a Ford executive engineer, later claimed. Inevitably Ford ran into the same problem that other concessionaires faced —the small percentage of profits that could be taken out of the country. This difficulty and the traditional labor and production problems of concessionaires, plus commercial expenses in addition to the original cost of the products sold, resulted in a loss to the company of $578,000 by 1935.

What was a small loss to Ford Motors was a large gain for the USSR. For "Automobilization" was an essential part of the First Five-Year Plan, and Ford contributed substantially to the goal of raising Russia's industrial production 136 per cent in five years and to the over-all success of Stalin's economic plan. It has been argued that Ford and other companies that began to deal with Soviet Russia in the late 1920s did the world a great service by building up a country that was to become a major opponent of fascism. It is true that the military importance of "Automobilization" was recognized by the architects of the Five-Year Plan, but there is no indication that Ford or such companies as International General Electric, United States Steel, DuPont de Nemours and Company, Underwood Typewriter, Standard Oil, the Caterpillar Company, International Harvester, and the Radio Corporation of America—all of whom contracted with the Soviets between 1928 and 1930 for goods and services—did so with any conscious realization that they were aiding a future ally "at a critical hour in world affairs."

It should be noted, however, that only one of the many Ford contracts with the Soviets in the 1920s, including the 1929 one, extended any credit. The significance, therefore, of this major Ford contract and GE's a year earlier was not in terms of long-term credit, but in terms of the vast amount of technology it placed at the disposal of the Soviets, who were granted the right, for example, "to use all Ford inventions or technical advances patented or unpatented."[1]

1. Wilson (St. Petersburg) to State Department, September 4, 1912, Coleman (Latvia) to State Department, July 16, 1925, August 7, 1926, June 23, 1929, White (Latvia) to State Department, June 16, 1926, DeWitt C. Poole (Division of Russian Affairs) to Secretary of State, November 19, 1928, Coleman to State Department, June 25, 1929, Schurman (Berlin) to State Department, April 17, 1929, U.S. Department of State, Records Relating to Internal Affairs of Russia and the Soviet Union, Record Group 59, Files 861.797, 861.797/3, 861.797/8, 861.797/13, 861.797/7, 861.797/9, 861.797 Ford Motor Co./1, 861.602 Hammer/4; Armand Hammer, *The Quest for the Romanoff Treasure*, pp. 102, 173; Allan Nevins and Frank Ernest Hill, *Ford*, Vol. 2, *Expansion and Challenge, 1915–1933*, pp. 673–74, 676–77, 679, 682–84n.8; Floyd James Fithian, "Soviet-American Economic Relations, 1918–1933: American Business in Russia during the Period of Nonrecognition" (Ph.D. dissertation, University of Nebraska, 1964); American-Russian Chamber of Commerce, *Handbook of the Soviet Union*, pp. 160–63; *Nation's Business* 18 (June 1930): 20–23.

APPENDIX D

NEW JERSEY STANDARD

The opposition of New Jersey Standard and of the Royal Dutch-Shell Company to Ivy Lee and to the New York Standard contract was somewhat hypocritical because both companies had been trying to monopolize the marketing of Russian oil since 1923. During the same time, both companies also conducted an anti-Soviet propaganda campaign throughout the 1920s in an attempt to obtain retribution for losses incurred as a result of nationalization. Thus the two companies vacillated between condemning the Soviets for stealing property and trying to negotiate lucrative oil contracts with them. New York Standard and Vacuum publicly did not take the same hard line about compensation while privately trying to deal with the USSR. New Jersey Standard's role in this complicated bargaining for Russian oil is particularly enlightening in terms of the relationship between U.S. Government officials and businessmen in the formulation of modern U.S. foreign policy.

No U.S. firms had been involved in Russian oil production on a large scale before the war. Standard Oil of New York and the Vacuum Oil Company did have minor holdings, and Jersey Standard had a small interest in the Nobel Brothers Petroleum Corporation, the largest foreign petroleum company operating in prewar Russia. The potential of the oil fields in the Caucasus and the disturbed conditions there following the Bolshevik Revolution tempted the board of directors of Jersey Standard to conclude that the time was ripe for a speculative investment in that part of the world, so the company bought half interest in the Nobel holdings in July 1920 *after the property had already been nationalized.* Convinced that the collapse of the Soviet regime was imminent, Jersey Standard took a calculated gamble that never paid off and then spent much time and effort in the 1920s trying to punish the Soviets for thwarting what might have been "among the most brilliant [transactions] ever consummated in the petroleum industry."

Jersey Standard's anti-Soviet campaign received the Government's backing. It began in 1920—the same year that the ill-fated Jersey-Nobel alliance was made—when the company turned down a Soviet offer of a fifty-year concession because it preferred to try to obtain direct compensation for what it deemed to be its confiscated property. Then the Soviets made the same offer to Standard Oil's major world competitor, Royal Dutch–Shell, and the efforts of Government and oil officials to prevent foreign domination of the rich Baku oil fields in the Caucasus led to the behind-the-scenes oil machinations at the Genoa and Hague conferences in 1922. At these talks the United States unofficially tried to apply the Open Door Doctrine to Russian oil. In essence, Hughes and Hoover wanted to keep all foreign oil companies from producing or buying Soviet oil until Jersey Standard received compensation for petroleum property nationalized by the Bolsheviks.

Thus, the Open Door position appeared to emerge victorious from both the Genoa and the Hague conferences of 1922, where the nations agreed for the time being not to make separate agreements with the Soviets for acquiring rights to confiscated property. While these conferences were going on the Royal Dutch–Shell and Jersey-Nobel interests agreed privately and very informally not to deal independently with Russia and to hold out for indemnification. This unsigned "London Memo" of July 24, 1922, was formalized in Paris on September 19, 1922, by sixteen oil companies. (Jersey Standard assented to, but did not actually sign, the September agreement.) Known as the *Front Uni*, the agreement was too negative and vague to be of long-lasting significance. It almost immediately began to disintegrate as the Soviets continued to play upon the self-interests of the larger firms. By the end of 1922, therefore, the Open Door position of the United States had produced a temporary stalemate over Russian oil reserves that the major international companies almost immediately tried to break.

In May 1923, for example, Teagle and Bedford of Jersey

Standard presented a plan to the State Department. It called for an agreement between three giant oil groups—Standard Oil, Royal Dutch–Shell, and the Anglo-Persian Oil Company —to market all "the oil which the Soviet people might be able to produce" because nationalization had removed any "basis for investment in Russia at this time." Such a combination of forces, according to the officials of Jersey Standard, would prevent any one of the three from taking advantage of the others. In keeping with his determination to keep economic and political foreign policy separated, Secretary of State Hughes initially refused to commit his department to the plan, saying that "it was purely an economic and business matter" for the companies involved to work out. He did intimate, however, that the pooling arrangement might be contrary to the Sherman Anti-Trust Act. At a second meeting between Bedford and Hughes on July 6, 1923, Bedford presented a more detailed draft of the big-three proposal. Hughes, having had more time to study the idea, now made three negative observations about the proposal: in all likelihood the pooling arrangement would "affect the freedom of trade in foreign commerce of the United States" and was therefore "contrary to the Sherman Act"; the combination would play into the hands of Soviet propagandists because it appeared monopolistic, and "unpleasant reaction" to it would "do much to offset the moral strength of the position [of the United States] with respect to the confiscation of property"; the agreement appeared to allow companies besides the original owners the use of confiscated property, and therefore, rather than "recognizing private property as sacrosanct," it seemed "to provide for its exploitation." Bedford replied that he had anticipated Hughes's position and "was personally in accord with it," and he promised that his company would not do anything "which would impair the policy of the Department."

This State Department opposition squelched the marketing deal between Jersey Standard, Royal Dutch–Shell, and Anglo-Persian at that time, but a marketing combination including these three oil groups and some of the smaller foreign oil companies did exist for a few months in 1923. The reason given publicly for its discontinuance was the desire of the companies involved to force the Soviets to compensate for their nationalization policies. Privately, however, Vacuum Oil Company, which was one of the participants, informed the State Department that it believed the real reason behind the dissolution of the combination was the desire of the larger companies to monopolize Russian oil exports by negotiating independent agreements with the Soviets.

The three big companies reached no agreement for the marketing of Russian oil until 1929, but a number of minor agreements were negotiated by the Vacuum Oil Company and Standard Oil of New York during the 1920s. Braving the protests of Jersey Standard and Royal Dutch–Shell about selling "stolen property," these two firms, which were to merge into Socony-Vacuum at the end of the decade, obtained the first of a series of small contracts in 1923 and then proceeded in 1926 to negotiate a five-year contract for purchasing an amount of oil worth $1,000,000 annually from the Soviet Oil Syndicate. President George P. Whaley of the Vacuum Company answered his critics by pointing out that "if the view should generally prevail that it would be unrighteous to buy petroleum from Russia on the theory that to do so would be to buy goods wrongfully confiscated from Russian subjects, Russia could export nothing." Referring to the increasing amount of trade between the United States and the USSR, he asked if it were "more righteous to buy from Russia than to sell to it."

During 1928 a private truce was effected between Jersey Standard, Royal Dutch–Shell, and Socony-Vacuum, and the following year on February 27 the Anglo-American Company (representing Jersey Standard, Royal Dutch–Shell and Anglo-Persian) signed a three-year contract with Russian Oil Products, Ltd. It guaranteed the Soviets 12.5 per cent of the British oil market in return for the right of Anglo-American to buy "considerable quantities" (estimated at $20,000,000 annually) of Russian oil at 5 per cent below the market price. Although the terms of the contract did not mention compensation, it was understood that the 5 per cent would be put aside for payment to those whose property had been nationalized. The agreement was described by a member of the U.S. foreign service as one that would "virtually eliminate Soviet Russia as an independent competitor from Europe and the Near East markets" by allowing Anglo-

American to monopolize the sale of Russian oil in these areas. This time the State Department raised no objections, even though this contract was part of a comprehensive understanding between Jersey Standard and Royal Dutch–Shell to allocate the international petroleum markets, which was in violation of the Open Door principle, and to control oil prices everywhere but in the United States.[1]

1. State Department, memorandum of conversation with Bedford, January 31, 1922, Sussdorff (The Hague) to State Department, July 27, September 19, 1922, Robert F. Kelley (chief, Eastern European Division), memorandum, February 8, 1927, Coleman (Latvia) to State Department, February 8, 1927, Vacuum Oil Company to Frank B. Kellogg, March 14, 1928, Atherton (London) to State Department, March 2, 1929, Harry Curran Wilbur to Kellogg, April 5, 1928, Schurman (Berlin) to State Department, May 1, 1928, Tobin (The Hague) to State Department, June 18, 1928, U.S. Department of State, Records Relating to Internal Affairs of Russia and the Soviet Union, Record Group 59, Files 861.6363/78, 861.6363/88, 861.6363/104, 861.6363/222, 861.6363/223, 861.6363/240, 861.6363/263, 861.6363 Standard Oil/1, 861.6363 Standard Oil/2, 861.6363 Standard Oil/4; Charles Evans Hughes, memoranda, May 8, June 6, 1923, U.S. Department of State, Memoranda of Conversations of the Secretary of State, 1921–1923, Record Group 59; George Sweet Gibb and Evelyn H. Knowlton, *History of Standard Oil*, Vol. 2, *The Resurgent Years, 1911–1927*, pp. 330–35, 338–41, 345–58; Harold F. Williamson, Ralph L. Andreano, Arnold R. Daum, and Gilbert C. Klose, *The American Petroleum Industry*, Vol. 2, *The Age of Energy, 1899–1959*, pp. 528–30; Frank A. Southard, Jr., *American Industry in Europe*, pp. 67–68; Peter G. Filene, *Americans and the Soviet Experiment, 1917–1933*, p. 118.

BIBLIOGRAPHY

Unpublished Documents

Newton D. Baker Papers. Manuscript Division, Library of Congress, Washington, D.C.

William E. Borah Papers. Manuscript Division, Library of Congress, Washington, D.C.

William R. Castle, Jr. Papers. Herbert Hoover Presidential Library, West Branch, Iowa.

Norman H. Davis Papers. Manuscript Division, Library of Congress, Washington, D.C.

Percival Farquhar USSR Papers. The Hoover Institution on War, Revolution, and Peace, Stanford University, Stanford, California.

John Hays Hammond Papers. Yale University Library, New Haven, Connecticut.

Herbert Hoover Papers. Herbert Hoover Oral History Program, Herbert Hoover Presidential Library, West Branch, Iowa.

————, Archives. Speeches and Addresses, 1915–1923; Herbert Hoover–Woodrow Wilson Correspondence, 1914–1919. The Hoover Institution on War, Revolution, and Peace, Stanford University, Stanford, California.

Charles Evans Hughes Papers. Manuscript Division, Library of Congress, Washington, D.C.

————. Memoranda of Conversations of the Secretary of State, 1921–1923. U.S. Department of State, Record Group 59. National Archives, Washington, D.C.

R. Walton Moore Papers. Franklin D. Roosevelt Library, Hyde Park, New York.

Henry Morgenthau, Jr., Diary. Franklin D. Roosevelt Library, Hyde Park, New York.

John Callan O'Laughlin Papers. Manuscript Division, Library of Congress, Washington, D.C.

George Foster Peabody Papers. Manuscript Division, Library of Congress, Washington, D.C.

George W. Perkins Papers. Butler Library, Columbia University, New York, New York.

Franklin D. Roosevelt Papers. Franklin D. Roosevelt Library, Hyde Park, New York.

Elihu Root Papers. Manuscript Division, Library of Congress, Washington, D.C.

U. S. Department of Commerce. General Records, 1918–1933. Record Group 40. National Archives, Washington, D.C.

————. Records of the Bureau of Foreign and Domestic Commerce, 1918–1933. Record Group 151. National Archives, Washington, D.C.

U. S. Department of State. General Records, 1918–1933. Record Group 59. National Archives, Washington, D.C.

————. Political Relations between the U.S. and Russia and the Soviet Union, 1918–1929. Record Group 59, Decimal File 711.61. National Archives, Washington, D.C.

————. Records Relating to Internal Affairs of Russia and the Soviet Union, 1918–1929. Record Group 59, Decimal Files 861.00–861b.6363. National Archives, Washington, D.C.

Frank A. Vanderlip Papers. Butler Library, Columbia University, New York, New York.

Published Documents

U.S. Congress, House, Committee on Ways and Means. *Hearings on H.R. 15597, H.R. 15927, H.R. 16517.* 71st Cong., 3d sess., January 27–28, 1931.

U.S. Congress, Senate, Committee on Foreign Relations. *Relations with Russia: Hearings on S.J.R. 164 for Re-establishment of Trade Relations.* 66th Cong., 3d sess., January 26, 1921.

————, Subcommittee of the Committee on Foreign Relations. *Russian Propaganda.* Senate Report 526. 66th Cong., 2d sess., April 14, 1920.

————. *Hearings on S.R. 50: Recognition of Russia.* Pts. 1–2. 68th Cong., 1st sess., January 21–23, 1924.

U.S. Department of Commerce, Bureau of Foreign and Domestic Commerce. *Foreign Capital Investments in Russian Industries and Commerce,* by Leonard J. Lewery. Department of Commerce Miscellaneous Series, no. 124. Washington, D.C., 1923.

————. *Russian Economic Notes, 1928–1933.*

U.S. Department of State. *Papers Relating to the Foreign Relations of the United States.* 1918–1933. Washington, D.C., 1931–1952.

U.S. Federal Trade Commission. *Report on Foreign Ownership in the Petroleum Industry.* February 12, 1923.

BIBLIOGRAPHY

Autobiographies, Memoirs, Correspondence, and Speeches

Barron, Clarence Walker. *More They Told Barron: Conversations and Revelations of an American Pepys in Wall Street.* New York, 1931.

Baruch, Bernard. *The Public Years.* New York, 1960.

The Bullitt Mission to Russia: Testimony before the Committee on Foreign Relations, United States Senate, of William C. Bullitt. New York, 1919.

Complete Presidential Press Conferences of Franklin D. Roosevelt. Vols. 1–2: *1933.* New York, 1972.

Ford, Henry. *My Life and Work.* New York, 1922.

———. *My Philosophy of Industry.* New York, 1929.

———. *Today and Tomorrow.* New York, 1926.

Hammer, Armand. *The Quest for the Romanoff Treasure.* New York, 1932.

Hammond, John Hays. *The Autobiography of John Hays Hammond.* New York, 1935. 2 vols.

Harper, Samuel N. *The Russia I Believe In: The Memoirs of Samuel N. Harper, 1902–1941.* Chicago, 1945.

Hendrick, Burton J. *The Life and Letters of Walter H. Page.* New York, 1922–1925. 3 vols.

Hirsch, Alcan. *Industrialized Russia.* New York, 1934.

Hoover, Herbert. *American Individualism.* New York, 1923.

———. *Campaign Speeches of 1932.* Garden City, 1933.

———. *A Cause To Win: Five Speeches on American Foreign Policy in Relation to Soviet Russia.* New York, 1951.

———. *The Challenge to Liberty.* New York, 1934.

———. *Memoirs.* New York, 1952. 3 vols.

———. *The New Day: Campaign Speeches of Herbert Hoover, 1928.* Stanford, 1928.

Hughes, Charles Evans. *The Pathway of Peace: Representative Addresses Delivered During His Term as Secretary of State, 1921–1925.* New York, 1925.

Hull, Cordell. *Memoirs.* New York, 1948. 2 vols.

Kahn, Otto. *Of Many Things: Being Reflections and Impressions on International Affairs, Domestic Topics and the Arts.* New York, 1926.

———. *Our Economic and Other Problems: A Financier's Point of View.* New York, 1920.

Kennan, George F. *Memoirs, 1925–1950.* Boston, 1967.

Lamont, Thomas W. *Across World Frontiers.* New York, 1951.

Lansing, Robert. *War Memoirs.* Indianapolis, 1935.

Liberman, Simon. *Building Lenin's Russia.* Chicago, 1945.

Lloyd George, David. *War Memoirs.* Boston, 1937. 6 vols.

Lyons, Eugene. *Assignment in Utopia.* New York, 1937.

Rockefeller, John D., Jr. *The Personal Relation in Industry.* New York, 1923.

Scheffer, Paul. *Seven Years in Soviet Russia.* New York, 1932.

Seymour, Charles. *The Intimate Papers of Colonel House.* New York, 1926. 2 vols.

Sloan, Alfred P., Jr. *My Years with General Motors,* Edited by John McDonald and Catherine Stevens. New York, 1964.

———. *Adventures of a White Collar Man.* New York, 1941.

Sorensen, Charles E. *My Forty Years with Ford.* New York, 1956.

Strauss, Lewis L. *Men and Decisions.* New York, 1962.

Thompson, Dorothy. *The New Russia.* New York, 1928.

Vanderlip, Frank A. *From Farm Boy to Financier.* New York, 1935.

———. *What Happened to Europe?* New York, 1920.

———. *What Next in Europe?* New York, 1922.

Newspapers, Periodicals, and Proceedings of Commercial Organizations

American Industries: The Manufacturers' Magazine. New York, 1918–1933. (From 1926 through 1928, it appeared under the title *Pocket Bulletin.*)

The Annalist: A Magazine of Finance, Commerce, and Economics. New York, 1918–1933.

Baltimore. Baltimore, 1918–1933.

Bankers Magazine. New York, 1918–1933.

Bradstreet's: A Journal of Trade, Finance and Public Economy. New York, 1918–1933.

Business Week. New York, 1918–1933. (In 1929, it superseded the *Magazine of Business.*)

Chicago Journal of Commerce and Daily Financial Times. Chicago, 1918–1933.

Cleveland Chamber of Commerce. *Annual.* Cleveland, 1918–1933. (It contains proceedings of annual meetings and board of directors' reports.)

Coast Banker (and California Banker). San Francisco, 1918–1933. (In 1922, it absorbed the *Western Banker and Financier;* by

1924, it was the official organ of the state banking associations of Utah, Arizona, and Nevada, and it carried banking and financial information about eleven Western states.)

Iron Age. New York, 1918–1933.

Journal of the American Bankers Association. New York, 1918–1933.

The Magazine of Wall Street. New York, 1918–1933.

National Association of Manufacturers. *Proceedings.* New York, 1918–1933. (It contains proceedings of annual conventions.)

National Foreign Trade Council. *Proceedings.* New York, 1918–1933. (It contains proceedings of annual National Foreign Trade conventions.)

Nation's Business: A Magazine for Businessmen. Washington, D.C., 1918–1933.

The New York Times. New York, 1918–1933.

Oregon Business. Portland, 1918–1933.

Pacific Banker. Portland, 1918–1933.

Philadelphia Board of Trade. *Proceedings.* Philadelphia, 1918–1933. (It contains proceedings of annual meetings.)

Southern California Business. Los Angeles, 1918–1933.

The Wall Street Journal. New York, 1918–1933.

Books

Adams, James Truslow. *Our Business Civilization: Some Aspects of American Culture.* New York, 1929.

Allison, Graham T. *Essence of Decision: Explaining the Cuban Missile Crises.* Boston, 1971.

American-Russian Chamber of Commerce. *Handbook of the Soviet Union.* New York, 1936.

Amtorg. *Soviet-American Trade Outlook.* New York, 1928.

Angell, James W. *Financial Foreign Policy of the United States: A Report to the Second International Studies Conference on the State and Economic Life, London, May 29 to June 2, 1933.* 1933. Reprint. New York, 1965.

Apter, David E., ed. *Ideology and Discontent.* New York, 1964.

Bass, Herbert, ed. *The State of American History.* Chicago, 1970.

Bauer, Raymond, Ithiel de Sola Pool, and Lewis Anthony Dexter. *American Business and Public Policy: The Politics of Foreign Trade.* New York, 1963.

Baykov, Alexander. *Soviet Foreign Trade.* Princeton, 1946.

Bennett, Edward M. *Recognition of Russia: An American Foreign Policy Dilemma.* Waltham, Mass., 1970.

Benson, Lee. *Turner and Beard, American Historical Writing Reconsidered.* Glencoe, Ill., 1960.

Berkhofer, Robert F., Jr. *A Behavioral Approach to Historical Analysis.* New York, 1969.

Bernstein, Barton J., ed. *Towards a New Past: Dissenting Essays in American History.* New York, 1968.

Berthoff, Rowland. *An Unsettled People.* New York, 1971.

Bishop, Donald G. *The Roosevelt-Litvinov Agreements: The American View.* Syracuse, 1965.

Black, Cyril. *The Dynamics of Modernization.* New York, 1966.

Blaisdell, Thomas C., Jr. *The Federal Trade Commission: An Experiment in the Control of Business.* New York, 1932.

Blum, John Morton. *From the Morgenthau Diaries: Years of Crisis, 1928–1938.* Boston, 1959.

Bowen, Ralph. *German Theories of the Corporative State.* New York, 1947.

Brady, Robert. *Business as a System of Power.* New York, 1943.

Braeman, John, Robert H. Bremmer, and David Brody. *Twentieth-Century American Foreign Policy.* Columbus, 1971.

Brandes, Joseph. *Herbert Hoover and Economic Diplomacy: Department of Commerce Policy, 1921–1928.* Pittsburgh, 1962.

Bron, Saul G. *Soviet Economic Development and American Business.* New York, 1930.

Browder, Robert Paul. *The Origins of Soviet-American Diplomacy.* Princeton, 1953.

Budish, J. M., and Samuel S. Shipman. *Soviet Foreign Trade: Menace or Promise?* New York, 1931.

Bullitt, Orville H., ed. *For the President: Personal and Secret Correspondence Between Franklin D. Roosevelt and William C. Bullitt.* Boston, 1972.

Campbell, Thomas D. *Russia: Market or Menace?* London, 1932.

Carr, Edward Hallett. *The Bolshevik Revolution, 1917–1923.* New York, 1951. 3 vols.

————. *Socialism in One Country.* New York, 1958. 3 vols.

————. *The Soviet Impact on the Western World.* New York, 1947.

Chamberlin, William Henry. *Soviet Russia: A Living Record and History.* Boston, 1931.

Chandler, Alfred D. *Strategy and Structure: Chapters in the History of American Industrial Enterprise.* Cambridge, 1962.

Chase, Stuart. *The Nemesis of American Business and Other Essays.* New York, 1931.

————, Robert Dunn, and Rexford Guy Tugwell, eds. *Soviet Russia in the Second Decade.* New York, 1928.

Cohen, Bernard C. *The Influence of Non-Governmental Groups on Foreign Policy-Making.* Boston, 1959.

Dennis, Alfred L. P. *The Foreign Policies of Soviet Russia.* New York, 1924.

DeNovo, John A. *American Interests and Policies in the Middle East, 1900–1939.* Minneapolis, 1963.

Diamond, William. *The Economic Thought of Woodrow Wilson.* Baltimore, 1943.

Dobbert, Gerhard. *Red Economics.* Boston, 1932.

Dorfman, Joseph. *The Economic Mind in American Civilization.* Vols. 3–5. New York, 1959.

Dougherty, James E. *Contending Theories of International Relations.* Philadelphia, 1971.

Elbow, Matthew. *French Corporative State.* New York, 1953.

Farnsworth, Beatrice. *William C. Bullitt and the Soviet Union.* Bloomington, Ind., 1967.

Fay, Charles Norman. *Business in Politics: Considerations for Business Leaders.* Cambridge, Mass., 1926.

Feis, Herbert. *The Diplomacy of the Dollar: First Era, 1919–1932.* Baltimore, 1950.

————. *1933: Characters in Crisis.* Boston, 1966.

Filene, Peter G. *Americans and the Soviet Experiment, 1917–1933.* Cambridge, Mass., 1967.

Fischer, Louis. *Oil Imperialism: The International Struggle for Petroleum.* New York, 1926.

————. *The Soviets in World Affairs.* London, 1930. 2 vols.

————. *Why Recognize Russia?* New York, 1931.

————. *The Life of Lenin.* New York, 1964.

Freidel, Frank. *Franklin D. Roosevelt.* Vol. 3: *The Triumph.* Boston, 1956. Vol. 4: *Launching the New Deal.* Boston, 1973.

Friedman, Elisha M. *Russia in Transition: A Business Man's Appraisal.* New York, 1932.

Galambos, Louis. *Competition and Cooperation.* Baltimore, 1966.

Gauld, Charles A. *The Last Titan: Percival Farquhar.* Stanford, 1964.

Gibb, George Sweet, and Evelyn H. Knowlton. *History of Standard Oil.* Vol. 2: *The Resurgent Years, 1911–1927.* New York, 1956.

Glad, Betty. *Charles Evans Hughes and the Illusions of Innocence: A Study in American Diplomacy.* Urbana, Ill., 1966.

Golob, Eugene. *The Isms*. New York, 1954.

Graber, Doris A. *Public Opinion, The President, and Foreign Policy: Four Case Studies from the Formative Years*. New York, 1968.

Graham, Otis L. *The Great Campaigns: Reform and War in America, 1900–1928*. Englewood Cliffs, N.J., 1971.

Haber, Samuel. *Efficiency and Uplift*. Chicago, 1964.

Haensel, Paul. *The Economic Policy of Soviet Russia*. London, 1930.

Hagedorn, Hermann. *The Magnate: William Boyce Thompson and His Times*. New York, 1935.

Harvard University, Research Center in Entrepreneurial History. *Change and the Entrepreneur: Postulates and Patterns for Entrepreneurial History*. Cambridge, 1949.

Hawley, Ellis W. *The New Deal and the Problem of Monopoly*. Princeton, 1966.

Hayek, F. A., ed. *Capitalism and the Historians*. Chicago, 1954.

Hays, Samuel P. *Response to Industrialism*. Chicago, 1957.

Heymann, Hans. *We Can Do Business with Russia*. Chicago, 1945.

Higham, John. *History: Professional Scholarship in America*. New York, 1973.

Hofstadter, Richard. *The Progressive Historians*. New York, 1968.

———, and Walter P. Metzger. *The Development of Academic Freedom in the United States*. New York, 1955.

Hoover, Calvin B. *The Economic Life of Soviet Russia*. New York, 1931.

Iriye, Akira. *After Imperialism: The Search for a New Order in the Far East, 1921–1931*. Cambridge, Mass., 1965.

Irwin, Will. *How Red is America?* New York, 1926.

Jones, Robert Huhn. *The Roads to Russia: United States Lend-Lease to the Soviet Union*. Norman, 1969.

Kennan, George F. *Russia Leaves the War*. Princeton, 1956.

———. *The Decision to Intervene*. London, 1958.

Kimball, Warren F. *The Most Unsordid Act: Lend-Lease, 1939–1941*. Baltimore, 1969.

Knickerbocker, H. R. *Soviet Trade and World Depression*. London, 1931.

Kolko, Gabriel. *The Roots of American Foreign Policy*. Boston, 1969.

Kuklick, Bruce. *American Policy and the Division of Germany: The Clash with Russia over Reparations*. Ithaca, 1972.

Lasch, Christopher. *The American Liberals and the Russian Revolution*. New York, 1962.

Layton, Edwin T., Jr. *The Revolt of the Engineers*. Cleveland, 1971.

Levin, N. Gordon, Jr. *Woodrow Wilson and World Politics: America's Response to War and Revolution*. New York, 1968.

Lewis, Cleona. *America's Stake in International Investments*. Washington, D.C., 1938.

Lichtheim, George. *The Concept of Ideology and Other Essays*. New York, 1967.

Loth, David. *Swope of G.E.: The Story of Gerard Swope and General Electric in American Business*. New York, 1958.

Lovenstein, Meno. *American Opinion of Soviet Russia*. Washington, D.C., 1941.

McConnell, Grant. *Private Power and American Democracy*. New York, 1966.

McKenna, Marian C. *Borah*. Ann Arbor, 1961.

Maddox, Robert James. *William E. Borah and American Foreign Policy*. Baton Rouge, 1969.

————. *The New Left and the Origins of the Cold War*. Princeton, 1973.

Mannheim, Karl. *Ideology and Utopia: An Introduction to the Sociology of Knowledge*. London, 1936.

Matz, Mary Jane. *The Many Lives of Otto Kahn*. New York, 1963.

Meiburger, Anne Vincent. *Efforts of Raymond Robins toward the Recognition of Soviet Russia and the Outlawry of War, 1917–1933*. Washington, D.C., 1958.

Mooney, James D. *The New Capitalism*. New York, 1934.

Morgan, H. Wayne. *The Gilded Age: A Reappraisal*. New York, 1963.

Moyer, George S. *Attitude of the United States toward Recognition of Soviet Russia*. Philadelphia, 1926.

Murray, Robert K. *The Harding Era: Warren G. Harding and His Administration*. Minneapolis, 1969.

Myers, William Starr. *The Foreign Policies of Herbert Hoover, 1929–1933*. New York, 1940.

Naess, Arne. *Democracy, Ideology and Objectivity*. Oslo, 1956.

Nelson, William H., ed. *Theory and Practice in American Politics*. Chicago, 1964.

Nevins, Allan, and Frank Ernest Hill. *Ford*. Vol. 2: *Expansion and Challenge, 1915–1933*. New York, 1957.

Nicolson, Harold. *Dwight Morrow*. New York, 1935.

Nixon, Edgar B. *Franklin D. Roosevelt and Foreign Affairs.* Vol. 1: *January 1933–February 1934.* Cambridge, Mass., 1969.

Parrini, Carl P. *Heir to Empire: U.S. Economic Diplomacy, 1916–1923.* Pittsburgh, 1969.

Pasvolsky, Leo, and Harold G. Moulton. *Russian Debts and Russian Reconstruction.* New York, 1924.

Paterson, Thomas G., ed. *Cold War Critics.* Chicago, 1971.

———, ed. *The Origins of the Cold War.* Lexington, Mass., 1970.

Prothro, James Warren. *The Dollar Decade: Business Ideas in the 1920's.* Baton Rouge, 1954.

Quint, Howard H., and Robert H. Ferrell, eds. *The Talkative President: The Off-the-Record Press Conferences of Calvin Coolidge.* Amherst, Mass., 1964.

Radosh, Ronald. *American Labor and the United States Foreign Policy.* New York, 1969.

———, and Murray N. Rothbard, eds. *A New History of Leviathan: Essays on the Rise of the American Corporate State.* New York, 1973.

Rosenau, James N., ed. *Domestic Sources of Foreign Policy.* New York, 1967.

Rothbard, Murray N. *For a New Liberty.* New York, 1973.

Saveth, Edward N., ed. *American History and the Social Sciences.* New York, 1964.

Schattschneider, E. E. *Politics, Pressures and the Tariff.* New York, 1935.

Schmalhausen, Samuel D., ed. *Behold America!* New York, 1931.

Schneider, Wilbert M. *The American Bankers Association: Its Past and Present.* Washington, D.C., 1956.

Schuman, Frederick Lewis. *American Policy toward Russia since 1917.* New York, 1928.

Schumpeter, Joseph. *Capitalism, Socialism and Democracy.* 2d ed. New York, 1950.

Shonfield, Andrew. *Modern Capitalism.* London, 1965.

Singer, J. David, ed. *Quantitative International Politics: Insights and Evidence.* New York, 1968.

Siracusa, Joseph M. *New Left Histories and Historians.* Port Washington, N.Y., 1973.

Smith, Daniel M. *Aftermath of War: Bainbridge Colby and Wilsonian Diplomacy, 1920–1921.* Philadelphia, 1970.

Southard, Frank A. *American Industry in Europe.* Boston, 1931.

Strauss, Lewis. *Men and Decisions.* Garden City, N.Y., 1962.

Strout, Cushing. *The Pragmatic Revolt in American History: Carl Becker and Charles Beard.* New Haven, 1958.

Stuart, Graham H. *American Diplomatic and Consular Practice.* New York, 1952.

Sutton, Anthony C. *Western Technology and Soviet Economic Development.* Vol. 1: *1917 to 1930.* Stanford, 1968. Vol. 2: *1930 to 1945.* Stanford, 1971.

Sutton, Francis X., Seymour Harris, Carl Kaysen, and James Tobin. *The American Business Creed.* Cambridge, Mass., 1956.

Thompson, John M. *Russia, Bolshevism, and the Versailles Peace.* Princeton, 1966.

Tompkins, Pauline. *American-Russian Relations in the Far East.* New York, 1949.

Tucker, Robert W. *The Radical Left and American Foreign Policy.* Baltimore, 1971.

Tulchin, Joseph S. *The Aftermath of War: World War I and U.S. Policy toward Latin America.* New York, 1971.

Ware, Louise. *George Foster Peabody: Banker, Philanthropist, Publicist.* Athens, Ga., 1951.

Weber, Max. *The Theory of Social and Economic Organization.* New York, 1947.

Weinstein, James. *The Corporate Ideal in the Liberal State.* Boston, 1969.

Wheeler, Harvey. *Democracy in a Revolutionary Era.* Santa Barbara, Calif., 1970.

Wiebe, Robert. *The Search for Order.* New York, 1967.

Williams, William Appleman. *American-Russian Relations, 1781–1947.* New York, 1952.

——. *The Contours of American History.* Cleveland, 1961.

Williamson, Harold F., Ralph Andreano, Arnold R. Daum, and Gilbert C. Klose. *The American Petroleum Industry.* Vol. 2: *The Age of Energy, 1899–1959.* Evanston, Ill., 1963.

Wilson, Edmund. *The American Earthquake: A Documentary of the Twenties and Thirties.* New York, 1968.

Wilson, Joan Hoff. *American Business and Foreign Policy, 1920–1933.* Lexington, Ky., 1971.

——. *Herbert Clark Hoover: Forgotten Progressive.* Boston, 1974.

Zinn, Howard. *The Politics of History.* Boston, 1970.

Articles

Austin, W. J. "Why Fear Russia?" *Scribner's Magazine* 90 (September 1931).

Bernstein, Barton J. "Our Empire's Roots." *The Progressive* 34 (June 1970): 45–48.

Boller, Paul F., Jr. "The 'Great Conspiracy' of 1933: A Study in Short Memories." *Southwest Review* 39 (Spring 1954): 97–112.

Bowers, Robert E. "American Diplomacy, the 1933 Wheat Conference, and Recognition of the Soviet Union." *Agricultural History* 11 (January 1966): 39–52.

——. "Hull, Russian Subversion in Cuba, and Recognition of the USSR." *Journal of American History* 52 (December 1966): 542–54.

Bridges, Hal. "The Robber Baron Concept in American History." *Business History Review* 32 (Spring 1958): 1–13.

Bruchey, Stuart. "The Inadequacy of the Profit Maximization as a Model of Business Behavior." *Business History Review* 34 (Winter 1960): 495–97.

Clubb, O. Edmund. "New Horizons in U.S.–Soviet Trade." *The Progressive* 37 (June 1973): 41–44.

Cuff, Robert D. "A 'Dollar-a-Year Man' in Government: George N. Peek and the War Industries Board." *Business History Review* 41 (Winter 1967): 404–20.

——. "Bernard Baruch: Symbol and Myth in Industrial Mobilization." *Business History Review* 43 (Summer 1969): 115–33.

Davis, G. Cullom. "The Transformation of the Federal Trade Commission, 1914–1929." *Mississippi Valley Historical Review* 49 (December 1962): 437–55.

Davis, Jerome. "Capitalism and Communism." *Annals of the American Academy of Political and Social Science* 156 (July 1931): 62–75.

DeNovo, T. A. "Movement for an Aggressive American Oil Policy Abroad, 1918–1920." *American Historical Review* 61 (July 1956): 854–76.

Feuer, Lewis S. "American Travelers to the Soviet Union, 1917–1932: The Formation of a Component of New Deal Ideology." *American Quarterly* 14 (Summer 1962): 119–49.

Fike, Claude E. "The United States and Russian Territorial Problems, 1917–1920." *The Historian* 24 (May 1962): 331–46.

Freyn, H. J. "An American Engineer Looks at the Five-Year Plan." *New Republic* 66 (May 6, 1933).

Galambos, Louis. "The Emerging Organizational Synthesis in Modern American History." *Business History Review* 44 (Autumn 1970): 279–90.

Garaty, John A. "The New Deal, National Socialism, and the Great Depression." *American Historical Review* 78 (October 1973): 907–44.

Goulder, Alvin W. "Metaphysical Pathos and the Theory of Bureaucracy." *American Political Science Journal* 49 (June 1955): 496–507.

Grin, Carolyn. "The Unemployment Conference of 1921: An Experiment in National Cooperative Planning." *Mid-America* 55 (April 1973): 83–107.

Hawley, Ellis W. "Secretary Hoover and the Bituminous Coal Problem, 1921–28." *Business History Review* 42 (Autumn 1968): 253–70.

Hays, Samuel P. "The Social Analysis of American Political History, 1880–1920." *Political Science Quarterly* 80 (September 1965): 373–94.

———. "The Politics of Municipal Government in the Progressive Era." *Pacific Northwest Quarterly* 55 (October 1964): 157–69.

Hopkins, George W. "The Politics of Food: United States and Soviet Hungary, March–August, 1919." *Mid-America* 55 (October 1973): 245–70.

Kaufman, Burton I. "Organization for Foreign Trade Expansion in the Mississippi Valley, 1900–1920." *Business History Review* 46 (Winter 1972): 444–65.

———. "The Organizational Dimension of United States Economic Foreign Policy." *Business History Review* 46 (Spring 1972): 17–44.

Koistinen, Paul A. "The 'Industrial-Military Complex' in Historical Perspective: World War I." *Business History Review* 41 (Winter 1967): 378–403.

———. "The 'Industrial-Military Complex' in Historical Perspective: The InterWar Years." *Journal of American History* 56 (March 1970): 819–35.

Maddox, Robert James. "Keeping Cool with Coolidge." *Journal of American History* 53 (March 1967): 772–80.

———. "Woodrow Wilson, the Russian Embassy and Siberian Intervention." *Pacific Historical Review* 26 (November 1967): 431–48.

Morris, Robert L. "A Reassessment of Russian Recognition." *The Historian* 24 (August 1962): 470–82.

Muchnic, Charles M. "A Business Man's View of Russia: Letters from an American Executive." *Harper's* 149 (September 1929): 437–53.

Nash, Gerald D. "Experiments in Industrial Mobilization: WIB and NRA." *Mid-America* 45 (July 1963): 157–67.

Olson, James. "The End of Voluntarism." *Annals of Iowa* 41 (Fall 1972): 1104–13.

Parry, Albert. "Washington B. Vanderlip, the 'Khan of Kamchatka.' " *Pacific Historical Review* 17 (August 1948): 311–30.

Radosh, Ronald. "John Spargo and Wilson's Russian Policy, 1920." *Journal of American History* 52 (December 1965): 548–65.

Redlich, Fritz. "The Business Leader in Theory and Reality." *American Journal of Economics and Sociology* 8 (April 1949): 223–37.

Rukeyser, Walter A. "Do Our Engineers in Russia Damage America?" *Scribner's Magazine* 90 (November 1931).

Snyder, J. Richard. "Coolidge, Costigan and the Tariff Commission." *Mid-America* 50 (April 1968): 131–48.

Stein, Herbert. "Pre-revolutionary Fiscal Policy: The Regime of Herbert Hoover." *Journal of Law and Economics* 9 (October 1966): 189–233.

Tipple, John. "The Anatomy of Prejudice: Origins of the Robber Baron Legend." *Business History Review* 33 (Winter 1959): 510–23.

Unger, Lewis. "The 'New Left' and American History: Some Recent Trends in United States Historiography." *American Historical Review* 72 (July 1967): 1237–63.

Vinson, J. Chal. "War Debts and Peace Legislation: The Johnson Act of 1934." *Mid-America* 50 (July 1968): 206–22.

Williams, William Appleman. "American Intervention in Russia 1917–1920." *Studies on the Left* 3 (Fall 1963): 24–48; 4 (Winter 1964): 39–57.

Wilson, J. H. "American Business and Recognition of the Soviet Union." *Social Science Quarterly* 52 (September 1971): 349–68.

Theses and Dissertations

Diggins, John P. "Mussolini's Italy: The View from America, 1922–1941." Ph.D. dissertation, University of Southern California, 1964.

Fithian, Floyd James. "Soviet-American Economic Relations, 1918–1933: American Business in Russia during the Period of Nonrecognition." Ph.D. dissertation, University of Nebraska, 1964.

Gray, Sister Gertrude Mary. "Oil in Anglo-American Diplomatic Relations, 1920–1928." Ph.D. dissertation, University of California, Berkeley, 1950.

Hurvitz, Haggai. "Notes on the Orientation Guidance Approach to the Analysis of Ideologies." M.A. thesis, Columbia University, 1968.

Layton, Edwin T. "The American Engineering Profession and the Idea of Social Responsibility." Ph.D. dissertation, University of California, Los Angeles, 1956.

Lloyd, Craig. "Aggressive Introvert: A Study of Herbert Hoover and Public Relations Management, 1912–1932." Ph.D. dissertation, University of Iowa, 1970.

McClelland, Robert Crawford. "The Soviet Union in American Opinion, 1933–1942." Ph.D. dissertation, West Virginia University, 1950.

Parrini, Carl Philip. "American Empire and Creating a Community of Interest: Economic Diplomacy, 1916–1922." Ph.D. dissertation, University of Wisconsin, 1963.

Solberg, Winton U. "The Impact of Soviet Russia on American Life and Thought, 1917–1933." Ph.D. dissertation, Harvard University, 1952.

Stalker, Nellis, Jr. "The National Association of Manufacturers: A Study in Ideology." Ph.D. dissertation, University of Wisconsin, 1950.

Weissman, Benjamin M. "The American Relief Administration in Russia, 1921–1923: A Case Study in the Interaction Between Opposing Political Systems." Ph.D. dissertation, Columbia University, 1968.

INDEX

Adamic, Louis, 77
Agricultural Adjustment Administration, 123
Agriculture. *See* Natural resources industries
Agriculture, Department of, U.S., 123
Allied American Corporation (ALAMERICO), 47, 71, 74–76
Allied blockade: against Central Powers, 32; against Russia, 32–33, 50. *See also* Embargo, U.S.; Trade, U.S.: commercial and financial restrictions
Allied Council of Four, 22
Allied Patriotic Societies, 41
Allied powers (Allies), 3, 5, 16, 32, 86
Allied Supreme Council, 32, 35
Allis-Chalmers Manufacturing Company, 63
All Russian Textile Syndicate (ARTS), 38, 73, 76, 77–79, 95
All Union Textile Syndicate of Moscow, 76
Amalgamated Bank of New York, 41
Amalgamated Clothing Workers of America, 117n.23
Amalgamated Trust and Savings Bank of Chicago, 41
American Automotive Club of France, 100
American Bankers Association, viii, 61, 96, 107, 119
American Car and Foundry Company, 63
American Commercial Association to Promote Trade with Russia, 52–58, 67, 152
American Farm Bureau Federation, 106
American Federation of Labor, 107, 117, 119
American Federation of Teachers, 117n.23
American Foundation, 115; Committee on Russian-American Relations of, 116, 117
American Industrial Concession, 155
American Industries, 59, 68n.34, 107
American Iron and Steel Institute, 106, 111
American Legion, 113, 119
American Locomotive Sales Corporation, 39–40, 63, 107
American Manganese Producers' Association, 106
American Manufacturers Export Association, 35n.26, 61, 63n.23
American Relief Administration (ARA), xivn.9, 21, 23–25, 27, 30, 32, 44, 97, 151, 152, 153
American Telegraph and Telephone (AT&T), 119
American Tool Works, 74, 107
Amrusco, 81
Amtorg Trading Corporation, 47, 79–89 *passim*; 91, 95, 97, 103n.1, 109, 121, 124, 126, 155, 161
Anaconda Copper Company, 120
Anglo-American Company, 167
Anglo-Persian Oil Company, 166
Annalist, 61, 66
Anticommunism, xiii, 85, 102, 130. *See also* Communism
Antitraders. *See* Bankers; Businessmen; Internationalists; Nationalists; Natural resources industries; individual businessmen; individual departments of government
Arcos, 73
Armistice, World War I, 23, 32, 34
Armsby, James K., 63
Assay Office, U.S., 41, 42
Avezzana, Baron Camillo, 14

Bakhmetev, Boris, 55n.10, 63n.22
Balance of trade. *See* Trade, U.S.: international balance of
Baldwin Locomotive Works, 117 n.22
Bank of Italy, San Francisco, 41
Bankers, 56, 60, 81, 87; antitraders, 54, 58–60, 86, 95, 153; German, 159; protraders, 107, 108, 112; and recognition, 67, 86; and Soviet credit, 66, 95–96, 103n.1, 109, 159, 162. *See also* Credit; Loans
Bankers Magazine, 61, 113
Baruch, Bernard, 63, 119
Beard, Charles A., 135, 136
Bedford, A. C., 63, 165, 166
Blockade. *See* Allied blockade
Boards of Trade: Chicago, 106; Philadelphia, 61, 66, 107; U.S., 112. *See also* Chambers of Commerce; Organizations, business
Bolsheviks, 6, 17, 19, 21, 22, 23, 28, 33, 34, 51, 59, 60, 61, 66, 67, 72, 94, 97, 112, 148, 153, 165
Bolshevism, viii, 5, 6, 7, 14, 20, 21, 28, 145, 148, 149, 150n.36

INDEX

Occidental Petroleum Corporation, 157
Oddie, Tasher L., 107
Oil companies, 88, 164–68. *See also* Natural resources industries; individual firms
Olds, Robert E., 99
Open Door policy, U.S., 165, 168
Organizations: business, viii, 1, 57, 64, 67, 107, 111, 113, 117n.22, 128, 152; labor, 117 and n.23; Soviet trading, 52, 73, 76, 80, 155. *See also* individual organizations
Oudin, Maurice, 63, 95n.42

Pacific Banker, 61, 67n.33
Packard Motors, 120
Page, Walter Hines, 3
Palmer, A. Mitchell, 21
Parrington, Vernon Louis, 135
Parrini, Carl P., 136
Patents, 82
Perkins, George W., 64
Petrograd Telegraph Agency, 77
Pittman, Key, 107
Populist era, 135
Products Exchange Corporation, 73, 79
Progressive era, xi, 135
Progressives, 113, 133, 136, 137
Propaganda, 6, 20, 29, 48, 50, 61, 87, 98, 122, 147
Protraders. *See* Bankers; Businessmen; Internationalists; Natural resources industries; individual businessmen
Provisional Government, of Russia. *See* Russia
Public, 3, 29, 100, 128, 144, 152
Public opinion, vii, 99, 131, 132; polls, 114–16

Radicalism, 20
Radicals, 23, 66
Radio Corporation of America (RCA), 94, 97, 111, 163
Rand, J. H., 177n.22
Ranke, Leopold, 134, 135
Rawack and Grünweld Metal Company, 159
Recognition policy, vii, xi, 1, 8, 13, 14, 30n.19, 35, 44, 47, 57, 69, 70, 78, 89, 90, 99, 100, 112, 119, 127, 129, 131, 148; bureaucratic and/or organizational influence on, vii, xi, 34, 70, 85, 102, 130, 132, 134; and business pressure, vii and n.1, viii, 112; contradictions of, 29–30, 32, 69, 131; economics of, 113–32 *passim*, 134; geographic divisions over, 67, 116; ideological

influence on, mentioned *passim*; political reasons for, 120, 132
—relationship to trade: 8, 30, 59, 65n.28, 67, 71, 75, 82, 92, 97, 103, 110–11, 112, 113, 114–15, 116, 120, 122, 123, 127, 130, 143, 153. *See also* Hoover, Herbert; Hughes, Charles E.; Non-recognition policy
Reconstruction Finance Corporation (RFC), 84, 102, 126, 128
Red Cross, 33
Red Scare (1919–1920), 5, 7, 21, 55, 101
Redfield, William C., 33
Redlich, Fritz, 135
Relief, U.S.: "bread and butter" type of, 6–8; to Europe, 6; famine, 4, 6, 22, 74; farm, 24, 123, 128; to Russia, 7, 21–25, 44, 51, 74, 101; relation to recognition and revolution, 23. *See also* American Relief Administration; Hoover, Herbert
Remington Rand Corporation, 177n.22
Republicans: and recognition, 18, 66, 70, 78, 121
Revolutions: Bolshevik (November, 1917), vii, xi, 1, 3, 4, 32, 51, 60, 72, 86, 95, 164; Russian (March, 1917), 2, 3, 76
Reynolds, George M., 64
Robins, Raymond, 77; prorecognition, 65n.28, 66, 76, 114, 127, 128n.38
Robinson, Joseph T., 107
Rogers Bill (1921), 30–31
Ropes, E.C., 81, 83, 121, 153
Roosevelt, Franklin Delano, 14, 48, 70, 90, 91, 111; and recognition, 112–32 *passim*
Root, Elihu, 66, 98; mission of, 2n.4, 76–77
Rosen, Baron, 2n.4
Rowell, Chester H., 113
Royal Dutch-Shell Company, 99, 164, 165, 167, 168
Rukeyser, Walter A., 118
Russia: mentioned *passim*; Bolshevik-dominated, 1, 101, 150; dismemberment of, 15–18 *passim*; disruption of production in, 4, 20, 50, 150; Provisional Government in (1917), 2, 16, 44, 55n.10, 63n.22; similarities to U.S., 9–10; First World War effort of, 3, 5, 16
Russian-American Industrial Corporation, 71
Russian Corporation, of the War Trade Board. *See* State, Dept. of, U.S.

190